The Isle of Man

A SOCIAL, CULTURAL, AND
POLITICAL HISTORY

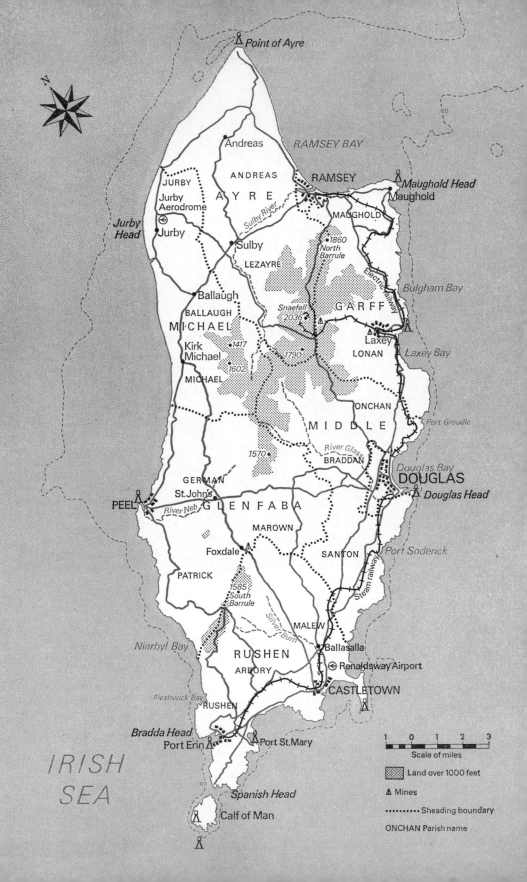

N

Point of Ayre

RAMSEY BAY

Andreas

ANDREAS

JURBY

AYRE

RAMSEY

Maughold Head

Jurby
Aerodrome

Maughold

MAUGHOLD

*Jurby
Head*

Jurby

Sulby

•1860
North
Barrule

LEZAYRE

Sulby River

Electric Railway

Bulgham Bay

GARFF

Ballaugh

BALLAUGH

Snaefell
•2036

Laxey

MICHAEL

Kirk
Michael

•1417

•1790

Laxey

Laxey Bay

LONAN

•1602

MICHAEL

ONCHAN

Port Groudle

MIDDLE

River Glass

•1570

BRADDAN

Douglas Bay

GERMAN

St.John's

DOUGLAS

PEEL

River Neb

GLENFABA

Douglas Head

MAROWN

Foxdale

SANTON

Port Soderick

PATRICK

Steam railway

1585
South
Barrule

MALEW

Silver Burn

Niarbyl Bay

Ballasalla

RUSHEN

Ronaldsway Airport

ARBORY

Fleshwick Bay

CASTLETOWN

RUSHEN

Bradda Head
Port Erin

Port St.Mary

*IRISH

SEA*

Spanish Head

Calf of Man

Scale of miles
1 0 1 2 3

Land over 1000 feet

⚒ Mines

•••••••• Sheading boundary

ONCHAN Parish name

The Isle of Man

A SOCIAL, CULTURAL, AND POLITICAL HISTORY

R. H. KINVIG

Late Emeritus Professor of Geography in the University of Birmingham

CHARLES E. TUTTLE CO., INC.—PUBLISHERS
RUTLAND, VERMONT

Published by the Charles E. Tuttle Co., Inc.,
Rutland, Vermont, U.S.A.

Library of Congress Catalog Card Number: 75-15412
International Standard Book Number: 0-8048-1165-2

First Tuttle edition, 1975

Printed and bound in Great Britain

TO MY WIFE

Preface

THE FIRST EDITION OF THIS WORK WAS PUBLISHED BY OXFORD University Press in 1944. In 1950 a second, enlarged, and revised edition was published by Liverpool University Press under the title *A History of the Isle of Man*, with the help of a grant from the Trustees of the Manx Museum, funds having been made available for this purpose by Tynwald.

These earlier editions of Robert Kinvig's work did much to make the history, geography, and cultural richness of the Island far better known throughout the British Isles and the English-speaking world. In them the author revealed his strongly held belief in the value of detailed area studies and in the relationship between geography and culture. These convictions sustained his lifelong interest in the Island of his forebears and of his wife.

He was born in Liverpool and graduated there after reading modern history. Three years later he was awarded a Ph.D. degree for his studies of the historical geography of the West Country woollen industry. In 1919 he was appointed by Professor P. M. Roxby as a lecturer in the Department of Geography in the University of Liverpool, and in 1924 he was appointed Reader in Geography and Head of Department in the University of Birmingham. In 1948, reflecting the growing status of his subject and the contribution that his department had made both locally and nationally, he was elected to the newly created Chair of Geography, which he held until his retirement ten years later.

Outside his own university he was held in equally high esteem. He was Secretary and, from 1929 to 1932, Recorder of Section E (Geography) of the British Association for the Advancement of Science, and President of the Section in 1953 when, very appropriately, the Annual Meeting was held in Liverpool. He was President of the Institute of British Geographers in 1957 and was a keen supporter of the activities of the Geographical Association, particularly of its Birmingham Branch. He was a Fellow of the Society of Antiquaries and in 1967 the Royal Geographical Society elected him an Honorary Fellow.

Robert Kinvig's interests took him to many parts of the world including North and South America, India, and South Africa, but he always had a special concern for studies in his own part of Britain, the West Midlands. He made some notable contributions to the geographical literature of that area and he encouraged many research students to work there. At the same time he maintained his lifelong involvement with the Isle of Man. In 1952, he visited the United States as a Smith-Mundt Fellow and Fulbright scholar and pursued his interest in the Island by making a special survey of Manx settlement in North America. His Presidential Address to the Institute of British Geographers in 1958, entitled *The Isle of Man and Atlantic Britain: A Study in Historical Geography*, showed his continuing interest in the geography of the Island, and he was also for many years President of the Birmingham Manx Society.

Following his retirement, the author was asked to prepare a third edition of this book. He agreed to do so, and was concerned that it should take into account the many changes that had taken place on the Island, ranging from archaeological discoveries to modern developments in commercial life and changes in social structure. It has saddened his friends that Robert Kinvig died before this work of revision could be completed to his satisfaction, and I am sure that he would have appreciated the care with which Mrs. Alison Quinn has compiled the index and the continuing concern of Mr. J. G. O'Kane and Mr. M. V. Holland, of Liverpool University Press, that the book should appear in the form in which the author would have wished.

All who knew him, as a colleague or a friend, are glad that this work, in its new format, will introduce another generation of readers to the life and history of a unique Island community, and will serve as a lasting memorial to the attainments and the affections of an outstanding son and scholar of the Isle of Man.

ROBERT W. STEEL

John Rankin Professor of Geography,
University of Liverpool, 1957–74

Contents

Illustrations

Frontispiece: Map of the Isle of Man, showing some principal physical features

Acknowledgements

THE AUTHOR AND PUBLISHERS ARE GRATEFUL TO THE MANY people who have helped in the preparation of this work for publication. Mr. P. S. Gelling and Dr. R. L. Thomson devoted a considerable amount of time to reading the earlier chapters and offered much useful advice. Professor D. M. Wilson kindly loaned a number of drawings and photographs.

Among all those on the Isle of Man who have helped with this revised edition, special thanks for their enthusiasm are due to Mr. J. R. Bruce, of Port Erin, and to Mr. J. A. Quilleash, of the Treasury, and Mr. J. Tulip, the former Government Statistician, who both helped expand the chapters devoted to modern developments on the Island. Many other former and present Government officers helped the author with detailed advice, particularly Mr. T. E. Kermeen, the Clerk of Tynwald.

In the Manx Museum, the source of many of the photographs reproduced in this book, the Director, Mr. A. M. Cubbon, and the Librarian, Miss A. R. Harrison, have been unfailingly helpful and generous with their time.

Many institutions and individuals have supplied illustrative material, given permission for its use, or otherwise assisted in bringing together the photographs and drawings used in this work. Plates 1, 2, 21, 22, and 29 were specially photographed for the publishers by Manx Technical Publications. Plates 47, 52, 55, and 56 are reproduced by permission of Manx Press Pictures. Plate 12 was kindly supplied by the Viking Ship Museum, Roskilde, Denmark, and Plate 13 by Universitetets Oldsaksamling, Oslo. Plates 39 and 41, showing coins and notes from the collection of Mr. Ernest Quarmby, were specially photographed for this edition. Plates 51 and 54 were selected from Mr. A. Earnshaw's collection of mining photographs. All other illustrations are reproduced by courtesy of the Trustees of the Manx Museum.

CHAPTER ONE

The Physical and Human Background

PLACED AS IT IS IN THE MIDDLE OF THE IRISH SEA, THE ISLE of Man has received many influences from neighbouring lands—England, Scotland, Ireland, and Wales—from all of which it is often clearly visible. At the present day, English influence is the most important, as it has been for many centuries, but in some of the earlier periods of Manx history, Ireland, particularly Northern Ireland, has played a very significant part, while south-west Scotland, which is nearest of all to the Island, has also been extremely important at various times.

The Irish Sea opens southward through St. George's Channel and beyond Land's End to the shores of western France, Spain, and Portugal; and there is no doubt that in prehistoric times traders from the Mediterranean followed this route and brought ideas from that distant region to the Isle of Man as well as to the other lands surrounding it. There is another open sea passage through the North Channel to the Western Isles of Scotland, and on round the north of that country to Scandinavia; by this route from the end of the eighth and the following centuries came the Norse Vikings to conquer Man and to settle in it.

Many varied streams have therefore entered into the main current of Manx life, and the characteristics of that life have tended to vary in consequence. The details will be examined in the following chapters of this book; in the present chapter it will be helpful to think a little further not only about the general position of the Island in relation to the British Isles, but also about some important features concerning the nature of the land and its people in the past and at the present.

Most people are familiar with the geographical division of Great Britain into two broadly contrasted zones, a north-western and a south-eastern, by a diagonal line drawn from the mouth of the Tees to the lower Exe. The first of these, which would include the whole of the Isle of Man, constitutes the so-called 'highland' zone since it contains much land of considerable elevation, reaching 1,000 ft. and over, while the south-eastern section is 'lowland', or 'continental Britain', where the relief is much more gentle and the hills, such as the chalk downs, are generally smooth and low. This distinction has some significance since it brings out certain differences in the physical and human characteristics of the two zones. At the same time such a broad division has many short-comings, and it can indeed be very misleading, especially in the case of the Isle of Man which has to be included entirely within the highland zone although obviously the Island also has some true lowland areas, for example those in the south as well as in the north where the soils are quite deep and fertile, very different from those in the uplands. More-over, there is the almost inevitable implication that this north-western or 'highland' zone now associated with the 'Celtic fringe' has always been a relatively backward and more old-fashioned section culturally and economically, as contrasted with south-eastern or lowland Britain which is in more direct contact with the main streams of European life.

Although there may be some justification for such a belief in more modern times, there have been periods when life was more vigorous in the west and culture more advanced there than in the south-eastern zone. Such a period was that known as the Neolithic, during the third millennium before Christ, when trade was very active throughout the Irish Sea and along the western seaboard generally. Again, during the Age of the Celtic Saints from the fourth to the eighth centuries A.D., it was the Celtic west that shone forth as a great centre of learning and of the arts while the lowland zone of Britain during much of this period was being occupied by the Anglo-Saxons, who were still barbarians.

There is need, therefore, for a closer examination of this 'highland' division, and certainly a better understanding of both our history and our geography can be attained if it is divided into two parts: an Atlantic zone, comprising the lowlands and also the low plateaux, up to about 650 ft. fringing the coastline; and a Moorland zone backing the littoral belt, comprising all the land above about 650 ft., much of it being over 1,000 ft. It is this which is the real highland area in its physical and human qualities. Conditions vary throughout the long stretch of western Britain, but in the Isle of Man the contrast is well marked, and it provides good illustrations of the varying reactions within the two environments. Thus Cregneash in the south of the Island is an excellent example of a moorland village, or rather *clachan*, which formed one of the last strongholds of old Manx country life and traditions, where Old Christmas (5 January) was kept up to the beginning of this century because the people thought it to be the 'right Christmas' despite the eighteenth-century reform of the calendar. In contrast, the coastal belt resembles in certain respects the lowland sections of England rather than the highland zone.

Historically, far from being the isolated, passive area waiting to absorb the more backward or traditional elements, this Atlantic belt has at times been in a very real sense a primary 'receiving' zone of cultures rather than a 'preserving' zone, which was the function of the moorland area. On the other hand, the whole Island has experienced periods of relative isolation and backwardness, as during the later phases of the Bronze Age (about 650 B.C. and succeeding centuries) when a deterioration in climate is believed to have occurred, or during parts of the Stanley regime, from the early fifteenth to early eighteenth century, when official policy tended to isolate the Island in cultural and economic affairs from other parts of the British Isles.

It is thus not surprising that many old ideas and customs have survived into modern times, one such practice being the long-continued use of white quartz stones. These had some mystical or religious significance far back in pagan times since they were used in the burial monuments of megalithic peoples. They continued to be used in Christian times, being found, for instance, in the portion of the floor underneath the altar in one of the old 'keeills' (or early chapels) in Maughold churchyard. Later, white stones came to be associated with various superstitions and charms so that their use persisted. They are, indeed, still widely used in the Island as decorations on walls, as may be noted in many parts. Another example of a different kind is provided by the Tynwald ceremony held annually on 5 July. At one time it was believed that this ceremony was introduced solely by the Scandinavian conquerors of the Island; but although the actual name is Norwegian and some of the observances may owe their origin to the Norse, there can be no doubt whatever that the idea of an annual midsummer assembly at St. John's goes back to a very early period and that this tradition has been maintained by the Manx people right up to the present day.

GENERAL PHYSICAL PLAN

The map of the Island's topographical features shows that its central
mass consists of a moorland plateau over 750 ft. in height above which
rise a number of peaks, most being over 1,500 ft. The dominant line of
such peaks extends from north-east to south-west, beginning in North
Barrule, then through Snaefell (2,034 ft.), the highest of them all, on
through Beinn y Phott, Garraghan, Colden, and Greeba, whence the
line is continued on the other side of the central valley between Peel and
Douglas, in South Barrule, and Cronk ny Arrey Laa to terminate in
Bradda Hill. This main axis is of great importance because it divides
Man into what were originally two distinct portions, the 'Northside'
and the 'Southside' (strictly north-east and south-west), whose significance will be discussed later. The boundary between these divisions can
be traced by the main line of water-parting which is closely related to this
belt of uplands, though it does not usually follow the peaks themselves.

On the eastern and western sides of the central uplands the land
usually takes the form of a lower plateau ranging in height between
about 300 ft. and 600 ft. The best example is the belt running south from
Maughold through Lonan and Onchan into Santan, although throughout this stretch the level is broken and glens are formed where the
larger rivers cut across to the sea. Further south-westward this plateau
is separated from the coast by the southern lowland, but it can be
distinguished in areas surrounding Ronague in Arbory and the adjoining stretches in the parish of Rushen. On the western side of the
Island a somewhat similar, if smaller, coastal plateau extends south-
wards from Kirk Michael, being continued south of the River Neb in
the coastal belt of Kirk Patrick.

Cutting right across the upland mass is the central valley between
Douglas and Peel, which is followed by both a railway and a main road
despite the narrowness in the middle, particularly near Greeba. Nowadays this valley is often regarded as the line separating 'North' from
'South', but in earlier days it was not so important, partly on account of
its narrow character and partly because its floor was, and still is in part,
swampy. Trackways from east to west formerly tended to keep to the
higher ground outside the valley. On the other hand, at St. John's,
where the valley is opening out towards Peel, is situated the most
obvious meeting-place in the whole Island, since routes from all direc-
tions—from the south via the Foxdale river, from the north via Glen

Helen, as well as from east and west—converge at this point. From very early times, therefore, this has been the scene of a national assembly, and the spot has acquired a sanctity which has persisted to the present day.

The Island contains two principal lowland areas: (1) that extending north of a line between Ballaugh and Ramsey to the Point of Ayre, and (2) the smaller one surrounding Castletown in the south-east. The northern lowland is by no means uniform since it includes a low range of hills reaching over 300 ft. extending roughly east–west through Bride. The southern section of this lowland, where it borders on the main upland mass, forms the Curragh, and there were formerly a number of shallow meres extending from Ballaugh to Ramsey. These have now been largely drained, chiefly by means of the Sulby and Killane rivers and the Lhen trench, but they are still liable to flooding in the winter. Formerly, also, the Castletown lowland contained some stretches of water surrounding the Silverburn and in the Great Meadow, but these have also been drained.

Chief rock formations

Three-quarters of the Island's area consists of hard slates and grits belonging to a very early period in the earth's history known as the Primary. These are the rocks that form not only the mountain mass but also the coastal plateaux, the only exceptions being the rather small but interesting areas made of igneous rocks, chiefly granite, including the Granite (or Stoney) Mountain, near Foxdale, and the quarries at the Dhoon and Oatland. The grits and slates must have been originally horizontal, but owing to frequent earth movements since they were made the beds have been twisted into various forms, as may be seen in many quarries and particularly around the headlands which provide such glorious coastal scenery, a good example of which is the Marine Drive between Douglas and Keristal.

In the Castletown lowland, on the other hand, the underlying rocks consist of beds of shale and limestone, which may be seen along the coast at Scarlett as well as in the Billown quarries. This rock has not only provided lime, so necessary for agricultural purposes, but has proved to be a valuable building stone, as may be observed in many of the houses as well as in the famous Castle Rushen. On the other side of the Island surrounding Peel the local rock is a red sandstone which was also much used at one time for building houses and hedges, giving this district an aspect quite different from that in other parts.

The glacial period

Rocks similar to the Castletown limestone and the Peel sandstone, both
of which belong to roughly the same period in the earth's history, are
known to exist below the northern lowland but they are covered by
thick deposits of up to 150 ft. or more of glacial drift, consisting of soft
clays, sands, and gravels. These materials are significant almost everywhere in the Island and they owe their origin to the great glacial period
which occurred only fairly recently in relation to the long history of
the earth. Yet it ended about 20,000 years ago after having lasted
for many thousands of years. The glacial period was certainly not a
continuously cold one; indeed, three successive glaciations are now
believed to have affected the Island, during the earliest of which the ice
entirely covered the upper slopes of the Manx mountains and produced
the rock scratches, or striae, still in evidence. Then came an interglacial
(and much milder) spell to be followed by another general glaciation
when the ice rose to about 1,300 ft. on the hills. The latter resulted in
the thick smooth blanket of drift which swathes the intermediate and
lower slopes of the hills, generally below 1,000 ft. It may also have
caused the steepening of the valley sides of certain streams as, for example, in Laxey Glen, where the existing river flows as a misfit stream
at the bottom of a broad rounded valley, although this feature may
date from the first glaciation. It was during the gradual retreat of these
conditions produced by the second glaciation that a re-advance of the
ice-front from Scotland brought about a third glaciation which affected
only the lowland areas of Man.

    The ice-sheets came essentially from south-west Scotland and north-
east Ireland, and boulders from each of these areas, as well as from the
Cumbrian region of England, have been found in drift from outside the
Island. Northern Ireland and the floor of the Irish Sea are of special
significance as the sources of the flint carried in the chalk from those
areas to the coastal deposits north of Kirk Michael which were used by
early man to be chipped into arrowheads, knives, chisels, and so on.
Apart from the northern lowland much of the drift is from sources
within the Island, and a very good example of this is provided by the
masses of granite from the Foxdale Granite or Stoney Mountain which
can be traced right down to the Sound, and which have been used,
when available, in buildings and hedges throughout the southern part
of Man. Many of the soils on which agriculture depends, both on the

plateaux and in the lowlands, are the result of the glacial epoch. Above about 600 ft. there is barely any soil, but below this there is usually a covering of glacial drift mainly derived from the local slates, which, although stony, produces some fair crops. In the more fertile lowlands the deposits are usually deeper, and of a finer and more mixed nature. Conditions vary, of course, especially in the northern lowland where some of the sandy patches are very light and other, clayey, patches very heavy. An interesting feature of this lowland is the lack of suitable building stone owing to the absence of solid rocks, so that much use has been made of glacial boulders for building houses and walls—such boulders, often well smoothed and rounded, usually being obtained from the shore where they are very plentiful. Much of the stone in Bride Church consists of granite boulders carried by ice from southern Scotland. Bricks made from local boulder clay at Ballacorey, Andreas, are also frequently seen in the older buildings of the area.

An interesting aspect of the ending of the glacial period is the appearance of the Irish elk or great deer (*Cervus giganteus*) whose remains have been found in many localities including St. John's, from which came the magnificent specimen, with a spread of antlers extending to about 9 ft., now exhibited in the Manx Museum. This must have been one of the earliest immigrants into the area after the retreat of the ice when it was covered with subarctic grassland with some birch woods; no doubt the animals reached Man before it became an actual island by the land bridge which linked it with north-western England. Clearly it was an animal which frequented open ground rather than forest since the spread of its gigantic antlers would be a serious encumbrance amongst trees. It appears to have died out here more than 8,000 years ago when very cold conditions temporarily returned. Another animal which came at an early date was the Manx pony, a member of the Celtic pony group whose ancestors came from north-western Europe into Britain after the last glaciation. They were very tough and hardy animals favouring a cold climate, and those that reached Man via the land bridge from Cumberland became separated from other groups after the severing of these land links so that a distinctive breed of Manx pony came to be established. These animals were later domesticated and they survived until the beginning of last century when, owing to changing economic conditions favouring the use of larger animals, the small Manx pony was allowed to die out.

Finally, in the extreme north of the Island occurs a barren strip of shingle, known as the Ayre, having a width of nearly one and a half miles at its widest in the east but tapering westwards to 50 yards or less. It forms a raised beach now standing 10 or 12 ft. above high-water mark while formerly it lay below it, and it indicates an uplift in the level of the land since the glacial period. Evidence of a similar movement also occurs in the neighbouring regions of Scotland, Ireland, and England, and the uplift seems to have occurred during the early history of man in the Island.

PERIODS OF HUMAN HISTORY

There are two principal divisions in the story of human development, the *prehistoric* and the *historic*, the difference between them being that in the case of the latter the evidence is based primarily on written documents, whereas in the prehistoric period such written material did not exist. Knowledge of that age is obtained from relics left by man in the shape of domestic utensils, particularly pottery, ornaments, weapons, buildings, and monuments of various kinds often associated with the burial of the dead. At the present much valuable information concerning those far-off days is being revealed by careful excavations, but it must be pointed out that there are many gaps in our knowledge and many problems still waiting to be solved.

In Britain it is customary to regard the coming of the Romans in 55 B.C. as the dividing-line between prehistoric and historic times, since it is with Caesar that there is a definite beginning of written accounts. But much of our knowledge of the Roman period itself and even of the succeeding Anglo-Saxon period is obtained not from written documents but from archaeological evidence. As regards the Isle of Man this date cannot be adopted since there is no proof that the Romans settled in the Island, although they undoubtedly knew of its existence, referring to it under various names including Mona (Caesar, 54 B.C.), Monapia (Pliny, A.D. 77), and Mevania (Orosius, A.D. 416). The same is true of Ireland, where the historic period may be said to begin about the middle of the fifth century A.D., or the period which marks the great extension of Christianity in that country as a result of the work of St. Patrick. This same date may be adopted for the Isle of Man, since there is no doubt that it was deeply influenced by the same religious and cultural movements.

Thus the Island had a long prehistoric age beginning some thousands of years before Christ and extending up to about A.D. 450. From that date until about A.D. 800 there was what may be called the Early Christian period or the Age of the Celtic Saints. Then followed the Scandinavian period when Man was conquered and colonized by the Vikings or Norsemen. This was a very important phase in the Island's history, despite the fact that it began with plundering and destruction and a partial return to paganism, since it brought a very virile people who proved to be good organizers and administrators. The Scandinavian period ended in 1266, three years after the defeat of the Norwegians by the Scots under King Alexander III. Then came a very confused and troubled time during which the Island was alternately under Scottish and English rule, until finally in 1405 it came into the hands of the Stanley family (later known as the Earls of Derby), who, with their connections the Dukes of Atholl, ruled it until the eighteenth century. Since 1765 the Island has had no independent ruler, but has come directly under the British Crown while still retaining its ancient constitution and the right (perhaps, at times, more nominal than real) to make its own laws.

ADMINISTRATIVE DIVISIONS

The Island is divided for the purposes of government into sheadings and parishes, there being six sheadings, all except one containing three parishes each. On the west, from south to north, there are the sheadings of Glenfaba, containing the parishes of Kirk Patrick, Kirk German, and Kirk Marown; Michael, with the parishes of Kirk Michael, Ballaugh, and Jurby; and Ayre, with the parishes of Kirk Bride, Kirk Andreas, and Kirk Christ Lezayre. On the eastern side, from north to south, there are the sheadings of Garff, now containing only two parishes, Kirk Maughold and Kirk Lonan; Middle, with the parishes of Kirk Onchan, Kirk Braddan, and Kirk Santan; and Rushen, with the parishes of Kirk Malew, Kirk Arbory, and Kirk Christ Rushen.[1] Before 1796 the parish of Marown was included in the sheading of Middle, while Onchan was part of Garff. It is thus evident that the original boundary between the sheadings of the 'North'—Glenfaba, Michael, and Ayre—and those of the 'South'—Garff, Middle, and Rushen—was

1. Here the full name of each of the ancient parishes is given, but elsewhere the prefix Kirk will be omitted. Onchan was formerly Conchan (after the saint of that name) but the latter form has become archaic. The name Arbory (after St. Cairbre) originally also had an initial C, but this disappeared long ago.

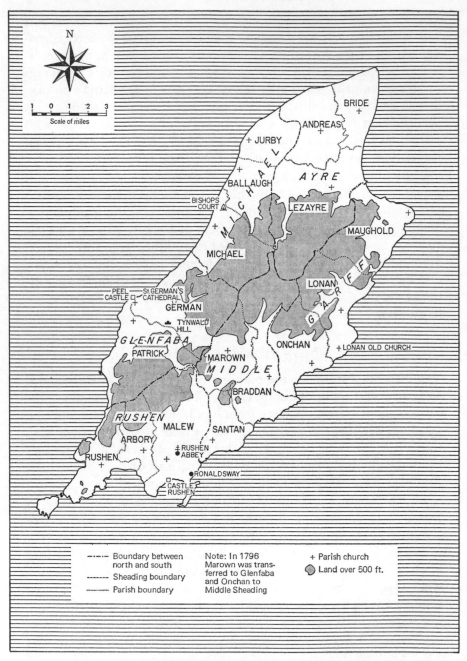

N

1 0 1 2 3
Scale of miles

BRIDE +

ANDREAS +

+ JURBY

A Y R E

BALLAUGH +

BISHOPS
COURT △

LEZAYRE +

M I C H A E L

MAUGHOLD +

MICHAEL +

PEEL ⊡ St.GERMAN'S
CASTLE CATHEDRAL

LONAN +

GERMAN +

TYNWALD
HILL

G A R F F

G L E N F A B A

ONCHAN +

+ LONAN OLD CHURCH

PATRICK +

MAROWN +

M I D D L E

BRADDAN +

R U S H E N

MALEW

SANTAN +

ARBORY +

RUSHEN +

‡ RUSHEN
● ABBEY

● RONALDSWAY

⊡ CASTLE
RUSHEN

—·—·— Boundary between
north and south

-------- Sheading boundary

———— Parish boundary

Note: In 1796
Marown was trans-
ferred to Glenfaba
and Onchan to
Middle Sheading

+ Parish church

◗ Land over 500 ft.

1. Administrative divisions before 1796.

the line of water-parting following the main upland belt.[1] This division existed not only on the map but in the minds of the people, and there were many points of difference between the 'Northside' and the 'Southside' dialects and customs. At present, with our quick and easy transport, it is difficult to realize what a distance it seemed from one side of the mountains to the other; but in early days the north and the south were like independent countries and they were occasionally in conflict, as recorded, for example, in the year 1098. This feeling of separateness and remoteness is well expressed in one of T. E. Brown's verses in which he muses about *Braddan Vicarage*:

> I wonder if the hills are long and lonely
> That North from South divide;
> I wonder if he thinks that it is only
> The hither slope where men abide,
> Unto all mortal homes refused the other side.

Each region had its own capital, its own chief, and various officers connected with laws, defence, and so forth. Where the original capitals were it is difficult to say—probably there have been various places— but in the end Castletown came to be the chief place in the south and Peel in the north; when the Island was really united in one kingdom Castletown came to be the only capital until it was displaced by Douglas in 1869. One interesting survival of these two primary divisions is the fact that there are still two deemsters, or judges. Each division had its chief man-of-law who has been known by different names at different periods. In pre-Norse times he was called the *Briw*,[2] which was the name always used in Manx, but the Norse called him *Lagman* (or *Lawman*), and then the English introduced the term *Deemster*, the name which has continued until the present day. Until 1918 there was a Northern Deemster and a Southern Deemster, but since that date these officials have been known as the First Deemster and the Second Deemster respectively.

The modifications in the administrative divisions introduced in 1796 had the effect of blurring the original significance of the terms north

1. See, for example, *The Manorial Roll of the Isle of Man, 1511–1515*, translated by the Revd. T. Talbot (Oxford University Press, 1924). This valuable document illustrates, amongst other things, the ancient division of the Island into north and south, and gives the names of sheadings and parishes, with lists of treens, and names of property owners, in the early sixteenth century.

2. See p. 74, n. 1.

and south since it was decreed that for legal purposes the northern district should include Michael, Ayre, and Garff sheadings while the southern district should include Glenfaba, Middle, and Rushen sheadings. These divisions still hold good for the Common Law Courts, except that for some purposes Glenfaba is included within the northern district.

On the other hand, the Petty Sessions and the High Bailiff's districts are more modern and are based on the four towns and the parishes adjoining them. Hence with the borough of Douglas are included the parishes of Onchan, Braddan, Lonan, and Marown. With the town of Ramsey are included the parishes of Maughold, Bride, Andreas, Jurby, and Lezayre; while with Peel go the parishes of Patrick, German, Michael, and Ballaugh. Lastly, with the town of Castletown go the parishes of Malew, Santan, Arbory, and Rushen. These divisions also serve as districts for the Licensing Acts, and under the names of the Eastern, Northern, Western, and Southern divisions they are often used at the present day for a variety of purposes. Individual Boards of Tynwald, e.g. the Highway and Transport Board and the Electricity and Water Boards, adopt other divisions which are more suited to their own particular needs.

Sheadings and parishes

Nowadays the sheadings form electoral districts for the return of sixteen out of the twenty-four members of the House of Keys. The meaning of the word sheading and the period when such divisions came into being have been much disputed. Some writers argue that the word means a 'sixth part', and that it may be either Celtic or Norse. Others have urged that it means a 'ship-division', and that it was introduced by the Norse with the intention that each such district should provide a certain number of ships or war galleys (called *skeid* in Norwegian) for the service of the king. A more recent view is that the word sheading was derived from a Middle English word, *scheding*, meaning 'a division', and that it was introduced by Sir John Stanley when he became king of Man in the early fifteenth century.[1]

1. This last interpretation is accepted by the *Oxford English Dictionary* and would be a regular derivative of *shed* in the now dialectal sense of 'divide, part (the hair)' and which survives in *watershed*, but there appears to be no positive Middle English evidence for the use of the word in the sense of 'division'. On the whole it is more likely to be a Manx technical term, like *treen*, taken over into English, and to be of Norse origin. There is reason to doubt whether either *skip-* or *skeid-* compounds would produce a Manx form with *sh-* rather than *sk-*, and Norse *séttung(r)* 'a sixth part' seems to fit the phonology best. See also W. Cubbon, *Island Heritage*, p. 28.

Whatever the precise origin of the word, there is reason to believe that the divisions now called sheadings originally corresponded to the chief tribal units of the Island. Each had its principal meeting-place, something like a local Tynwald. During the Norse period these areas came to be better organized, and their boundaries more precisely defined, very much as they have persisted to modern times. It is quite likely also that the Norse introduced their custom of making each of the divisions provide one or more ships towards the defence of the Island. But the earlier functions of the sheading also continued, and these persisted long after the Scandinavian period, since each had its own Sheading Court which settled questions concerning revenues and land tenures, while it also had power to deal with private disputes. Sheading Courts are no longer held, but all cases formerly dealt with in them are heard at sittings of the Courts of Common Law held regularly for the three Northside and the three Southside sheadings.

The divisions known as parishes were for long the basis of the military and civil organization, as well as the religious life in the Island. Nowadays they are linked mainly with ecclesiastical and civil matters, but at first their function was probably more of a military character. Although precise proof is lacking, there is every likelihood that originally there were sixteen parishes—not seventeen as at present—each having a frontage on the seaboard, and there is good evidence for the belief that Santan and Marown were one. The centre of each parish was the church, and we find that almost every parish in the Island has the prefix Kirk, derived from the Norse word *kirkja* meaning church.[1] When the parishes were created there were quite a number of *keeills* or chapels in each division, and the one selected to serve as the parish church was apparently that which occupied the most convenient site at the time. Occasionally the choice was for reasons not quite so obvious, such as a tradition of special sanctity. This has sometimes meant that the parish church is now rather inconveniently situated for the parish as a whole, as in the cases of Maughold and Santan; but in other examples the church is placed more centrally, as in Rushen or Andreas.

Treens and quarterlands

The divisions known as treens have given rise to a great deal of discussion, and all the problems connected with them have not yet been

---

1. To the English *kirk* here corresponds Manx *skeeyley* or *skeerey*, the latter found also in Gaelic Scotland as *sgire* 'parish', while the former is possibly a blend of *skeerey* and *keeill*.

solved. The treens were fairly small units of land, usually varying in size from about 200 to 400 acres. In earlier days they formed quite important administrative divisions, especially for the fixing of land taxes, but nowadays these units hardly exist. It has been generally assumed that the word is of Celtic origin and that it has reference to the figure 'three'. But if it meant a third part of some bigger unit, nobody has ever discovered what the bigger unit was; on the other hand, the treen was not normally divided into thirds but into fourths, and in fact the name quarterland (or *kerroo* in Manx) is still used for these subdivisions of the old treens. A more recent and very probable view is that it had a similar origin to the Irish word *tirunga* ('ounceland'), used in the Hebrides for a land unit which the Norse in the Orkneys called *urisland*. Whatever the actual origin of the term, there is every likelihood that these units have had a very long history, and that they initially represented the areas of cultivated land which were occupied and developed for agricultural and pastoral purposes by individual families or tribes in very early days. Naturally the heads of such estates would be very influential men, and it is probable that they were the original freeholders who claimed the privilege of choosing the members of the House of Keys in early times. Another interesting point relating to the former importance of the treen is that, in the early days of Christianity in the Island, it appears to have been customary to build a small chapel (or *keeill*) on each of these units, which was maintained by the owner of the estate. Moreover, during Norse times, it is believed that each treen had the duty imposed upon it of supplying four fully equipped men, one from each of the quarterlands, to serve in the war-galleys.

THE HUMAN BACKGROUND

It is obvious that the Manx population today is by no means uniform from the racial, that is to say the physical, point of view, and the degree of mixture has been increased by the immigration that has taken place during the last ten or twenty years. It is thus quite wrong to speak of a Manx 'race'; and it might, perhaps, be as well to point out in this connection that it is also quite incorrect to speak of a Celtic race since the term Celtic has reference to language and culture, and not to physical characteristics.

Some of the Manx are very fair, others are very dark, the latter usually being shorter in stature than the former. Moreover, certain districts tend, or rather tended, to have more people of one type than of another, the northern parishes of Andreas, Bride, and Jurby having a majority of fair-haired people, while Onchan, Braddan, and Santan have a higher percentage of darker folk. These and other facts emerged from a survey made some thirty years ago, during which measurements were taken of about 1,200 men whose four grandparents belonged to the Island by descent, and whose family names were known in the Island before 1800. According to these data the two more important race types found are the Mediterranean and the Nordic. People belonging to the first type have dark brown or black hair, brown eyes, and a long narrow head, and are of medium stature. It is very probable that these first came to Britain before 2000 B.C. during the Neolithic period from the western Mediterranean area via France, and although originally fairly widespread throughout the British Isles they are now chiefly found in the western fringes, including Ireland, Wales, Cornwall, and the Isle of Man. In the Island itself these 'little dark people', as they are often called, are found everywhere, but they are most numerous in Onchan, Braddan, and Santan, while they occur as frequently as fair people in Rushen and Patrick. The Nordic type, distinguished by its fair hair, light eyes (usually blue), taller stature, long narrow head, long face, and long narrow nose, came to the Island later, and its presence is associated particularly with the Viking settlers. People of this type are most frequent in the north, notably in Bride, Andreas, and Jurby, as well as in the southern parish of Malew. It is significant that these parishes contain the largest areas of fertile lowland, and it seems clear that the Norwegians deliberately chose these richer districts for their own settlements.

Naturally much intermixture has taken place in the course of time, and now many Manx people have blended characteristics, such as dark hair and light eyes, so that it is impossible to describe them as pure Nordics or pure Mediterraneans.

It is believed that the Island also contains some representatives of two other interesting types. One is distinguished by its tall stature, spare build, dark colouring, with a long and often very narrow head and face. It is sometimes referred to as the Plynlimmon type from the fact that it is usually found in the higher moorland areas of Wales and west Scotland; and the evidence seems to suggest that the type is very old, going back possibly to an early movement at the end of the Old Stone Age. The other type is broad-headed and dark, and strongly built.

Men with these characteristics are found in certain coastal districts in Wales and along the western fringe of Britain generally. Some writers have suggested that these people came as traders or prospectors from the eastern Mediterranean to Britain, perhaps during the early Bronze Age.

There is one race type usually known as the Beaker, found fairly frequently in eastern Britain but apparently very rare in the Isle of Man. Beaker people are fair and tall but broad-headed, with strong brows and powerful faces, and entering Britain from central Europe during the early Bronze Age, they brought with them the particular form of pottery known as beakers or drinking cups. Finds of these vessels in early burial mounds become less and less in going westwards from the eastern half of England and Scotland, and the fact that only one beaker has been found so far in the Isle of Man goes to prove that the Island was not affected directly by either this culture or the distinctive physical type initially associated with it.

THE MANX LANGUAGE

The language which was formerly widespread in the Island but which has decayed so rapidly during the last hundred years that it threatens to become extinct,[1] is a branch of the Celtic group of languages, one of the oldest of the great Indo-European family. This also includes the Germanic, Slavonic, and Romance languages of Europe, as well as the languages of northern India.

Prior to the Anglo-Saxon invasions, Celtic in one form or another was the dominant language throughout the British Isles. Since then it has receded steadily westwards until now it survives only in the highlands and islands of Scotland, Ireland, Wales, and the Isle of Man. Within this Celtic area there are two forms of the language distinguished as *Goidelic* (or *q*-Celtic) comprising Manx, Irish, and Scottish Gaelic, and *Brythonic* (or *p*-Celtic) including Welsh, the extinct Cornish, and Breton, the existing Celtic tongue of Brittany. It has generally been considered that Goidelic is the older form which came from central Europe probably during the later Bronze Age; but as against the earlier view that this language entered via eastern England to be pushed westwards later on by Brythonic Celtic, it is now thought more likely that the Goidelic form bypassed Britain to go to Ireland direct by sea-

1. The number of Manx speakers according to the 1961 Census was only 160.

routes from western France. From Ireland it then spread to the Isle of Man and western Scotland at the end of the fifth century A.D.[1] On the other hand, there seems no doubt that the Brythonic speakers entered south-east England from the Continent in pre-Roman days and that this speech form spread over the greater part of Britain. Later on it was pressed westwards as a result of the Anglo-Saxon invasions from the fifth century A.D. onwards.

The differentiation into the Goidelic and Brythonic forms of Celtic resulted from certain sound-changes which had possibly taken place in their continental home, and the effects of these changes are significantly expressed in the use of the alternative terms of q- and p-Celtic. Thus, whereas in Manx the word for five is *queig*, in Welsh (which is p-Celtic) the word is *pump*. The same kind of difference is visible in many of the characteristic surnames, several of which in Manx begin with a Q, or hard C or K, and this initial letter is frequently an abbreviation of the original *mac* meaning 'son of'. Thus the well-known surname Quilliam (the Manx form of Williamson) was originally MacWilliam, and in the Isle of Man the *Mac* was abbreviated at a relatively early date, although in Ireland and Scotland it has often persisted down to the present date (as, for example, in names like Macalister and Maclean). In Welsh, on the other hand, where *mab* corresponds to Manx *mac*, names of this type, also with loss of the first syllable, are Bowen for *mab Owain*, and, before a voiceless consonant or *h-*, Powell for *mab Hywel* and Prothero for *mab Rhydderch*.

As will be seen in Chapter 3, there is definite evidence regarding the existence of Gaelic speech in the Island as early as at least the fifth century A.D., while it is also likely that some Brythonic speech was present at the same period, although the latter did not survive. In the tenth and succeeding centuries the Celtic tongue was temporarily subordinated to the Norse language as a result of the Viking conquest, but Gaelic gradually re-established itself and after 1266 it again became the chief speech of the Manx. In view of the events during that period it is not surprising that henceforth the Celtic tongue in Man was more closely related to Scottish than to Irish Gaelic, and a present-day Manx Gaelic speaker is readily able to converse with a Gaelic speaker, say, of the Ardnamurchan area of western Scotland or the Western Isles.

1. According to the views expressed by Dr. Anne Ross, in *Pagan Celtic Britain* (London, 1967), p. 16, q-Celtic is represented only in Ireland, apart from slight traces in Spain and Gaul in place-names and inscriptions.

Nowadays Norse survives in such important terms as Tynwald (see p. 72), but some evidence of its one-time significance is to be found in a number of place-names;[1] even in this sphere, however, Celtic became so fully restored that in existing names the proportion of Norse to Gaelic in the Isle of Man is roughly only 1 to 6 whereas in the island of Lewis it is nearer 4 to 1.

THE NAME OF THE ISLAND

There are still a number of unsolved problems regarding the origin of the name, but on the philological side it is now recognized by leading Celtic scholars that there are a number of ancient island-names in western Britain which in their earliest forms are parallel to Man in declension. Thus Erin (the ancient name for Ireland) comes from *Eriu*, of which the genitive form is *Erenn*, while Arran is from *Aru*, of which the genitive is *Arann*. Similarly the earliest form of Man is *Manu* (or *Mana*) of which the genitive is *Manann*, whence is derived *Mannin* and also the common Manx form of the name, *Ellan Vannin*. In the last-named there is no difficulty concerning *ellan* which is Gaelic for island, while *Vannin* is the mutated form of *Mannin*; but no satisfactory explanation has ever been given of Man itself and it still remains a puzzle. Most likely it is of pre-Celtic origin (as implied by its membership of the group of island-names mentioned above) and it may represent an early tribal name in view of its survival in the names *Clackmannan* and *Slamannan* in central Scotland. These border on the old British territory round Edinburgh and the Firth of Forth known as *Manaw Gododdin*, and in later Welsh *Manaw* is the name for the Isle of Man.

Another name derived from *Manann* is *Mananán*, the mythological character who appears in so many guises, superhuman and otherwise, in Manx folklore (see p. 37). It used to be suggested that he gave his name to the Island, but this is highly improbable, and indeed such an implication should be rejected as an unscientific conjecture, while it is much more likely that he obtained his own name from Man.

At this point it may be recalled that Julius Caesar in his well-known description of Britain after his brief visits in 55 and 54 B.C. refers to 'an

1. A peculiarity of Manx place-names is the way in which anglicized versions of Norse names coexisted with gaelicized versions and modern usage has adopted sometimes one, sometimes the other; for example, the gaelicized *Barrule*, not the anglicized *Wardfell*, but the anglicized *Snaefell* (earlier the even more English *Snowfield*) not *Shniaul*, and *Ronaldsway* not *Runnysvie*.

island called Mona which lies midway across the sea separating Britain from Ireland', and this statement has been the source of controversy ever since. The position so described is certainly that of the Isle of Man, but there is no doubt that the name Mona was applied to the island of Anglesey in Roman times and until the Scandinavian period. It is, for example, significant that on the modern Ordnance Survey map of Roman Britain (3rd edition, 1956), the Latin names finally adopted for the island of Anglesey and Man respectively were *Mona* (Anglesey) and *Monavia* (Man), the latter being a variant of the latinized form (*Monapia*) used by Pliny the Elder in the first century A.D. In this connection it is worthy of note that the native Welsh name for Anglesey is *Môn*, which is not unlike the early name of Man (i.e. *Manu*) and indeed the Irish goddess *Danu* appears in Welsh as *Don* so that the correspondence may even be regular. Caesar, who reports all this at second hand, no doubt refers to Man and his informants may not have been aware that Anglesey was an island if the Welsh habit of referring to the straits as the River Menai is of such antiquity.[1]

In the Icelandic sagas the name of Man is *Mön*, while in the Island itself the first written name-form occurs on the famous tenth-century Gaut cross from Kirk Michael where it is written in Scandinavian runes as *Maun*, both of which imply earlier *Manu*.

1. Another Graeco-Latin name for the Island was *Eubonia*, possibly to be connected with the Irish *Eamhian* (see p. 94, n. 1); this is the term used by Nennius in a Latin context (chap. 8, 'Eubonia, id est Manau'), and the Welsh Annals (anno 684, 'Terrae motus in Eubonia factus est magnus'), and much later by Archdeacon Rutter in the seventeenth century (*Manx Ballads*, p. 198). Bede (*Hist. Eccl.* ii. 5) lumps Man and Anglesey together as *Menauiae insulae*.

CHAPTER TWO

The Prehistory of Man

AS ALREADY SEEN IN THE PREVIOUS CHAPTER, THE STAGE OF human existence called prehistoric is that which has left no ordinary written documents. Evidence of what happened in those days must therefore be gleaned from the actual remains of man himself and of his handiwork in the shape of weapons of stone or metal utensils, ornaments, and monuments of various kinds. Just how long this period lasted it is impossible to say, but, as far as this area is concerned, it began at least 5,000 years before Christ and ended somewhere about the fifth century A.D. Nevertheless, it should be stressed that our knowledge of this period is, in many cases, still very slender, and it may quite well turn out that some suggestions which are put forward here will have to be given up or modified in the light of fresh facts that will be discovered in future years.

The first division is that called the Palaeolithic, or Old Stone Age, when man was dependent on stones of various kinds (including flint) for making his weapons—fashioning them into various forms, e.g. knives, chisels, and scrapers, by patient and often very skilful chipping. People in that age had no knowledge of agriculture, but relied for their food on hunting and collecting, so they could not make permanent settlements but were forced to lead some kind of nomadic life in search of food.

It used to be thought that the Old Stone Age was followed directly by the Neolithic, or New Stone Age, when man acquired a knowledge of agriculture and of the domestication of animals which ultimately enabled him not only to live a more settled or sedentary life, but in addition to develop arts and crafts such as the making of pottery and weaving. It is now known that the Neolithic period was really separated from the Palaeolithic by what is called the Mesolithic, or Middle Stone Age, during which conditions of life did not show any marked advance on those of Palaeolithic times. It is also believed that this Mesolithic Age of north-western Europe was quite a long one, extending from the ninth to the fifth millennium B.C. There were probably neolithic cultures in the British Isles by about 4000 B.C., and the Neolithic Age lasted until about 2300 B.C., when the first metal users began to appear in the country.

The Bronze Age receives its name from the fact that bronze, an alloy of copper and tin, came into general use for the making of tools and weapons. But the use of stone axe-heads and flint knives and arrow-heads still persisted, especially in the poorer or more isolated districts. The Bronze Age saw further developments in agriculture and in pottery, while trade appears to have been quite active during much of this period, and such conditions led to the spread of ideas and to the development of culture.

The last big division of prehistory is called the Early Iron Age, when bronze was gradually superseded by iron as the material for making weapons, although it remained in use for the making of ornaments. The use of iron probably began to spread into south-east Britain in the sixth century B.C., but it is likely that one or two centuries passed before it had much influence in Man. Since the Island had no definite Roman period, the prehistoric division of the Early Iron Age has to be carried on to at least about A.D. 450.

THE STONE AGES

In the Palaeolithic Age climatic conditions must have been very severe, and for long periods the area was covered by vast glaciers and ice-fields which marked the stages of the great Ice Age. Although there is some evidence of early man in southern England at this period, it seems that he did not reach the Island. There is clear proof, on the other hand, that he arrived here during the next stage, that called the Middle or Meso-lithic, which witnessed the spread of forests, first of pine and hazel and later of oak with associated trees, over western Europe as a whole. The first people of whom there is any definite knowledge were primitive food collectors similar to those called Sauveterrians, who lived in England and other parts of western Europe at the same period. Most likely they reached the Island from north-west England well before

5000 B.C., when the land link still existed. In Man evidence of temporary settlements has been found in several coastal sites, such as Glen Wyllin and Cronk Urleigh in Kirk Michael and on Peel Hill and the slopes near Ramsey; while in the south of the Island similar evidence has been found at Port St. Mary, Rhenwyllan, Poyllvaaish, Cass ny Hawin, and Port Grenaugh. These settlements of hunter-fishermen are on light gravelly soils which would not support a dense woodland in Mesolithic times, and probably a family, or a small group of families, settled for a season or so at each of these until they had exhausted the means of getting food. Finds have been made of quite small pieces of flint, called microliths, which have been deliberately chipped, and most likely they were fastened as barbs on wooden spears for use on hunting expeditions.

Later on in the Mesolithic period, or shortly after it, there is proof that another culture reached the Island. Flints of a different kind have been found on many of the sites used by the Sauveterrian folk, and also at places on the hills further inland, such as Kirkill, and on the slopes of Slieau Whallian. A very interesting feature about this culture is that it seems almost certainly to have come from northern Ireland, since the people chipped their flint implements in precisely the same way as folk living along the banks of the River Bann in Ulster. Since there cannot have been any land connection between these two areas at that time, it is evident that people must have been able to travel across this channel in boats. Quite possibly these Bann hunter-fishers continued to live in the Island contemporary with the New Stone Age settlers who began to spread into the Irish Sea region in the fifth millennium B.C.

As time went on more advanced ideas began to reach Man, including knowledge about the cultivation of the land, so as to produce grain, and about the domestication of animals. Also the methods of making pottery and polished stone implements came to be acquired by the people, so that mankind passed gradually into that stage of development which is called Neolithic. How did these new ideas reach the Island? This is not yet known for certain; but it is known that the new knowledge developed first of all in the countries around the eastern Mediterranean and that it spread slowly to north-west Europe. It came partly overland across central Europe and partly by sea through the Mediterranean, thence along the western seaboard of Europe via Iberia and France so as to reach Britain.

There are good reasons for thinking that it was by the latter route that the knowledge of agriculture and the pastoral life reached the Island. Firstly, it has already been seen in the previous chapter that most of the population at that period came from the western Mediterranean region. Moreover, there can be no doubt that sea-trade from the Mediterranean round the coasts of Spain, Portugal, and France and into the Irish Sea was going on during this Neolithic period, as it continued during much of the Bronze Age. Indeed, there is strong evidence that trade-routes which approached the Irish Sea in this way continued on northwards by western and northern Scotland so as to reach Scandinavia and the Baltic.

It might be wondered why travellers from the western Mediterranean to the Baltic region did not prefer to go up the English Channel and via the Straits of Dover into the North Sea. There are various reasons for this, one being that the Straits of Dover may not have existed in their present form, probably being too narrow and dangerous. Moreover, south-eastern England, or the lowland region of Britain as it has been called in Chapter 1, was not quite as suitable for settlement then as it became later on, since much of the clayey land was covered with dense forest or was marshy.

On the other hand, the western part of Britain, including Man, offered certain advantages since many areas were not quite so heavily forested but were rather more open and so more attractive to early man. This Atlantic zone had further advantages which became more obvious in the Bronze Age, because it was nearer greater supplies of copper and tin than the lowland region, the former in Wales, western Scotland, and Ireland, and the latter in Cornwall. In addition, the fact that Ireland possessed supplies of gold, particularly in the Wicklow area, which were prized at quite an early stage, made that country a very great centre of attraction.

The megalithic culture

In the light of the conditions just sketched it is now possible to appreciate the significance of a highly important and interesting group of Manx monuments called 'megalithic' because they are constructed of 'large stones'. Usually they are known by somewhat fanciful names such as the Druid's Circle, Cregneash, or King Orry's Grave near Laxey, or the Giant's Grave at Kew in Kirk German, and these names are apt to hide the true origin of the structures. Unfortunately many of these monuments have been so badly damaged, their stones having

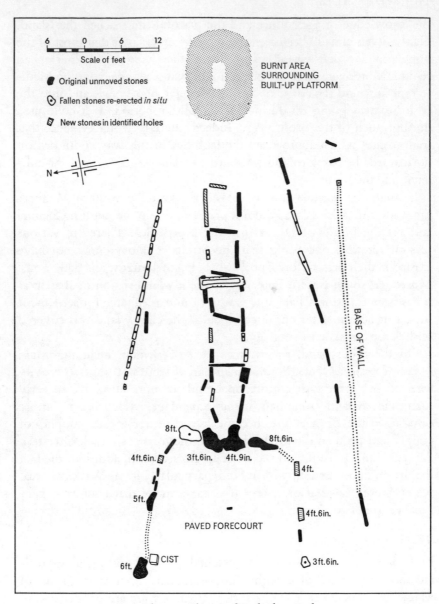

Original unmoved stones

Fallen stones re-erected *in situ*

New stones in identified holes

N

BURNT AREA
SURROUNDING
BUILT-UP PLATFORM

BASE OF WALL

8 ft.

8 ft. 6 in.

4 ft. 6 in.

3 ft. 6 in.

4 ft. 9 in.

4 ft.

5 ft.

4 ft. 6 in.

PAVED FORECOURT

6 ft.

CIST

3 ft. 6 in.

2. The central area of Cashtal yn Ard.

been removed to make hedges or houses, that it is now practically impossible to say what they were like originally. Happily, some have been better preserved and these are now being carefully guarded, while some have been excavated, such as the one known as Cashtal yn Ard, Maughold, so that we have a truer idea of their earliest form.

Most of these megaliths were certainly places for the burial of the dead, the remains being placed inside stone chambers (or cists). Sometimes only one or two such chambers survive, or there may be several of them arranged in some definite scheme, as can be seen at Cashtal yn Ard and the Meayl Circle at Cregneash. There can be no doubt that the original idea of these collective tombs, and of the plans on which they were constructed, came from the Mediterranean, and that knowledge of them was brought along the western trade routes which existed during Neolithic and Bronze Age times. Thus, these monuments can be traced throughout the Atlantic zone of Britain where many of them belong to the later part of the Neolithic Age, although some are earlier, others being constructed during the Bronze Age, while no doubt all of them continued to be used for some time after they were built.

In Man these elaborate stone tombs are limited to areas between about 300 ft. and 650 ft. They are almost entirely absent from the northern lowland, due very likely to the lack of suitable building stone there. On the eastern plateau running through Maughold and Lonan are three significant monuments having certain resemblances to one another, namely (1) Cashtal yn Ard, Ballachrink, Maughold; (2) King Orry's Grave, Gretch Veg, Lonan; and (3) the Cloven Stones, Garwick, Lonan. The first shows the essential features most clearly. It has indeed become a classic of the type, and here the burial chambers are arranged in the form of a long gallery, this gallery being approached from the western end through a crescentic forecourt, which is marked by a series of tall standing stones, and a porthole. Originally, no doubt, the whole structure apart from the forecourt was covered by a bank of earth, so that it would then have had the appearance of a long mound or horned cairn. Megalithic monuments very similar to these gallery graves are to be seen in adjoining countries, particularly north-east Ireland and south-west Scotland, in Galloway and round the lower Clyde, thus indicating that these parts were inhabited by people of the same culture, and possibly ruled by members of the same tribe or group of tribes. King Orry's grave is particularly interesting, as it appears to

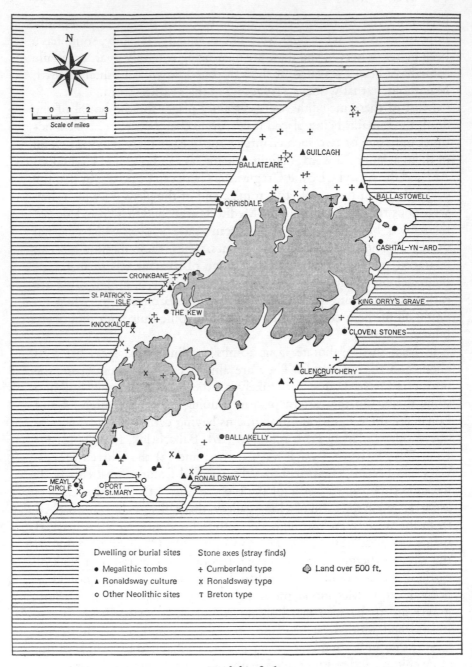

N

1 0   1   2   3
Scale of miles

GUILCAGH
BALLATEARE

BALLASTOWELL

ORRISDALE

CASHTAL–YN–ARD

CRONKBANE

St. PATRICK'S
ISLE

KING ORRY'S GRAVE

THE KEW

KNOCKALOE

CLOVEN STONES

GLENCRUTCHERY

BALLAKELLY

MEAYL
CIRCLE

PORT
St.MARY

RONALDSWAY

Dwelling or burial sites   Stone axes (stray finds)

● Megalithic tombs   + Cumberland type   ⬠ Land over 500 ft.

▲ Ronaldsway culture   x Ronaldsway type

○ Other Neolithic sites   ┬ Breton type

3. Neolithic finds.

belong to the rather rare type which has a forecourt and gallery at each end.

In the extreme south near Cregneash is the Meayl Circle (or the so-called Druid's Circle), which is different in form from any other megaliths on the Island. It has six pairs of chambers arranged in a more or less circular form. Such a plan cannot be exactly matched elsewhere in Britain, so that the monument is most interesting as illustrating the development of a rather new and special type in Man, most probably at a late date in the megalithic period. Another significant feature of this circle is that one of the potsherds from the graves has produced definite evidence of wheat cultivation at the period from a grain incorporated in the clay.

There are many other monuments consisting of just a single cist, such as the one near Tynwald Hill, about which little is known. Also, there are various circles of upright stones which do not seem to have any burial chambers associated with them. These stone circles are apparently limited to the British Isles and are not related to the Mediterranean area, but just what they represent and when they were built are problems still to be solved.

In addition to the megaliths there are various indications of settlements of Neolithic age in many parts of the Island, both north and south, and occupying sites with a more distinctive lowland character. By far the most striking to date have been those revealed at Ronaldsway in the south-eastern lowland during the excavations in connection with the airport in 1943. A unique feature here was the discovery of a primitive oblong dwelling-house about 24 ft. long by 12 to 14 ft. broad with a hearth near the centre. The roof was no doubt held up by a series of wooden posts, the bases of fourteen such posts having been definitely traced. Within the house were considerable amounts of pottery, tools, and bones; and the evidence seems to suggest that the site was occupied by a fairly large family group, throughout a continuous period of time, under what must have been relatively settled conditions. Stock-raising was apparently the chief occupation and the main source of food, as indicated by the bones of cattle (including the Celtic shorthorn, *Bos longifrons*), sheep, and pigs, especially the two first. Possibly the animals were kept at one end of the dwelling, as in the characteristic 'longhouse' of many parts of western Britain in later days, while the human beings occupied the other end. Although there is no precise evidence of cereal cultivation at Ronaldsway, more definite indications of this have been found at Ballateare, Jurby, where a site dating to the same period of the Neolithic Age has been discovered.

Amongst the stone tools found in the Ronaldsway house were several polished axe-heads up to 6 in. long, many of which were made of igneous rock from the Langdale area in the Lake District, as well as smaller flint axes, adzes, saws, and chisels, presumably used for tree-felling and carpentry. Other implements included stone hammers, flint scrapers, and polished flint knives—used for dressing the hides and skins—as well as flint arrow-heads. A fairly large amount of pottery was recovered, most of it very crudely made, and the more charac-teristic vessels appear to have been jars varying from 6 in. to 16 in. across the mouth, with straight sides and round bases. Far from being 'cinerary urns' as was formerly believed, these vessels are now thought to have been food-storage jars kept inside the house. Finally, amongst the most interesting finds at the site were five small oval-shaped slate plaques up to about 3 in. long and very thin, being only a six-teenth of an inch thick. Some of them show a lightly incised geometric ornamentation of chevrons and lozenges. So far nothing comparable to these decorated objects has been found in the British Isles, but the nearest parallels are the larger and more rectangular plaques of Portugal and Spain, while there are certain analogies, as far as the designs are concerned, with the Irish megalithic passage graves; and in both cases the links are with the Atlantic coastal routes whose significance has already been repeatedly stressed. So important are the Ronaldsway finds judged to be that this name has been given to what is recognized as a secondary culture of the Neolithic Age.

THE BRONZE AGE

It has already been implied that this period began in our area between 2300 and 1800 B.C. and that it lasted until a few centuries before Christ. The use of the alloy was known in the eastern Mediterranean much earlier, and it is quite probable that knowledge of it was brought along that same western sea-route by which had already come other new knowledge, such as the cultivation of grain. There was much activity in western Britain during the first part of the Bronze Age, particularly in Ireland, where the alloy was used very extensively. We have noted Ireland's supplies of gold in the Wicklow area; that country also had large supplies of copper, and was able to obtain tin quite easily across the Irish Sea from Cornwall.

Ireland attracted merchants from many countries and exported gold ornaments to France, Germany, and Denmark as well as to England and Scotland. At least one piece of gold of Irish origin has been found on the Isle of Man in the parish of Andreas. All this activity must have affected the Island, which stood as a convenient stepping-stone in the Irish Sea. The megaliths, which were described in the preceding section, must also have been in use during those times. Perhaps some were actually built then, and it is reasonable to suggest that they were used by groups of traders who were travelling about the Irish Sea a good deal at the time.

The Bronze Age may be subdivided into three periods, Early, Middle, and Late, each being characterized by particular types of implements and pottery. During the Early period the typical bronze tools were flat axes, of which at least half a dozen have been discovered in the Island, as at Surby in the south and at Andreas in the north. Three of these were of the decorated type which originated in north-eastern Ireland and were carried by trade across Britain to European centres, so that the Island was clearly playing its role as part of Atlantic Britain in the dissemination of such implements. It has, indeed, been said that the Isle of Man was one of the most active bronze-using areas in Britain.

Of the characteristic pottery belonging to this period the supposed drinking-cup called the beaker was the most distinctive in lowland Britain, having been introduced into eastern England from central Europe by a broad-headed race very early in the Bronze Age. So far only one specimen has been discovered in Man, namely at Barroose in Lonan. On the other hand, at the same period a type of pottery called the food-vessel—often very finely made and beautifully decorated in 'false relief' technique—was being produced extensively in Ireland and other parts of Atlantic Britain, including Scotland and Wales. Three examples have been found in the Island, at Gretch-veg (Lonan), Bishopscourt (Ballaugh), and Cronk Aust (Lezayre), the last being a particularly fine specimen.

During the Middle and Late Bronze periods people made more elaborate kinds of bronze axes, called palstaves and socketed axes, which could be fastened more securely to their wooden handles, while bronze swords and spearheads also came into use. Examples of all have been found in various parts of the Island. As far as pottery is concerned, the objects dating from these ages take the form of special types of burial urn in which the cremated remains of human beings were

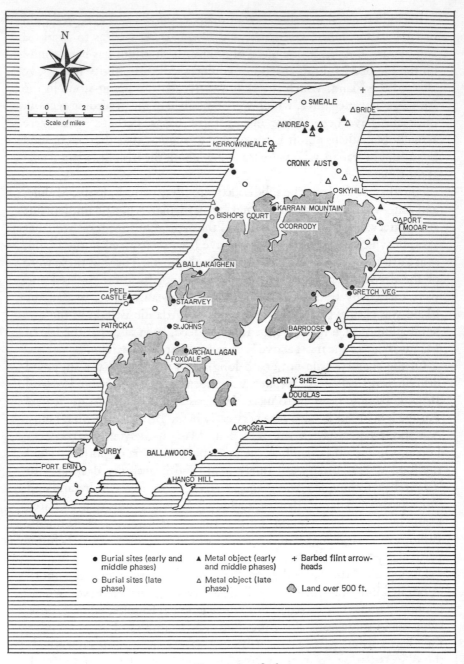

N

Scale of miles

SMEALE
BRIDE
ANDREAS
KERROWKNEALE
CRONK AUST
OSKYHILL
KARRAN MOUNTAIN
BISHOPS COURT
CORRODY
PORT MOOAR
BALLAKAIGHEN
PEEL CASTLE
GRETCH VEG
STAARVEY
PATRICK
St. JOHNS
BARROOSE
ARCHALLAGAN
FOXDALE
PORT Y SHEE
DOUGLAS
CROGGA
SURBY
BALLAWOODS
PORT ERIN
HANGO HILL

● Burial sites (early and middle phases)
○ Burial sites (late phase)
▲ Metal object (early and middle phases)
△ Metal object (late phase)
+ Barbed flint arrow-heads
⬭ Land over 500 ft.

4. Bronze Age finds.

placed. The Manx specimens that have so far been discovered have decorations very similar to those occurring in Ireland, thus indicating the persistence of connections with that country.

On the map (Fig. 4) the sites of all the objects belonging to the Bronze Age which have so far been found in the Island have been marked, so that some idea is given of the areas in which there must have been fairly permanent settlements during the period. Clearly the districts selected were the fertile lowlands and the coastal plateaux within fairly easy access of the sea, and this is not surprising since here was to be found the land best suited to agricultural and pastoral development. The northern lowland had a relatively large number of settlements, in marked contrast to the period of megalithic culture when evidences of settlement are few.

Some of the higher lands were probably occupied temporarily during the summer season for grazing purposes as they were in later times, as well as for hunting; it may be the case that the flint and stone tools which are found nowadays on the higher lands were used during the Bronze period for the latter purpose. No finds are shown in the central valley running between Peel and Douglas, and this might appear surprising in view of the existing importance of this route as the main link between east and west. But from what has been suggested in Chapter 1 it is likely that physical conditions in this valley were not such as to attract settlements or routeways in earlier days. Thus the map serves to emphasize the extent to which the Island was separated by the moorland belt into two main divisions, the Northside and the South-side, which have been such an important feature in Manx life through-out much of its history.

Life appears to have stagnated or even deteriorated in the Isle of Man as well as in Ireland and western Britain towards the end of the Bronze Age and the opening centuries of the Early Iron Age. It is now believed that a rapid worsening of climate during the seventh and sixth centuries B.C. onwards produced relatively cold, wet, blustery conditions which led to the diminution of the trading movements along the Atlantic sea-ways, and this makes it easier to understand why there should have been a period of relative poverty in the Island. Just when things began to improve it is difficult to say, but at least by the first century B.C. Celtic peoples possessing knowledge of iron-working were spreading to Man. Certainly by Roman times evidence of more activity exists, and there is no doubt that Atlantic Britain, including the Isle of Man, then entered upon a period of cultural development which witnessed some remarkable achievements during the succeeding centuries.

LIFE IN THE CELTIC IRON AGE

A settlement which may be regarded as transitional between the Bronze Age and the Iron Age is situated on the summit of South Barrule, a hill which reaches a height of 1,585 ft., and dominates the south of the Island. There seems to have been two quite separate phases of occupation of the hill-top, and it is the earlier which concerns us here. It consisted of a settlement of some eighty huts surrounded by a modest rampart. Excavation showed that at one point at least the rampart was reinforced by a timber *chevaux de frise*. A radiocarbon date derived from a sample of hearth material from one of the huts suggested that this phase of occupation belongs roughly to the sixth century B.C. Most of the pottery from the site reflected older Bronze Age traditions, but a little of it seemed to be influenced by early Iron Age styles, and this sums up very well the transitional nature of the settlement.[1]

The Roman settlers in Britain knew that the Isle of Man existed, just as they knew of the existence of Ireland. A certain amount of trading, or perhaps of mere raiding, went on between Britain and Ireland during the period, because various Roman relics including many coins have been found in Ireland; it is quite conceivable that traders with Roman Britain, or pirates who swooped down on the Romano-British coasts, made Man their centre. So far, however, the only specifically Roman finds to have been recorded in the Island consist of five coins, three having been found in Castletown, one in the parish of Santan, and one in Onchan parish.

On the other hand, the progress of archaeological research during the last twenty-five years has revealed very fascinating information regarding some aspects of life on the Island during, say, the last century B.C. and the first three or four centuries A.D. Thus it is now known that the

1. See P. S. Gelling in *Prehistoric Man in Wales and the West*, ed. Lynch and Burgess (1972), p. 285.

Plate 1. CASHTAL YN ARD, MAUGHOLD, looking east. The paved area, foreground, leads to the porthole giving entry to the gallery of cists beyond. See Fig. 2.

Plate 2. CASHTAL YN ARD, looking west towards the gallery of cists. The whole structure was originally covered by earth, the stones of the forecourt protruding to form a horned cairn.

circular type of dwelling was much in evidence during this period, and that in Man it grew, in certain instances, to assume hitherto undreamed-of dimensions. The site which now provides the exemplar of the single homestead of Celtic society, partly agricultural, but mainly pastoral during some of those centuries, was excavated by Professor Gerhard Bersu in 1942 in the meadowland of the Dumb River at Ballakaighen (Ballacagen) near Castletown. Earthworks described on earlier maps as a 'Fort' proved instead to be the remains of two large circular houses, each of which formed the dwelling-place of a chieftain and his family about, say, 1,700 or 1,800 years ago. The larger of these round, or 'Celtic' house types had a diameter of nearly 90 ft. and the whole space was covered by a continuous and slightly domed turf roof probably about 10 ft. high at the centre, and supported by a series of massive oak posts arranged in five concentric rings. Remains of such posts show them to have been up to 8 in. thick, and the trees from which they were made were at the time 100 or even 200 years old. The living-quarters round the central hearth of Poyllvaaish limestone were shut off from the rest by a circular wattle screen supported by more slender posts of elm or pine, and the remaining, and much larger, portions of the building were used for the stabling of animals and storage. The outer wall of the house consisted of a continuous wall of posts hidden by a bank of earth heaped against it. Outside this, about 10 ft. away, was a fence which prevented the animals from damaging the roof. A broad gap on the north-east opened on to a paved entrance-hall, and there was another smaller opening on the south. The Dumb River ensured a convenient supply of fresh water, while protection was afforded by the marshy ground, although otherwise there are no indications of defensive works.

Agriculture was carried on as shown by the discovery of granite rotary querns, but probably stock-raising was more important, and large numbers of animals' bones, including those of horses, cattle, pigs, sheep, and goats, were obtained. Spinning and weaving were carried on, while crucibles containing glass have been recovered. Glass beads, blue, yellow, and white, as well as bracelets were worn as ornaments;

Plate 3. CRONK AUST FOOD VESSEL from the Early Bronze Age. Although produced extensively in Atlantic Britain, this is one of only three examples of this type of pottery so far found in Man. The vessel is 11 cm high.

Plate 4. BEAKER FROM BARROOSE, placed in a grave together with the un-cremated body of a local chieftain. It is 18·3 cm high.

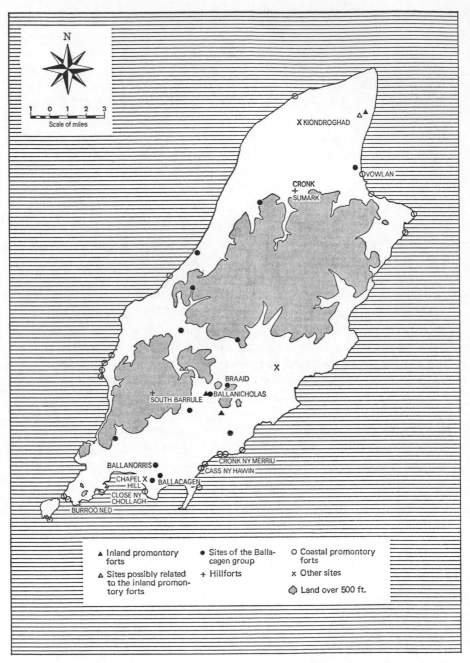

Scale of miles

X KIONDROGHAD

△▲

○ VOWLAN

CRONK
+
SUMARK

BRAAID
▲● BALLANICHOLAS
+
SOUTH BARRULE
▲

X

BALLANORRIS ●

CHAPEL X
HILL   ● BALLACAGEN
CLOSE NY
CHOLLAGH
BURROO NED

CRONK NY MERRIU
CASS NY HAWIN

▲ Inland promontory   ● Sites of the Balla-   ○ Coastal promontory
  forts   cagen group   forts

△ Sites possibly related   + Hillforts   x Other sites
  to the inland promon-
  tory forts   ⬠ Land over 500 ft.

5. Iron Age sites in Man.

a single amber bead was also found. Unfortunately, whatever iron implements were used have rusted away in the wet soil, but a few ornamented bronze articles have survived.

This dwelling-house was in existence from about the first to the third century A.D., and it was certainly in continuous occupation by several generations of people of the same type. Such long-continued use made renewals necessary from time to time and there is evidence of three distinct changes of plan. The size of the house, the single hearth, and the character of the finds—despite their small number—all indicate occupation by a family of social standing comparable to that held in England in later years by the squire in his manor-house. Since there appear to be a number of such sites widely distributed on the Island, the existence of numerous local chieftains seems to have been a feature of the insular social organization during this phase of Celtic times.

Houses of essentially the same plan also existed on the lower plateaux, where supplies of stone were more plentiful. In such cases the outer bank of earth could be faced with stones, not wooden posts, and circles of such stones would then form the last visible remains of what were originally timber-framed, earth-roofed houses. An excellent example of this occurs most likely at the Braaid where the stone circle (c. 420 ft. above sea level), which was formerly regarded as a megalithic monument, represents in reality the site of a Celtic round house.[1]

The fact that these Celtic round houses were undefended habitations which were in continuous occupation by several generations of people, indicates that conditions were undoubtedly peaceful for some length of time. Since this period corresponds to the heyday of Roman power in Britain, the Celtic population of Man in those days must have come to terms with the Romans, whose fleets would pass regularly within sight of the Manx coast plying from Chester with provisions for supplying the garrison of the Roman wall.

1. Amongst the first to suggest this was Professor G. Bersu who appears, however, to have changed his mind later on. This emerged from a lecture he gave in Switzerland in 1958, six years before his death in 1964. The lecture has now been published in the *J. Manx Museum*, vii (1968), 83–8, under the title, 'The Vikings in the Isle of Man', where he suggests that the Braaid circle, 'could very well have been the "Thing-place" of a sheading at the homestead of a sheading chief' (p. 88). Such an origin is not accepted by other authorities including Peter S. Gelling, who in a previous article in the same *Journal* entitled, 'The Braaid site', vi (1964), 201–5, thinks the stone circle is 'very probably a round house', but goes on to raise the interesting speculation whether 'there may not have been some sort of megalithic monument on the site long before either the round house or the long houses were built'.

Houses of a similar type are now known to have existed at the same period in other parts of Atlantic Britain, including North Wales where they are usually referred to as 'concentric circles', Ireland where they are called 'raths', and in western Scotland, and the Hebrides, where the same tradition is perhaps to be seen in the 'wheel-houses'.

Coastal forts

In the Isle of Man round houses of a smaller and less spectacular type are also known to have existed during the Celtic Iron Age and in locations which while being quite different from those just described were certainly not without significance in other respects. Evidence concerning these has been accumulating in recent years as a result of the important excavations carried out by Peter Gelling, but much work still remains to be done. Thus at Close ny Chollagh, Scarlett, about one mile south-west of Castletown, careful investigation has revealed a coastal fort containing four circular huts defended on its landward side by a rampart and fosse. It is uncertain when the occupation of this site began, but it probably came to an end in the first century A.D., after which it was left unoccupied until Viking times when a long house was built on the site. Of the huts used by the Iron Age inhabitants two were of quite solid construction, 18–20 ft. in diameter. The people living there were primarily breeders of cattle and sheep who also kept a few pigs, horses, and poultry, but there is no evidence that they raised any kind of crop, nor did they have any pottery apart from some small crucibles. Apparently only one hut was ever in use at a time so that the number of permanent inhabitants in the fort can hardly have been more than a dozen; yet the defences were so strong that it must have served a larger community, and thus it probably acted as a place of refuge for the surrounding area in times of stress.

The most exciting find recovered from the site was a La Tène III brooch of Colchester type, and we can therefore speculate on the possibility of a group of refugees from southern East Anglia moving to the Isle of Man towards the middle of the first century A.D. It cannot have been long after this that the Roman fleet appeared in the Irish Sea, and naval patrols may have enforced the abandonment of fortified positions of this kind. The forts may even have been abandoned spontaneously, with the establishment, at least for a time, of *pax Romana*. Other problems that await solution include the relationship between the Close ny Chollagh fort and the undefended Celtic round houses at Ballakeighan and Ballanorris barely a mile away, since, at least in part, their occupation was contemporary. Moreover, it would be very satisfactory to know how many of the coastal forts, of which twenty-two are known scattered round the Island, contain remains of dwellings similar to those at Close ny Chollagh. Most probably this is true of Burroo Ned, a precipitous promontory overlooking the Sound, but the site still awaits excavation. On the other hand, two other forts, one near Port Grenaugh known as Cronk ny Merriu and the other at Cass ny hawin, Santan, have revealed only long houses of Scandinavian type.

EARLY MANX LEGENDS

There are a number of legends which seem to date from later prehistoric times and particularly from the Early Iron Age. These legends are essentially bound up with those of Ireland, chiefly Northern Ireland, so that they indicate the continuance of that connection which was so strong during Bronze Age times. Moreover, these stories suggest trading and other links between Man and Ireland with the Western Isles of Scotland, thus pointing to a line of traffic which is known from other evidence to have been so important. The legends can be traced back to about the fifth century of the Christian era, but they must have been handed down by word of mouth for many generations previously. It may therefore be suggested that they belong roughly to the first century B.C. onwards, that is to the time when the knowledge and use of iron was slowly coming into the area.

The chief gods and heroes found in these myths are, of course, Manannan, as well as Conchobar, and Culainn. The first is often popularly supposed to have given his name to the Island, but it is much more probable that he obtained his own name from it. Manannan appears in so many different guises—as king, warrior, trader, navigator, and magician—that his original role can only be guessed at. He was, in any case, essentially bound up with the sea, whence he is often referred to as Manannan mac Lir, that is, the 'son of the sea'. Certainly the most interesting as well as the most likely explanation of his origin is that he reflected the vitally important part the Manx must have played in those early days as navigators and traders in the Irish Sea. Indeed, Cormac, an Irish writer, in the ninth century A.D., defines Manannan as 'a celebrated merchant who was in the Isle of Man (Manand). He was the best pilot that was in the west of Europe. He used to know, by studying the heavens, the periods which would be the fine weather and the bad weather, and when each of these two times would change.' This quaint explanation is, no doubt, as near as we are likely to get to the origin of the famous Manx hero and god.

The exploits of Conchobar, a mythical king of Ulster, in his search for some wonderful weapons from Culainn, illustrate the link between Northern Ireland and Man, but also serve to emphasize the importance of possessing good weapons of iron, such as were slowly coming into use in the area at that time. Culainn was, amongst other things, a famous smith and armourer, who is supposed to have lived for a time in Man, where he manufactured a sword, spear, and shield of such amazing quality for Conchobar that the latter invited Culainn to go and live in Ulster. This great smith, according to the story, had some secret place of manufacture in Man, and he was persuaded to make the weapons for the ambitious young Conchobar through the intervention of a lovely young maiden whom the warrior found asleep on the shore when he arrived. Once in possession of the weapons, Conchobar was able to become king of Ulster while quite a young man. How far it is true that iron weapons of such quality were actually made in the Island must remain doubtful until other more definite evidence is forthcoming.

Other stories of later date have also been handed down concerning the exploits of a hero named Finn and his son Ossian.[1] Finn is said to have been the chief of a band of soldiers, or robbers, called Fianns, who flourished in the second part of the third century A.D., and who had various adventures in northern Ireland, in Man, as well as in the Western Isles of Scotland. A Manx version of a story about Finn is all that remains of this line of traditional verse in Manx. It seems to present a mixture of Irish and Norse characters with Finn and his son Oshin appearing from the Irish side and Gorree from the Norse. This story of the burning of Finn's house is briefly narrated in the Irish *Colloquy of the Ancients*[2] where the arsonist is Garadh mac Morna, and this seems to be the name and character which Gorree has displaced in the Manx version.

---

1. For the text see A. W. Moore, *Manx Ballads* (Douglas, 1896), pp. 2–5. The ballad, which is incomplete, was recovered from oral tradition in the eighteenth century as part of the interest excited by the controversy over the genuineness of James Macpherson's Ossianic poems.

2. Edited and translated in S. H. O'Grady, *Silva Gadelica* (London, 1892), vol. i, p. 123, vol. ii, p. 134. An Irish poem giving a more elaborate, but recognizably the same account as the Manx appeared in *Eriu*, i. 13, edited by E. J. Gwynn.

CHAPTER THREE

The Early Christian Period
450-800

THERE IS ARCHAEOLOGICAL EVIDENCE THAT DURING THE LATER
Roman period, from the fourth century onwards, contacts between
various parts of Atlantic Britain not only continued but became intensified. This has been revealed by finds of distinctive pottery, including
large amphorae and cooking-pots, at the monastery of Tintagel and
other centres in Cornwall as well as in coastal areas along western
Britain, together with various sites in southern Ireland and the monastery of St. Mochaoi in the north-east of that country. The objects of this
trade included wine, oil, and possibly wheat from the Mediterranean,
along with smaller and more valuable objects of a religious nature or as
luxuries for the rulers, while the return trade probably comprised
Cornish tin, some Irish gold and copper, and dogs, slaves, and hides.

THE OGHAM STONES

Further indications of intercourse between different sections of Celtic
Britain is provided by the ogham-inscribed stones dating from the
fourth or fifth century to the seventh century. These memorials were
at one time thought to be Christian tombstones, but are now considered
to have been originally pagan, although in some cases they may have
been used by Christians after the addition of the symbol of the cross.

In the ogham script each letter is formed by a certain number of
strokes cut on the stone, and it is known that such a method of writing
developed in south-western Ireland, probably during the fourth or fifth
century A.D. (Pl. 7). The inscriptions on such stones normally give
nothing more than the name of the person buried and that of his
father, but they are, nevertheless, the oldest written records of the

early forms of Gaelic spoken in Ireland. It is in that country that by far the largest number of oghams have been found (more than 300 in all), while from there this method of writing was carried by colonists to Cornwall, Wales, Scotland, and also to Man so that some idea is obtained of the extent of Irish influence during the fifth and sixth centuries. Since Roman influence had penetrated into Cornwall and

6. The ogham alphabet.

Wales it is found that in addition to the ordinary ogham script over forty memorial stones in those areas also contain more or less the same inscription in Latin script. It is of great interest that of the five Manx ogham inscriptions so far discovered one is bilingual, i.e. in the ogham script in Irish and in Roman letters in Latin. This is the stone from Knoc y Doonee, Andreas, bearing the inscriptions in ogham *Abicatos maqi Rocatos* (for *Ambicatos*) and in Roman letters *Ammecati filius Rocati hic iacit* and dating from the late fifth or early sixth century. The names are Irish, later *Imchadh* and *Rochadh*, but the form in which they are recorded in Roman letters shows the influence of British pronunciation in the -*mm*- for -*mb*- and in the substitution of British *amb*- for Goidelic *imb*-. It seems that when Irish names were written in British territory in Roman letters they also underwent adaptation to the corresponding British form, a process which implies the presence of speakers of both languages living in contact with each other in the Island at that time. The conclusion can be drawn that the Island was originally British (in modern terms, Welsh-speaking) not Irish, but that here, as in Gaelic Scotland, the Irish immigrants eventually absorbed the previous population, whereas their colonies in Wales and Cornwall were absorbed by the population they found there.[1]

The other four oghams on the Island have inscriptions in Gaelic only, two of them being found in Rushen (at Ballaqueeney) and the others in Arbory (at the Friary).

1. These inscriptions, with the comparable material from Ireland and elsewhere, are collected by R. A. S. Macalister in his *Corpus Inscriptionum Insularum Celticarum* (Dublin, 1945–9). The Manx inscriptions are nos. 500–5 and 1066–8. The omission of *m*, a single stroke in ogham, in *Abicatos* is presumably an accident. The reading is that of K. H. Jackson, *Language and History in Early Britain*, p. 173.

CELTIC CHRISTIANITY

Against the background just outlined it is easier to appreciate the manner in which many of the features associated with Celtic Christianity came to Atlantic Britain and were then diffused throughout the area. First, it is well perhaps to make clear that Christianity originally entered Britain when Roman power was at its height, directly across the Channel to lowland Britain from which it gradually spread westward and northward. Evidence that it reached some parts of Atlantic Britain is forthcoming by the fact that St. Patrick (c. 389–461), the son of a minor official who was also a deacon, lived in some such locality, most probably in the south-west of the country. From here, at the age of sixteen, he was carried off to slavery in Ulster by Irish raiders. At the beginning of the fifth century Roman authority was waning in south-eastern Britain, leading, amongst other things, to the decay of Christianity and the coming of the pagan Anglo-Saxons there, while it was also linked with a correspondingly increased activity in the west where the Atlantic sea-routes gained in significance. Moreover, in Gaul Christians from the Mediterranean south-east were pressing towards the Gironde estuary or to the Loire and Brittany, thus repeating movements as old as megalithic days; it was by such routes that missionaries brought not only their beliefs but also some knowledge of Greek. It is now thought unlikely that Patrick himself, after his escape from slavery in Ireland, ever went to the Continent,[1] but it was by such routes also that other ideas now associated with Eastern or Orthodox Christianity, such as the method of calculating the date of Easter, came to be incorporated into Celtic Christianity at an early stage, while various art forms from the eastern Mediterranean were brought to Ireland by similar means.[2]

The name 'saint' has been given as a general title to the Celtic Christian missionaries who were active in spreading their religious beliefs and in establishing churches, oratories, and monasteries throughout western Britain from the fifth century onwards. The term 'monk' would probably have been a better name, but whatever word is used there is a tantalizing scarcity of reliable detail concerning their lives and travels;

1. The most recent authoritative study of Patrick's life is *St. Patrick* by R. P. C. Hanson (1968). For a balanced assessment of the Patrician question see also D. A. Binchy's article 'Patrick and his biographers' in *Studia Hibernica*, ii (1962), 7–173.

2. See below (p. 52) on the Calf of Man crucifixion.

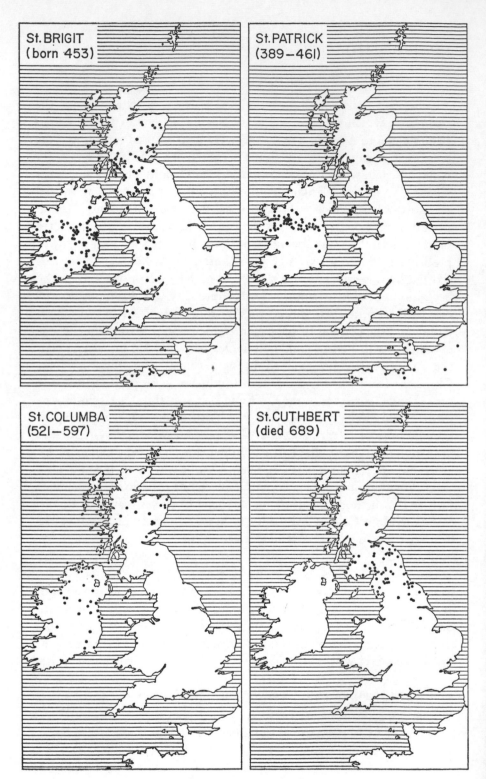

St.BRIGIT
(born 453)

St.PATRICK
(389—461)

St.COLUMBA
(521—597)

St.CUTHBERT
(died 689)

7. Celtic saints—areas of influence.

instead most accounts are full of supernatural occurrences or legendary material with very little or no historical foundations. In trying to assess the relative importance of these early missionaries an effective method is to consider the pre-Reformation dedications of the saints concerned since these provide good clues to the spheres of operations of themselves or of their immediate disciples. This arises from the marked contrast between the Celtic and Roman practice regarding dedication, so that whereas early Celtic churches or monasteries were, as a rule, called by the name of their original founders or by that of their monastic patrons, the Roman practice was to dedicate a church to a biblical saint or to a member of the Holy Family. Thus the maps shown in Figs. 7 and 8 give a very useful picture of the areas influenced by the saints named.

St. Ninian (who died *c.* 432), associated mainly with south-west Scotland, was one of the earliest of the Celtic missionaries to visit the famous monastery of Marmoutier established by St. Martin of Tours, who himself had links with Lérins, and then returned with some masons to Whithorn where he built the famous church called the *Candida Casa* towards the end of the fourth century. His influence was very localized, comprising only a few centres in north-east Ireland and northern England in addition to those in south-western and north-eastern Scotland, but many think he was the first to bring Christianity to the Island, which is not far from Galloway.[1]

St. Brigit (born *c.* 453) must have been an outstanding personality since the dedications linked with her range throughout the whole length of Atlantic Britain and into Brittany. No doubt her great popularity was based partly on the fact that she replaced a Celtic fire goddess of earlier times, and her cult was naturally most widespread in Ireland with an emphasis on the Kildare area where a perpetual fire was maintained near her church until the early thirteenth century. St. Patrick's influence was also very widespread throughout western Britain, and within Ireland his pre-Reformation dedications are especially numerous in the central lowland round Dublin and Meath in addition to the area round Strangford Lough where he landed about 432 to start his religious mission after his travels. His earlier experience in Ireland had filled him with a strong desire to go as a missionary to help the Christians already there, and to extend the new religion especially in the north where the Druids had great power. Between 432 and his death in about 461 he accomplished his great work of spreading the

1. On St. Ninian see J. MacQueen, *St. Nynia* (Edinburgh, 1961).

faith and organizing the Celtic Church in the land which he had first seen when taken there as a slave.

Schools were established in Ireland and learning was encouraged so that many scholars were trained, several of whom went forth as missionaries to carry their faith and learning to other lands surrounding the Irish Sea. The best known was St. Columba who was born in Donegal in 521. He had great influence not only on account of his piety and ability, but also because he was related to the royal family of Ulster and to the ruler of that part of western Scotland then known as Dalriada, now called Argyll. Columba undertook the task of converting the Picts of highland Scotland, and for this purpose he established in 563 the famous monastery on the remote island of Iona off the west coast of Mull. This hallowed spot, 'by the salt main on which the seagulls cry', became the great centre from which Columba and his disciples made many journeys to the far north of Scotland, to the Anglian kingdom of Northumbria, and to Man, so that by the time of the saint's death in 597 Celtic Christianity had spread far and wide throughout western and northern Britain. The results of these activities were strengthened at first by St. Cuthbert (d. 689) whose sphere of operations although primarily concerned with north-eastern England and southern Scotland, had a link with the Isle of Man where there is one dedication to him at Ballacuberagh in the lower part of Sulby Glen.

Meanwhile it will be recalled that the Roman form of Christianity had been reintroduced into south-eastern Britain following the mission of St. Augustine in 597, thus setting the stage for an ultimate head-on collision between the two forms of religion and of culture generally. This conflict actually reached its climax in the year 664 when the decision of the Synod of Whitby resulted in a victory for the Roman practice. Henceforth the Celtic ideas receded to the west where their influence continued to hold sway for many centuries although they ultimately succumbed before the full impact of the centrally organized rival system of Rome.

Celtic Christianity in Man

The map (Fig. 8) shows the various churches (or keeills) and other features, particularly holy wells, dedicated to the different Celtic saints. From this evidence it seems quite clear that the Island must have had an active role in assisting the travels of these missionaries, although there is no precise literary proof that any of the people in question ever visited these shores, nor is it known for certain just when Christianity was introduced here.

St. Ninian's church at Whithorn is very close to the Island, and his name survives in the name of St. Trinian's (a corruption of Ninian) that is given to the old church in Marown where the Priory of Whithorn for long held lands.

St. Patrick's name is widely and deeply honoured, being used for two parish churches (Kirk Patrick itself, and Kirk Patrick of Jurby) and also seven keeills, apart from various sacred wells, while it is associated with the two upright stone pillars bearing early Christian crosses, known as St. Patrick's Chair, in the parish of Marown. There are various legends that the saint actually visited the Island, but definite proof of this is lacking.

Many Manx churches and keeills are named after other Celtic saints who lived during St. Patrick's time, or not long after. They include Maughold, Lonan, and Brigit, 'the holy head of Ireland's nuns', who gave her name to the parish of Kirk Bride as well as to several keeills. Other parishes whose names are derived from Celtic saints are Arbory (from St. Cairbre), Santan (from St. Sanctan), Braddan (from a saint whose name is spelt in various ways including Brendan and Braddan), Onchan or Conchan (from St. Conchenn), and German (from a saint of the same name). Lastly, the parish church of Arbory is also dedicated to St. Columba, and *Laa Columb killey*, or St. Columba's Day, is still held as a fair day in the parish, having been revived in modern times. A keeill in Kirk Andreas is also dedicated to St. Columba. One of Columba's disciples was known as Molua or Moluoc, and it is to him that the parish of Malew is dedicated; while Marown is dedicated to Ronan, who was later than Columba but belonged to the Columban church.

Considerable confusion has been caused regarding some of these names from the fact that they appear in medieval documents in a Latinized form often far removed from the original, while the original form is usually preserved much more accurately in local place-names. Thus Maughold became 'Machutus' in the official medieval version, so that he actually became confused with the Breton saint of that name, whereas the real Maughold who was closely connected with St. Patrick was born either in Ireland or—still more likely—in the Isle of Man itself where he was the founder of the monastery named after him. Similarly the name Malew, which is derived from the Irish Mo-Lua, became mixed up with St. Lupus of Troyes who was a very different person,

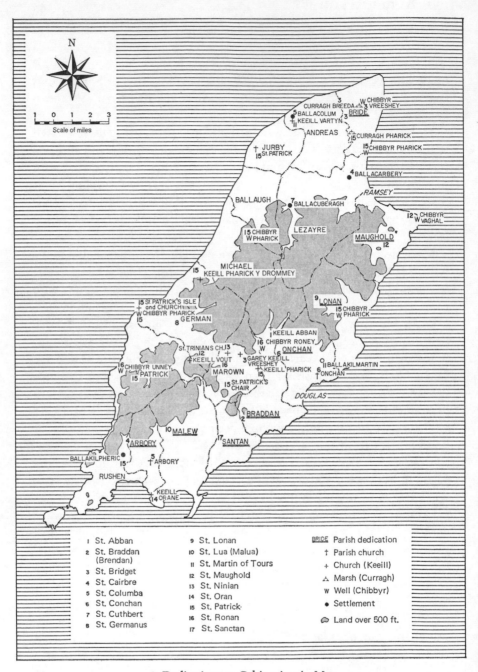

N

1 0 1 2 3
Scale of miles

W. CHIBBYR
CURRAGH BREEDA   3 VREESHEY
5 BALLACOLUM   BRIDE
KEEILL VARTYN   3
ANDREAS
15 CURRAGH PHARICK
JURBY   15 CHIBBYR PHARICK
15 St. PATRICK   W

4 BALLACARBERY

RAMSEY

BALLAUGH   7 BALLACUBERAGH
12 CHIBBYR VAGHAL
W
15 CHIBBYR   LEZAYRE
W PHARICK
MAUGHOLD
12
MICHAEL
KEEILL PHARICK Y DROMMEY
15   9 LONAN
St. PATRICK'S ISLE   15 CHIBBYR
and CHURCH   W PHARICK
W CHIBBYR PHARICK
15   8 GERMAN
KEEILL ABBAN
St. TRINIANS CH. 13   16 CHIBBYR RONEY
12   W   ONCHAN
4 KEEILL VOUT   16
16 CHIBBYR UNNEY   3 GAREY KEEILL   6 BALLAKILMARTIN
W   PATRICK   VREESHEY   ONCHAN
15   MAROWN   KEEILL PHARICK
15   6
15 St. PATRICK'S   DOUGLAS
CHAIR
BRADDAN
2
10 MALEW
4 ARBORY   17 SANTAN
BALLAKILPHERIC   5 ARBORY
15   RUSHEN
KEEILL
14 ORANE

1 St. Abban	9 St. Lonan	BRIDE Parish dedication
2 St. Braddan (Brendan)	10 St. Lua (Malua)	† Parish church
3 St. Bridget	11 St. Martin of Tours	+ Church (Keeill)
4 St. Cairbre	12 St. Maughold	⚐ Marsh (Curragh)
5 St. Columba	13 St. Ninian	W Well (Chibbyr)
6 St. Conchan	14 St. Oran	• Settlement
7 St. Cuthbert	15 St. Patrick	☁ Land over 500 ft.
8 St. Germanus	16 St. Ronan	
	17 St. Sanctan	

8. Dedications to Celtic saints in Man

and the Manx saint German was wrongly linked with St. Germanus of Auxerre, who was actually St. Patrick's teacher.

The keeills

Possibly the very earliest churches in Man were built of sods, or of wattle and mud, and there is now no trace of them. Graves have been found together with crosses which scholars ascribe to the fifth century, and it is probable that they mark the sites of buildings which have disappeared. Later stone buildings were erected, the stones at first being held together with earth. Afterwards clay was used as a cement, and finally lime or shell-mortar. The foundations of many of these structures still remain, now being carefully preserved by the Manx Museum trustees. They date from the seventh to the twelfth centuries, many later keeills dating from Norse times, after the Norsemen were converted to Christianity, and prior to the establishment of a parochial system during the twelfth century. They were simple structures and usually quite small, the keeill at Ballachrink, Marown, being, for example, as small as 10 by 6 ft. inside. The simple rectangular plan, with no apse or rounded end, and with no clear division between the nave and the chancel, became a kind of 'Manx style' in church-building, and may still be seen in many of the existing parish churches.

The earliest keeills, being so small, could not have been intended for congregational worship but rather as places in which the first Christian missionaries could offer up their simple service of prayer and praise.[1] Preaching would have been conducted out of doors, and so too would baptism, for a holy well, or *chibbyr*, is usually found near these old chapels. Many of the keeills that have been examined are known to have been built on sites that had been sacred for a long time previously, thus illustrating that respect for tradition which was noted earlier as a marked characteristic of the Celtic area of Britain.

So far some 200 keeill sites have been discovered in Man, all districts being represented except the higher mountain lands and the marshes. As previously stated, there appears to have been one on every treen, and a very recent survey shows that about 174 of such treen-chapels are known to have existed. Most probably the Celtic missionaries had a small church set up on each family estate, or treen, to counteract the

1. For the probable form of service see F. E. Warren, *Liturgy and Ritual of the Celtic Church* (Oxford, 1881), and for an Old Irish commentary on the action see W. Stokes and J. Strachan, *Thesaurus Palaeohibernicus* (Cambridge, 1903), vol. ii, pp. 252-5.

influence of ancestor-worship which had previously existed. Also the people gradually gave up worshipping the various pagan gods such as Lugh, the great sun god, Ler, the god of the vast ocean, and Manannan, the god of wind and storm and mist, who had formed the chief deities of the Celtic world.

THE MONASTERY OF ST. MAUGHOLD

Pre-eminent amongst the Manx religious centres during this period of Celtic Christianity was Maughold, where the existence of a monastery founded not later than the early seventh century and continuing until the eleventh century, is now accepted by B. R. S. Megaw after reviewing all the available evidence. The term monastery in this context does not imply a large edifice such as the word would now evoke, but rather a cluster of small churches and dwellings which formed in effect a mission station, a centre around which students gathered and from which the saints went forth on their labours. Probably the area of the Maughold monastery broadly coincided with the present churchyard, within which exist the ruins of three ancient keeills and the site of another, apart from the parish church of Kirk Maughold. The latter building, with its well-known doorway in the style of the Irish Romanesque architecture, has no part which is earlier than the eleventh century, but there are indications that it was not the first on the site.

Extremely little is known of Maughold himself, the founder of the monastery, but as already stated he was not Machutus, nor was he MacCuil with whom he was long associated as the result of incidents related in an early life of Patrick. The MacCuil legend has now been dismissed as a pagan folk-tale originally unconnected with the great saint;[1] but whether Maughold was an Irishman or a Breton or a Manxman is still unresolved.[2]

1. For the MacCuil story see W. Cubbon, *Island Heritage*, pp. 16–17.
2. Modern opinion appears to favour the Manx origin of both Maughold and Conchan. Regarding the latter see B. R. S. Megaw, 'Who was St. Conchan?', *J. Manx Museum*, vi (1962–3), 187–92.

Plate 5. CELTIC ROUND HOUSE, modelled under the supervision of Professor Bersu, after his excavation work at Ballacagan. The inner area contained hearth and living quarters; the outer area was used for storage and housing animals.

Plate 6. THE BRAAID SITE, MAROWN, showing the remains of a Celtic round house and rectangular and boat-shaped homesteads of the Norse type.

Plate 7. OGHAM STONE FROM BALLAQUEENEY, RUSHEN.
The inscription up the edge of the stone reads '(the stone) of Bivaidu, son of the tribe of Cunava(li)'—that is, Connell or Cannell. The ogham alphabet is shown in Fig. 7.

Plate 8. IRNEIT'S CROSS-SLAB from Maughold, the site of an important Celtic monastery. The inscription within the circle records a certain bishop Irneit. The Latin inscription below reads 'In the name of Christ, a figure of the cross of Christ'.

This famous Celtic religious centre has produced a number of early, or pre-Norse, inscribed stone monuments, some of which are not only remarkable in themselves but which, taken as a whole, confirm the high position occupied by the area during the period. The earliest of these is a cross-slab dating to the second half of the seventh century, and this stone contains a circle enclosing a hexagonal design, while inside the circle is a Latin inscription commemorating a certain *Irneit* who was, no doubt, a bishop in the Celtic monastery but about whom nothing else is known from literary sources. This monument also has two early *chi-rho* crosses below the circle with another Latin inscription reading: 'In the name of Christ, a figure of the cross of Christ' (*In Christi Nomine Crucis Christi Imagenem*). Another cross, found in the church-yard in 1948, is unique in commemorating the action of a person named *Branhui* who 'led off water to this place' (in Latin, *huc aqua(m) dirivavit*). This slab, one of the earliest in the 'Celtic' form is dated to about A.D. 820, and presumably refers to a monk of Kirk Maughold who achieved what was regarded as the almost miraculous feat of providing the monastery with a supply of running water for domestic use. It may be noted in this connection that traces of a stone-lined open conduit found in the churchyard some years ago suggest how this feat was probably accomplished. Another headstone is inscribed with the Saxon name *Blakman* in runic letters of a type used by the Angles, thus indicating how cultural influences originating in the English lowland had penetrated into the Celtic west. In conclusion it is a significant fact that of the 65 or so pre-Norse slabs so far found in the Island at least 25 have come fom the parish of Maughold, and of the latter figure 20 are from the area of the churchyard or the village immediately adjoining it.

THE ARTS DURING THE EARLY CHRISTIAN PERIOD

Accompanying the great religious movements there were vitally important developments in learning as well as in the arts and crafts. In Ireland the period from about A.D. 650 to 800 is often spoken of as the Golden Age. Beautiful things were created in architecture, the illumination or adornment of the pages of sacred books, metalwork, and in sculpture. The Isle of Man contains no examples of the first two of these arts, possibly because of its smallness and relative poverty in natural resources; or if any records did exist here they have disappeared,

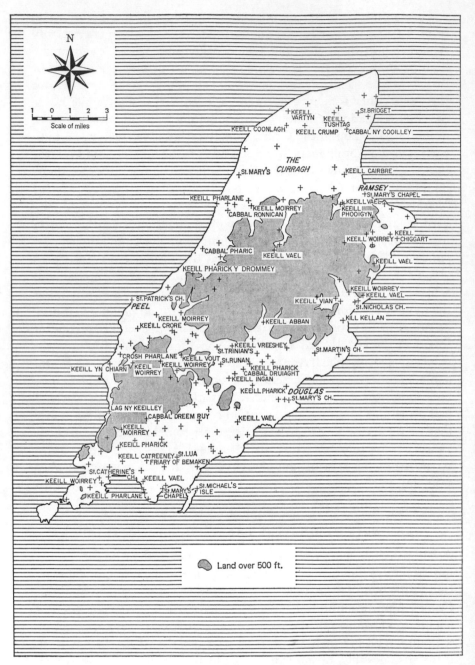

N

1 0 1 2 3
Scale of miles

+KEEILL
VARTYN   +KEEILL   +St.BRIDGET
              TUSHTAG
KEEILL COONLAGH+ +KEEILL CRUMP CABBAL NY COOILLEY
              +

THE
ST.MARY'S CURRAGH
+KEEILL CAIRBRE

RAMSEY
KEEILL PHARLANE   +St.MARY'S CHAPEL
+KEEILL MOIRREY   +KEEILL VAEL
CABBAL RONNICAN   KEEILL
              PHOOIGYN
+CABBAL PHARIC   +KEEILL
KEEILL WOIRREY +CHIGGART
KEEILL VAEL
KEEILL PHARICK Y DROMMEY   +KEEILL VAEL

+St.PATRICK'S CH.   KEEILL WOIRREY
PEEL   KEEILL VIAN +KEEILL VAEL
+KEEILL MOIRREY   St.NICHOLAS CH.
KEEILL CRORE   +KEEILL ABBAN   KILL KELLAN

CROSH PHARLANE   +KEEILL VREESHEY   +St.MARTIN'S CH.
              St.TRINIAN'S
KEEILL YN CHIARN +KEEIL KEEILL VOUT
KEEILL WOIRREY   St.RUNAN
WOIRREY   KEEILL WOIRREY   KEEILL PHARICK
CABBAL DRUIAGHT
+KEEILL INGAN
KEEILL PHARICK DOUGLAS
LAG NY KEEILLEY   +St.MARY'S CH.
CABBAL DREEM RUY
KEEILL   +KEEILL VAEL
MOIRREY
+KEEILL PHARICK
KEEILL CATREENEY St.LUA
FRIARY OF BEMAKEN
St.CATHERINE'S
CH. KEEILL VAEL
KEEILL WOIRREY   St.MICHAEL'S
KEEILL PHARLANE   St.MARY'S ISLE
CHAPEL

Land over 500 ft.

9. Keeill sites in Man.

perhaps being destroyed by the Norsemen who also destroyed many books in Ireland. In regard to metalwork a very significant discovery— the first of its kind—was recently made by Peter S. Gelling who between 1962 and 1967 excavated a metalworker's site at Kiondroghad. It is close to the Lhen Trench, and is described on the one-inch Ordnance Survey map as a Round House. In fact the site turned out to have been mainly open, with just one small oblong hut. It produced various pattern-stones, one of which bore a design characteristic of the Irish metalworking school, and, most important, fragments of crucible and an enamelled bronze disc of distinctly Irish type which had been the head of a latchet. There is a suggestion, therefore, that some work of this kind was really produced on the Island, and further evidence may be forthcoming.[1]

But as regards sculpture, the last of the arts mentioned, there is of course already abundant evidence of work in this field, and very notable progress took place during this period; a fine collection of inscribed and decorated monuments has been the result. Copies of these monuments, as plaster-casts or as drawings, form one of the most valued departments of the Manx Museum. As will be seen later this form of art was developed still further during the Scandinavian period, so that the Island is very fortunate in possessing a wonderfully rich series of stone crosses. The task of collecting, interpreting, and arranging this famous collection was initially accomplished by the late P. M. C. Kermode, who in 1907 described and illustrated the stones in his great work entitled *Manx Crosses*. Since then, of course, various other studies have been written regarding some of these crosses, while additional stones have also been found.

As already seen, the first inscribed stones in the Island are pagan and are marked merely with ogham characters belonging to the fifth and sixth or succeeding centuries. As Christianity made its influence felt slabs of stone were engraved with simple representations of the cross and set up as memorials to the dead. This practice dates from about A.D. 650, one of the earliest examples being the cross from Ballamanagh, Lezayre, and from such simple beginnings custom led to the carving of intricate and beautiful patterns of the later Manx crosses. The stones themselves were mainly of local origin, the vast majority being the comparatively soft slate-like stone of the Island's main rock formation;

1. See P. S. Gelling in *Medieval Archaeology*, xiii (1969), 67–83.

only occasionally were other rocks such as limestone or even granite used for the purpose.

The so-called 'Celtic' form with a circle surrounding the form of the cross, particularly associated with the Irish church, began to appear during the eighth century and one of the earliest as well as the most interesting example of these, dating to about A.D. 800, has already been mentioned as the 'Branhui' cross found in Maughold. In this parish, it will be recalled, have been found a relatively high proportion of all the known pre-Norse cross-slabs of the Island. Another quite famous and historic one is that bearing the inscription *Crux Guriat* (Pl. 9), belonging to the early ninth century, which commemorates a Welsh prince Gwriad, who is believed to have taken refuge in the Island before the year 825. This slab, now in the churchyard cross-house, formerly stood at a keeill near Port y Vullen about a mile from the Maughold parish church and it exhibits a bold plain form of the 'Celtic cross' while also having five heavy bosses. According to tradition Guriat, or Gwriad, while in the Island had a son named Merfyn known in Welsh history as *Merfyn o dir Manaw* (Merfyn from the land of Mannin) who returned to north Wales, there to found the ruling dynasties of Gwynedd and Deheubarth which were powerful until the end of the thirteenth century.

An outstanding and unique cross dating to the later eighth or early ninth century is that known today as the Calf of Man Crucifixion (Pl. 10), found in 1773 when the ruins of a Celtic chapel were being demolished on the Calf island. Until recent years this important stone was in the finder's family, but now it has been presented to the Manx Museum after being bought by the National Art-Collections Fund. When complete it was probably less than 3 ft. high and served as a kind of altar-frontal. Now, although broken, it displays a fine 'Celtic' interpretation of the Crucifixion in which Christ appears alive, head erect, fully and elaborately robed in a manner found in the art of the eastern Mediterranean at least as early as the sixth century A.D. and significantly different from what became the usual Roman representation of the theme in north-west Europe. The spear-bearer has been preserved; flanking him the missing portion of the carving would have shown the sponge-bearer, while two angels would have been depicted above the outstretched arms of Christ.

This particular Crucifixion theme must have travelled via the Mediterranean and reached Ireland early since it made one of its first appearances on a faded page of the illuminated manuscript called the *Durham Gospels*,[1] which was the work of one of the Irish monasteries of Northumbria during the late seventh century. The first completely 'Celtic' version is seen in a bronze plaque from Athlone now in the National Museum of Ireland and dating from the early eighth century (Pl. 11). The figure of Christ is very stylized and there are two inelegant winged cherubim on either side above, with renderings of the spear- and sponge-bearers below. The Manx carving appears to have been a more or less direct copy in stone of this metal version as shown particularly by the ornamentation of Christ's cloak, and indeed it is probably the earliest of all the Celtic representations of the Crucifixion in stone. Certain differences are also visible on the Calf version as compared with the Athlone one; for example, in the former Christ has long hair parted in the middle and a forked beard, whereas the Irish figure has a fringe of hair across the forehead and a clean-shaven face.

Although there is a great lack of ordinary historical records for the period between 450 and 800 it is clear that much of importance was then taking place. Trade and cultural relations were maintained with Ireland, Scotland, England—particularly the northern part—and Wales. Christianity spread over the whole Island, and the foundations were laid of that art which produced the exquisite Manx crosses.

1. Also known as the *Lindisfarne Gospels* or *Durham Book*; reproduced in colour in the Urs Graf edition, 2 vols., 1956–60.

CHAPTER FOUR

The Scandinavian Settlement 800–1266

TOWARDS THE END OF THE EIGHTH CENTURY THE ERA OF quiet prosperity which has been described in the previous chapter was shattered by the coming of the Norsemen from Scandinavia. Those great sea-warriors were also called Vikings, the usual derivation of the name being from the numerous creeks and bays along the Scandinavian coast known as fjords or *viks*. At first they were known as peaceful fishermen and traders. Then, encouraged by the unsettled conditions prevailing in their own country and in other countries of Europe at the time, they became pirates, harrying the coasts of Britain and western Europe, even penetrating the Mediterranean to Italy and Sicily. In eastern Europe they followed the great rivers into the heart of Russia and ultimately reached the city of Constantinople.[1]

The Scandinavians included three groups of peoples, Norwegians, Swedes, and Danes, but only the Norwegians (or Norse) and the Danes came to Britain in large numbers, since the Swedes were mainly interested in eastern Europe. As to the area of the Irish Sea with which we are particularly concerned, it may be stated that the people who came were almost wholly from Norway, particularly the south-western districts of that country. The Danes made settlements on the eastern side of England, and some went round the south and so got into the Irish Sea that way; but since only a few groups did this they can be disregarded.

The arts of shipbuilding and seamanship were more advanced in Scandinavia than in other parts of Europe at the time, so that its peoples were able to accomplish the long journeys for which they were famous,

1. A good general book on the Vikings is that by J. Brøndsted, *The Vikings* (Penguin Books, 1965).

not only to Britain but also to far-off Iceland and Greenland, and even to America itself. Much is known of their ships not only from Norse sagas, but also from the remains of actual ships. It was common for a chief to be buried in his ship, the whole 'grave' being covered with a mound or *how*, and several such vessels have been discovered.

The ships were shallow, narrow in the beam, and pointed at both ends, and thus were very suitable for handling in creeks and bays, while they could easily be run up on the beaches. Each ship had but one large and heavy square sail, and when a naval battle was in progress it depended for its movement on the rowers. The number of the latter varied with the size of the vessel, but on the average each ship had ten rowers on either side. Since these ships would often have to be rowed both day and night against a contrary wind many more men would be needed, while others would be required to fight. The Gokstad ship (Pl. 13) was an oak vessel with seats for sixteen pairs of rowers, and was 78 ft. long and 16 ft. broad amidships. A rather different type of ship, used to transport settlers and carry goods over longer distances, is shown in Plate 12.[1]

The warriors were well armed. For defence they had a helmet, mail-shirt of iron rings, leather or thick wool clothing, and a light round shield with an iron boss in the centre. For offensive purposes they used a sword, spear, or battle-axe.

These Norsemen were strong and fearless on both sea and land. The thrill of battle gave them immense joy, and they believed that open plundering was honourable, although to steal secretly was shameful. Such were the men who controlled Man for some hundreds of years. As can easily be imagined it was an age crowded with many thrilling incidents, while it also included much cruelty and futile strife; but when the results of the Viking rule are weighed it will be seen that the period produced much that was good and enduring.

The Norsemen appeared in the Irish Sea during the latter part of the eighth century and began plundering the coasts of Ireland and Man.

1. The discovery of this vessel, raised recently from Roskilde fjord, Skuldelev, Denmark, has contributed to the current reinterpretation of the nature of the Viking achievement. It is increasingly being emphasized that the pursuit of trade was an integral part of Viking expansion. For example, recent important archaeological discoveries in Dublin have shown that the city was an extremely wealthy and important trading settlement in ninth- and tenth-century Western Europe. It must be added that the Viking sagas, in which completeness was often sacrificed to the demands of the story-teller, are themselves largely responsible for many of the traditional judgements on the Norsemen.

They particularly sought the churches and monasteries since they were pagan and had scant respect for Christianity, while they knew that such places usually yielded rich spoil. The fear that the Norsemen inspired is shown by the following translation of a Gaelic verse written by an Irish scribe. Seated in his little hut near the sea, he is glad that a terrible storm is raging because it will prevent the pirates from approaching the shore:

> The wind is boisterous to-night;
> The white hair of the ocean is tousled.
> I do not fear that there may come across the
> Irish sea hordes of fierce Vikings.[1]

The earliest literary record of Viking raids in this part of the Irish Sea is that contained in the *Annals of Ulster* for the year A.D. 798 in the following entry: 'The burning of Inis Patrick by the heathen, and plunder taken from the districts, and the shrine of Dochonna was broken into by them, and great devastations on their part between Eire and Alba.' It was formerly assumed that the *Inis Patrick* (or *Inis Padraig* in the Gaelic) referred to was the Manx St. Patrick's Isle on which the ruins of Peel Castle stand, but modern opinion favours its identification with Inispatrick, or St. Patrick's Isle in the Skerries off the Dublin coast.[2] The nature of Dochonna's (or St. Conna's) shrine is not definitely indicated, but quite possibly it was a stone tomb built in the form of a small chapel. This is more likely than an earlier suggestion that the

1. A. K. Porter, *The Crosses and Culture of Ireland* (New Haven, 1935), p. 75.

2. Professor Brøndsted (see p. 54, n. 1) still accepts the older interpretation (op. cit., p. 33), but 'between Ireland and Scotland' is an over-literal rendering for what should read 'both Ireland and Scotland', as rightly translated by A. O. Anderson, *Early Sources of Scottish History, A.D. 500–1286*, vol. i, p. 257.

Plate 9. CRUX GURIAT, a monumental cross-slab of the early ninth century, 7 ft. high by almost 3 ft. wide. The face of the stone has been tooled down to leave five heavy hemispherical bosses to indicate the cross head.

OVERLEAF

Plate 10. THE CALF OF MAN CRUCIFIXION, re-discovered on the small island off the south-west coast of Man in the eighteenth century, illustrates the quality of Celtic artistic endeavour just before the Viking invasions. The eastern Mediterranean style of Christ's elaborate robes is quite different from the usual Roman representation of this theme in north-west Europe.

Plate 11. THE ATHLONE CRUCIFIXION. This eighth-century Irish bronze plaque was riveted to a wooden book-cover, and would appear to be an earlier model for the Calf of Man Crucifixion.

Plate 12. VIKING VESSEL FROM SKULDELEV. This broad solid vessel with high sides is the only example yet found of a seagoing cargo ship which would have sailed into the waters of the Irish Sea and beyond.

shrine was a small metal casket such as the one now preserved in the Museum at Copenhagen.[1]

For two centuries after 798 there is very little definite record of events in Man, although rather more is known of what was happening in surrounding lands, especially eastern Ireland. It is evident that its important strategic position must have made Man a vitally significant base of operations for the Norsemen. In support of this it is frequently stated in one of the sagas—the *Orkneyinga Saga*—that the Vikings would set off from the Island in the spring or early summer to raid the adjoining coasts, after which they would 'fare home to Man' in the autumn before the winter storms began.

The effective occupation of Man, following the period of pirate expeditions, seems to date to the later ninth century and earlier tenth century when the new masters seized the most fertile districts for their own use. The northern lowland still bears impressive evidence of this process in the form of a number of circular earthen mounds which probably mark the burial places of the more important farmer-warriors belonging to the first generation of Norse settlers. Such, at any rate, is the conclusion suggested as the result of careful excavations of typical mounds at Knoc y Doonee overlooking the Ayre in Andreas in 1927, as well as Ballateare and Cronk Mooar in Jurby between 1944 and 1946, and supported by chance finds from others. The Knoc y Doonee grave, excavated by P. M. C. Kermode, had the form of a low mound, 7 or 8 ft. high, and it proved to be a ship-burial. The local landowner had been placed in his own boat, about 20 ft. long, the whole being then covered with earth. In the boat were also placed his sword, spear, shield, and battle-axe, while his fishing-gear and his hammer and tongs were added. Finally his horse and dog were sacrificed so that they might accompany their master in his journey to the next world. Few ornaments were found in the grave, but significantly a small bronze brooch of Irish type was discovered, and this had no doubt been made by some local Celtic metalworker.

The Ballateare and Cronk Mooar excavations were carried out by Professor G. Bersu. The former consisted of a mound 45 ft. in diameter and 7 ft. high, and in its centre was the body of a Viking warrior within

1. While there is no clue as to the precise origin of this casket, it was in all probability stolen from Ireland where the greater part of such metalwork was produced. It is claimed to be of certain Irish origin by Dr. A. Mahr in his *Christian Art in Ancient Ireland*, vol. i (Dublin, 1932), pls. 16 and 17; vol. ii (1941), p. 109.

a wooden coffin. In accordance with the pagan beliefs of the period the man's armour, including spears, sword, and shield, had been buried with him after being broken, either to prevent the robbing of the grave or in the belief that a man's weapons had to be made useless to prevent him from haunting the living. As a sacrifice to the dead man the grave also contained, in addition to the body of a woman between 20 and 30 years of age, the bones of oxen, horses, sheep, and dogs—these symbolizing the livestock of the farmer-warrior, just as the sods of the mound bear witness to the fertile soil of the fields.

Again, on the Castletown lowland at Balladoole (Arbory), Bersu in 1945 discovered another ship-burial on the low rise of Chapel Hill, half a mile from the sea. Here a pagan Viking had been laid to rest in his clinker-built boat some 35 ft. in length, the keel of which had been placed directly above the graves of some early Celtic Christians. The latter, incidentally, had been buried within the decayed ramparts of an earlier fortress of Iron Age date. The Balladoole Norse chieftain of more than a thousand years ago had been buried with his full work-a-day equipment, including his shield, spurs, stirrups, and highly ornamented harness-mounts. The variety of these grave goods bears eloquent witness to the wide trade contacts of the Vikings, since they indicate links not only with workshops in Scandinavia, Ireland, and England but also with those of central and southern Europe. Finally, the mound had been capped by a heap of stones covered by a layer of cremated bones. Amongst these have been identified bones of horse, ox, pig, sheep or goat, dog, and cat, such presumably, as in the case of other burials, representing an offering of livestock to accompany the dead man to the other world.[1]

THE KINGDOM OF MAN AND THE ISLES

Meanwhile Scandinavian conquests and settlements took place around the coasts of Ireland, where Dublin was the centre of Norse power, as well as along the whole of western Scotland and parts of north-west England and Wales. All districts conquered by the Norse were claimed by the king of Norway as being under his control, but in practice powerful Viking chieftains fought each other for supremacy. Thus at one time Man might be ruled by a king who lived in Dublin, at another

1. See Bersu and Wilson, *Three Viking Graves in the Isle of Man* (London, 1966), pp. 1–45.

time by a king who lived in the Island itself. There were other occasions when the Earls of Orkney claimed to rule the Island, especially during the eleventh century.

As time passed Man came to be linked particularly with the other Norse islands of the Hebrides along the west coast of Scotland, and the whole domain was called the Kingdom of Man and the Isles. There are in fact several hundred islands in the area if each islet is counted separately, but officially they were together reckoned as thirty-two in the days of the kingdom, Man being the most important of all.

For the purposes of administration the Hebrides were divided into four groups, based on the main islands of Lewis, Skye, Mull, and Islay. These were further subdivided into two groups, a northern and a southern, by the promontory of Ardnamurchan Point, and a fact of much interest which may be noted here is that the North Isles, namely, Lewis and Skye, were regarded as the Out Isles, that is, from the Manx point of view. The significance of this will become apparent in the next chapter when the origin of the Keys is discussed.

Godred Crovan 'King Orry', 1079–95

With this king, who obtained the Manx throne in 1079, the history of the Island assumes a more continuous pattern, still, it is true, somewhat faint or blurred, instead of being the mere collection of unrelated scraps that it had previously been. But while Godred is the first king about whom anything very definite is known it must be admitted that much concerning him is very obscure. His nickname Crovan is supposed to be due to the fact that he always wore white gauntlets when he went to war. Godred's home was possibly Islay, though he is said to have spent part of his youth in Man. He fought with the Norwegians under Harold, king of Norway, against Harold of England at Stamford Bridge in 1066, and fled to Man following the English victory. Nothing is heard of him for some years, but he then appears on the scene as the leader of three expeditions against Man, having somehow gathered together an army and a fleet. His first two attacks were unsuccessful, but in 1079 he made an attack which gave him possession of the Island.

The way in which he succeeded in this final attempt is described in the *Chronicle of Man and the Isles*, compiled later by the monks of Rushen Abbey. Godred landed at Ramsey during the night and hid 300 men on the slopes of Scacafell, now called Skyhill. At daybreak the Manx fiercely attacked the invaders, but during the heat

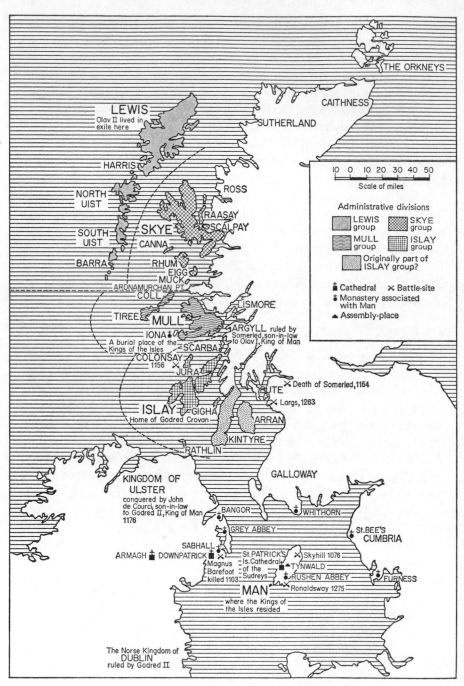

THE ORKNEYS

CAITHNESS

SUTHERLAND

LEWIS
Olav II lived in
exile here

HARRIS

ROSS

NORTH
UIST

RAASAY
SCALPAY

SKYE

SOUTH
UIST

CANNA

BARRA

RHUM
EIGG
MUCK
ARDNAMURCHAN PT.
COLL

LISMORE

TIREE

MULL

ARGYLL ruled by
Somerled, son-in-law
to Olav I, King of Man

IONA
A burial place of the
Kings of the Isles

SCARBA

COLONSAY
1156

JURA

Death of Somerled, 1164

BUTE

Largs, 1263

ISLAY
Home of Godred Crovan

GIGHA

ARRAN

KINTYRE

RATHLIN

GALLOWAY

KINGDOM OF
ULSTER
conquered by John
de Courci, son-in-law
to Godred II, King of Man
1176

BANGOR

WHITHORN

GREY ABBEY

St.BEE'S
CUMBRIA

SABHALL

ARMAGH DOWNPATRICK

St.PATRICK'S
Is.Cathedral
of the
Sudreys

Skyhill 1076

TYNWALD

Magnus
Barefoot
killed 1103

RUSHEN ABBEY

FURNESS

MAN
where the Kings of
the Isles resided

Ronaldsway 1275

The Norse Kingdom of
DUBLIN
ruled by Godred II

Scale of miles
10 0 10 20 30 40 50

Administrative divisions
LEWIS group
SKYE group
MULL group
ISLAY group
Originally part of
ISLAY group?

Cathedral   ✕ Battle-site
Monastery associated
with Man
Assembly-place

10. The Kingdom of Man and the Isles.

of the fray the 300 men in ambush attacked the natives from the rear. Disheartened, the Manx attempted to flee, but the tide was in flood, and as it came further up the Sulby river then than it does now, they were cut off on all sides. They piteously begged Godred to spare their lives as he had been reared amongst them, and taking compassion on them he forbade his army to attack them further. Thus Godred became king of Man and reigned for sixteen years, and except for short intervals his descendants ruled it until 1265. This great warrior can hardly have spent much time in the Island since his dominions included Dublin, where he resided a great deal, in addition to the Western Isles of Scotland. He died in the island of Islay in 1095.

Godred was the ruler who was responsible for the union of Man and the Isles into one kingdom, and to administer this great maritime unit he devised an ingenious political system which will be discussed in the next chapter. True, as will be seen, his great plan fell to pieces in less than two centuries after its creation, but there is reason to believe that in one respect at least, that is, as regards the number of the Keys, his system had a very important bearing on subsequent developments.

The Manx form of Godred (Irish *Gofraidh*) was *Gorree*; in the English phrase 'King Gorree' (when the -*g* of *king* was still pronounced) the words became misdivided as 'King Orree', hence the Orry of the anglicized tradition though, as the *Fin as Oshin* fragment and the *Traditionary Ballad* show, Gorree remained the Manx form of the name. Tradition says that when he first came to Man he landed at the Lhen on a bright starry night. Those who were gathered on the shore asked him whence he had come, and, pointing upwards to the Milky Way he said: 'Yonder is the road whence I came, and along that star-spangled dome is the way that leads to my country.' Ever since that time the Milky Way has been called in Manx *Raad Mooar Ree Gorry*, or 'the Great Way of King Orry'.

Magnus of Norway visits Man, 1098–1103

After the death of Godred Crovan came a period of conflict in which the two divisions of the Island, the north and the south, fought against one another. In 1098 a conflict took place which is referred to in the *Chronicle of Man*. According to the story there were two rival chieftains, Ottar and Macmarus, about whom nothing else is known. In their struggle for supremacy a great battle took place at a ford called Santwat which is thought to have been near Peel. Traditionally the north gained victory owing to the assistance of their women, but the leaders of both sides perished in the struggle.

Just after this battle Magnus Barefoot, king of Norway, came to assert his supremacy over the various Norse conquests. In 1098 he arrived at St. Patrick's Isle with a fleet of 160 ships, and he was so pleased with the Island's fertility that he chose it as his chief residence. Like other ambitious monarchs, he conquered as much as possible of other lands around the Irish Sea. After humbling the men of Galloway, who were compelled to supply timber for the erection of three forts on the Island,[1] he set off to subdue Anglesey. Next he turned his attention to Ireland, where he lost his life in 1103.

Olaf I, 1113–53

After the death of Magnus there was apparently another period of confusion until the accession of Olaf I, probably in the year 1113. He was the youngest son of Godred Crovan and had lived at the English court of Henry I since his father's death. His long reign of about forty years was one of the most memorable in the Island's history. Described in the *Chronicle* as a man of peace he showed such wisdom and skill, and kept on such friendly terms with the rulers of England, as well as those of Ireland and Scotland, that no one ventured to disturb his own kingdom of Man and the Isles until he had grown old and feeble. During his reign the foundation of the Cistercian monastery at Rushen Abbey took place, Olaf having granted the site to the Abbot of Furness. Tragedy marked the end of Olaf's reign since he was treacherously murdered by his nephews who came over from Dublin to demand a share of his kingdom.

Godred II, 1153–87

Olaf's son Godred was in Norway doing homage to the Norwegian king on behalf of his father at the time of the latter's death. Returning immediately to Man he dealt sternly with Olaf's murderers. Shortly afterwards he set sail for Dublin with a number of ships and a large army, since he had been offered the throne of the Scandinavian kingdom there. Despite stiff opposition Godred obtained possession of Dublin and then returned to Man. Here he so offended the chiefs of the Isles who had helped him on this Irish expedition that they rebelled against

1. Dr. Bersu believed he found traces of a fort built by Magnus on St. Patrick's Isle, this presumably being one of the three forts.

him with the aid of his brother-in-law, Somerled, the ruler of the Scottish coast of Argyll; Somerled was of Norwegian extraction as his name indicates. In 1156 Godred was defeated in a great naval battle off Colonsay, and was forced to share the kingdom of Man and the Isles with Somerled. The latter took the islands of Mull and Islay off the coast of Argyll, which formed the southernmost of the Hebrides, while Godred retained Man and the northern group of Lewis and Skye. As a result of this curious arrangement the hold of the Manx kings on their other island possessions was permanently weakened, although they retained the title of King of the Isles. The monks of Rushen Abbey, mournfully recording these events in the *Chronicle of Man*, wrote: 'thus was the Kingdom of the Isles ruined from the time the sons of Somerled got possession of it'. Godred seems to have felt his throne in danger, for after his struggle with Somerled in 1156 he put himself under the protection of Henry II of England.

Godred and Somerled quarrelled again in 1158 when the latter appeared off Ramsey with a fleet of fifty-three ships. He drove Godred out of the Island and then plundered the area before retiring to Scotland. In 1164 Somerled was slain in an attack against Scotland. Meanwhile Godred, who had gone to Norway to seek assistance, returned to resume possession of his island kingdom; he ultimately died in 1187. It is significant that although he died in Man his body was carried next year to Iona, the island made holy by the work of St. Columba.

Reginald I, 1187–1228

Godred left three sons, Reginald, Olaf, and Ivar, and while Reginald was the eldest he was not strictly the heir to the throne since he had been born many years before the marriage of his parents. The lawful heir was Olaf, but as he was then only ten years old the nobles preferred his older brother as their king. Reginald, who thus succeeded his father, stood out as one of the most warlike princes of his age, having spent much of his time in the manner of the ancient sea-kings. In proof of this, one of the sagas declares that he had passed three successive years always on board his ship, never being for one single hour beneath the roof of a house! Just where he performed his exploits is not quite clear, but probably most of them were in northern Scotland and the Orkneys.

As king of Man he had to face many troubles, most of which were due to the inevitable quarrels between his brother Olaf and himself and their various supporters. The details of such quarrels are wearying, so we need concern ourselves only with the main incidents. To begin with, Reginald gave his brother Olaf the island of Lewis, one of the northern Hebrides. Despite its size it was much poorer than Man, since it consisted mainly of moorland, and its inhabitants lived chiefly by hunting and fishing. Olaf therefore complained that he was unable to support himself and his retinue on such a poor island and asked for a larger share of the dominions. Reginald's reply was to have his brother imprisoned in Scotland. In the end Olaf escaped, and in 1224 he gathered a fleet of thirty-two ships from the Isles and came to Man, landing at Ronaldsway. Reginald now gave his brother many more islands but kept Man for himself. Neither was satisfied and so Man was again plunged into civil war. The north was on the side of Olaf, while the south supported Reginald. The opposing forces met in 1228 at Tynwald Hill, where Reginald was slain and his followers routed. The unfortunate southerners had a very unhappy time on this occasion, for not only did they lose the battle but just afterwards their land was visited by pirates and the area was devastated!

Apart from all these squabbles Reginald's stormy reign had one other feature of significance, namely, that it showed the increasing power of the English king in the Irish Sea, with the correspondingly waning power of the Norwegian king. Like previous ambitious rulers Reginald could not resist the temptation to interfere in Irish affairs, particularly in northern Ireland. This considerably annoyed the English King John, because England was anxious to extend her own power in Ireland, since the previous king, Henry II, had assumed the title of Lord of Ireland in 1171 when he added to his possessions by annexing Dublin and some other ports. Hence Reginald was sharply summoned to appear before the English king in 1206 to do homage to him.

The king of Norway was also trying to assert his former authority over the Manx ruler, and indeed Reginald set off to Norway to do homage there. This so irritated John of England that in 1210 he sent an expedition against the Isle of Man while its king was away, and on his return Reginald had to appear before John once again.[1] Reginald's career as a monarch can thus hardly be described as a happy one!

1. Reginald also paid homage to Rome in 1219. See *J. Manx Museum*, vii (1966), 9.

Plate 13. VIKING SHIP FROM GOKSTAD. The Norseman's high standards of ship design and construction put the known world within their range.

Olaf II, 1228–37

After the death of his brother in 1228 Olaf gained possession of Man, although he was not able to regain all the other isles that had formerly belonged to the kingdom. Since he had received some help from Norway, the English king, now Henry III, showed his annoyance by bringing Olaf before him and making him promise to defend the Irish Sea against intruders, and if necessary to place fifty ships at the disposal of England. This naturally displeased the Norwegians, and Olaf was on the point of setting out for Norway to try and make his peace there when he died.

Harald I, 1237–48

Olaf II's son Harald was only fourteen when he succeeded his father, and his reign witnessed still more rivalry between England and Norway for the control of Man and the Isles. At first Harald refused to recognize the Norwegian monarch as his overlord, with the result that he was deposed and the revenues of the country were collected by King Haakon of Norway. In the end Harald submitted, and received back his kingdom which gave him a friendly welcome. Then the English ruler, Henry III, showed his favour by knighting him, but this of course aroused the jealousy of Norway. Once more Harald set off to the latter country where he received such a warm reception that he married King Haakon's daughter. Tragedy befell him on his return journey, for he and his queen were shipwrecked and drowned near the Shetlands. His brother succeeded to the throne as Reginald II, but his reign was only to last a few weeks since he was assassinated by one of his knights, Ivar, in a meadow near Rushen Church.

Magnus, 1252–65

A period of confusion and strife followed the tragic death of Reginald II, but finally in 1252 Magnus, youngest son of Olaf II, secured the

---

Plate 14. CHAPEL HILL, BALLADOOLE, a Celtic Iron Age hillfort. Near the entrance, stone markers outline a Viking ship burial; excavations made by Bersu revealed a richly clothed Viking, with his horse harness beside him, together with the body of a woman, probably his wife, and cremated animal bones to accompany him to Valhalla.

Plate 15. VIKING JEWELLERY from the ship at Balladoole. The two long thin strips in the centre are bridle mounts from the horse harness, and the four bronze enamel discs to the right may also belong to the bridle. To the left are three buckles and strap ends; that on the extreme left is of silver-gilt, and fastened the belt; the other two pairs (top and bottom) fastened the spurs.

Manx throne, and he was fated to be the last King of Man and the Isles. It has already been seen that England and Norway were competing for the control of Man. Meanwhile Scotland had been growing in strength, and its king, Alexander III, was anxious to obtain possession of the Western Isles. By this time only some of these islands (Lewis and Skye with their 'pertinents') belonged to Man, the others being in the hands of the descendants of Somerled.

After vainly trying to get them by bargaining Alexander attacked the Hebrides. King Haakon of Norway arrived off the Scottish coast with a large fleet to defend the islands, but in 1263 he suffered a reverse at the battle of Largs on the Firth of Clyde. Meanwhile the Manx king, Magnus, had also taken a fleet to oppose the Scots, but he was not present at the battle of Largs, having proceeded up Loch Long to attack that coast. Upon the retreat of the Norwegians, Magnus returned to Man with Alexander in pursuit. After a truce the two kings met in Dumfries, where Magnus was allowed to keep the Isle of Man after doing homage to King Alexander and promising to supply him with ten war-galleys— five 24-oared, and five 12-oared—whenever he needed them. Thus for the last two years of his life Magnus was King of Man only; and he was the last of the dynasty founded by Godred Crovan to hold that position, since in 1266, a year after the death of Magnus, a treaty was signed between Norway and Scotland by which not only the Western Isles of Scotland, but also Man, were handed over to the king of Scotland.

CHAPTER FIVE

Life under Scandinavian Rule

WE ARE INCLINED TO THINK OF THE NORSE SEA-ROVERS AS ruthless and cruel, with an insatiable passion for warfare and plunder. It is true that at first they were enemies of Christianity; but they were a fine virile people with a great love of freedom, and they gave life and vigour to the regions in which they settled. They were not barbarians. They had the art of writing and a great appreciation of beauty, as they showed in their love of ornaments (for example, Pl. 15) and fine clothing and in the decoration of their wonderful carvings in stone and wood. Their weapons show their skill in working iron, as their clothing, often with very graceful patterns, shows their skill in weaving. They were practical, resourceful men and great organizers. In this connection the essential thing to remember is that when they entered a country with old and settled traditions, such as Man at that period, they came under the influence of the local culture and devoted their skill and power of organization to developing and improving what they found.

In their physical make-up, as already seen in Chapter 1, the Vikings are thought to have been mainly fair, tall, and long-headed, belonging to what is called the Nordic race type, and there are many people of this kind in Man at the present day as a result of the Norse invasions. As previously stated, there are rather more people of this type in the parishes of the northern lowland and in the parish of Malew than elsewhere, partly because these areas contain so much of the richer agricultural land. It should also be remembered that these parts offered the best low-lying shores on which the shallow and flat-bottomed boats could be pulled up when they came to stay for the winter or for longer periods, so that they were the most attractive areas for the Norsemen.

Generally speaking, it was only the younger men who came from

Norway, possibly bringing with them a few slaves. Thus from the beginning there must have been constant intermixture between the Norsemen and the native women inhabitants of the Island, so that there would soon be a fusion of the two elements to form a new Manx type. Since the Vikings were known to the Gaels as 'Strangers' (Galls) the mixed population of Man came to be called the Gael-Galls by the other Gaelic people in districts unaffected by Scandinavian immigration.

The Norse language was naturally introduced into Man; since it was the language of the conquerors it came to be the speech used by the upper classes and also in the government of the country. Gaelic must also have been used by the women, who would teach it to the children. When the kingdom of Man and the Isles came to an end the Norse language gradually died away and the Celtic tongue once more became the chief speech of the Manx. Owing to the close connection that had existed between Man and Scotland, particularly the south-west and the Western Isles, the native tongue of Man had become influenced by the Scottish form of Gaelic—and, in fact, it continued to be so affected—so that henceforth Manx had a greater resemblance to Scottish Gaelic than to Irish. Surprising as it may seem, the Norse language had scarcely any effect on modern Manx.[1]

Survivals of the Norse occupation still persist in many place-names ending in *by*, which was a Scandinavian word for farm or homestead, so that Sulby originally meant Solli's farm, Colby meant Colli's farm, and so on. The Scandinavian word for mountain was *fell*, and thus Snaefell is pure Norse for snow-mountain. The Norse name *dalr*, meaning a dale or valley, is found in the names of many glens in the Island, as in Foxdale, meaning waterfall-dale, while Dalby means the farm in the dale or glen. Many names of places on the coast are also of Norse origin, although as the names are written now it is not always easy to see this. Thus the Norse word *vik*, meaning creek, is now found in the form *wick*, as in the case of such bays as Fleshwick and Perwick.[2]

1. This contrast between the very small proportion of words of Norse origin in the Manx vocabulary (apart from sea terms) and the rather large proportion of place-terms, especially major names of administrative significance, has sometimes been explained by the assumption that after the Norse period there was substantial immigration into Man from some other Gaelic-speaking area, most probably south-west Scotland. Cf. Gelling, Nicolaisen, and Richards, *Names of Towns and Cities in Britain* (London, 1970), p. 84. The linguistic situation in the Isle of Man during the Norse period has been discussed by Dr. M. Gelling in *J. Manx Museum*, vii, nos. 86 and 87.

2. This fascinating but complicated subject can be studied in more detail in the well-known books by A. W. Moore and in *Place Names of the Isle of Man*, by J. J. Kneen, and

WAY OF LIFE: BUILDINGS, CLOTHING, FOOD

Records dealing with the Isle of Man at this time tell nothing of how the people lived. There are, nevertheless, descriptions of life in Iceland and the Western Isles, and it may be assumed that the Vikings who settled in Man wore the same kind of dress and lived in the same kind of homes. Their houses were rather long and narrow, with low walls built of stones and earth and a very steep roof covered with turf, straw, or rushes. The rooms had open hearths in the centre of the floor from which the smoke escaped through a hole in the roof, and the people slept on beds made of straw placed round the walls. The chiefs and prominent men lived on their own estates with their families, followers, and servants. On such an estate there would be a dwelling-house and a series of farm buildings, the whole arranged so as to form a quadrangle. The buildings were all detached from one another, and often even the different parts of the dwelling-house—the kitchen, the dining-hall, and so on—were under separate roofs, although later people were able to erect larger houses with more rooms under one roof.

It appears to have been customary for more than one family to live in the same household, since the married son or sons, and in some cases the married daughters, remained on the farm with their families doing their share of the work. The result was to form large family units consisting of two or more generations, all under the strict control of the patriarch, or head of the whole group.

A certain amount of information regarding actual buildings of the Norse period in the Island has been obtained by excavations carried out in recent years by Peter Gelling, particularly in the coastal promontory forts at Cronk ny Merriu (Port Grenaugh, Santan) and Cass ny Hawin. The houses revealed a typically oblong form with raised benches on either side; and since such sites were not those of ordinary homesteads but rather, in all probability, watch-posts set up by the Norse kings to control the use of secluded coves overlooked by them, they lacked the space for normal domestic activities. In the case of Cronk ny Merriu the walls of the house were mainly of turf with stone facings, but the walls of the house in the other fort must have been almost exclusively of turf.

most reliably in C. J. Marstrander's article, *Det norske landnåm på Man* (see Bibliography, p. 186), all of which deal not only with Norse, but with Celtic and English place-names also. See also the Appendix, p. 177, giving a glossary of Gaelic and Norse words most often found in Manx place-names.

Of quite a different character are the two buildings standing beside the round house at the Braaid already mentioned (see p. 35 and Pl. 6). These are the remains of rectangular Norse houses, and the larger must have been quite an imposing house about 70 ft. long; and while this is perhaps not exceptional the maximum width of about 30 ft. certainly is. Normally the distance between the two long walls would be not more than 20 ft. since the builders wished to avoid erecting a roof with a wider span. It is, however, an interesting fact that the Celtic round house was apparently still in existence at the Braaid when the Norse long house was being built, and when it is recalled that such circular houses could have a roof span of up to 90 ft., as in the case of the Balla-keigan dwelling, it is very tempting to think that the Celtic skill of roofing wide areas was actually brought into play in the construction of this very wide Norse long-house. Unfortunately in the lack of any records nothing is known of the history of this house, but it must have been the home of a prominent Viking settler.

A small Norse farmstead has recently been identified, and partly excavated, near Doarlish Cashen at Dalby. It is situated at a height of about 700 ft., on the edge of what is today moorland. The dwelling-house was very small, but of unmistakably Norse type. It occupied part of one side of a small enclosed farmyard, while on the other side was a large kiln for drying corn. Outside the farmyard, but in the immediate vicinity, there were eight small huts or pens. Some field-banks could be traced nearby, at one point forming a funnel-shaped entrance to facilitate the driving of sheep or cattle. Whereas at the Braaid we probably have the home of a prosperous landowner, this farmstead represents the opposite end of the social scale. Not all the settlers were well-to-do; certainly not the family which attempted to farm this marginal land.[1]

The men wore grey woollen trousers, kept in position by a belt, and often had the socks knitted on to them. They also wore a linen shirt or woollen tunic, a cloak, and shoes made of raw hides like the former Manx *carranes*, or sandals. The most important piece of women's clothing was the long gown, or *kyrtil*, made very wide and fastened round the waist by a belt. They were very fond of ornaments. Brooches, finger-rings, and bracelets are often mentioned in the sagas, while elaborate ornaments in silver and bronze have often been found in their graves. When they could obtain them, by plunder or other means, the

1. See P. S. Gelling in *Medieval Archaeology*, xiv (1970), 74.

Vikings loved fine clothes in many colours. One account of 968 speaks of the Norsemen in Limerick possessing 'woven cloths of every kind and colour, silk and satin raiment, beauteous and variegated, both scarlet and green'.

Their bread was made of rye, oats, or barley, as little wheat was sown. In the summer herrings would be plentiful, and there would be meat as well as milk, butter, and cheese from the cattle. Curds and whey seem to have been very popular. The problem of curing food for winter consumption must, on the other hand, have been difficult, since salt was scarce and had to be imported, unless it was obtained by boiling sea-water.

During the summer months many of the people went up into the mountain pastures since good natural grazing existed there for the animals, both cattle and sheep, while turf could also be obtained for winter fuel. The Manx term for these summer grazing pastures is *earys* (equivalent to the Scottish word *shielings*), and this word can be found very frequently as an element in the place-names in many upland areas of the Island.[1] The existence of this seasonal up-and-down movement of population—now referred to under the general term of *transhumance*— has been a well-recognized feature of several European countries for a very long time, and in all likelihood it became intensified in Man as a result of the Norse occupation. Evidence for its existence has been obtained by excavation and field-work by Peter Gelling on the groups of mounds found in many parts of the Manx mountains, about 48 such groups in all having been identified. These are generally situated around the 1,000-ft. contour on dry ground close to a stream, and one of the most characteristic groups is that around Block Eary at the head of Sulby valley on the northern slopes of Snaefell, where about 37 mounds have been recognized.[2] Again, at the head of Glen Dhoo in Ballaugh there are 33 mounds, while around Injebreck there are 23. It is very interesting to reflect that this mode of life, which must have existed in

1. The word *eary*, Irish *áirghe*, was sufficiently characteristic of Gaelic practice to be borrowed into Norse as *erg*, and appears also in northern England in areas where the Norse-Irish settled; see A. H. Smith, *English Place-Name Elements* (Cambridge, 1956), vol. i, p. 157.

2. For a map showing distribution of these mounds see P. S. Gelling, 'Medieval shielings in the Isle of Man', *Medieval Archaeology*, vi–vii (1962–3), 168. These mounds should be distinguished from the hut-circles which also exist in the mountain areas, although in rather smaller numbers. It is possible they represent the forerunners of the *earys* going back to prehistoric times, but they have not been properly excavated.

the Isle of Man for very many centuries, has now disappeared entirely, and it appears that it had ceased to exist by the seventeenth century since Blundell, the well-known writer on the Island in the middle of that century, makes no reference to the practice.

Trade appears to have been more important than is usually thought. The Norseman with his great love for, and his great skill on the sea could and did become a great trader when not engaged in some raiding enterprise. It is, indeed, known that active trading took place between Norway, through the various Norse settlements in the west, such as those in western Scotland and around the Irish Sea, and France and the countries of southern Europe. From the north came fish, hides, and furs, while to the north went woollen and linen cloths, as well as corn, honey, and wine. There was also a great trade in slaves who had been made prisoners in war. Just what part the Island played in all this traffic it is impossible to say at the moment, but there can be little doubt that the existence of these trading movements definitely contributed to the persistence of the kingdom of Man and the Isles for some two centuries.

GOVERNMENT AND ADMINISTRATION

The Manx system of government illustrates very strikingly two things, firstly the influence of ideas introduced by the Norsemen, and secondly the genius of these people for turning to account customs which were in existence amongst the people they had conquered.

The Tynwald Court

An essential feature of the Norse life was the annual open-air assembly of all the freemen at some central place where new laws were announced, disputes settled, and other necessary business dealt with.[1] This assembly was called the *thing*, a word which forms the first part of the Manx term Tynwald. The second half is Norse for field or meeting-place, so that Tynwald (or *Thingvöllr*) was originally the place at which the assembly of freemen met. This is the meeting which is still held every Tynwald Day, 5 July, for the purpose of announcing new laws that have been passed during the preceding year. Until the First World

---

1. Norse analogies suggest that law-making was only an exceptional part of the business, but that a recital of the traditional laws or part of them by the lawman was an essential part of the proceedings. The law might or might not be written, but this was how the knowledge of it was spread.

War it was true to say that laws did not become effective until they had been approved at this ceremony.

As had been said, the mound called Tynwald Hill (Pls. 35 and 36) is much older than the Scandinavian period and, although not itself a burial mound, it has been placed on the site of an earlier mound of the Bronze Age, and has pre-Christian graves in the vicinity. Long before the coming of the Norse a national assembly, or fair, had been held on this site, which is the natural meeting-place for the whole Island. The date of the fair was originally Midsummer Day, a day associated with much rejoicing from very early pagan times.[1] With the coming of Christianity into the Island, the fair was linked with the name of a Christian saint, John the Baptist, whose place in the Church's calendar, 24 June, was as near as possible to Midsummer Day. Then, with the alteration of the calendar that took place in the eighteenth century, the date was changed to 5 July, the present date. Further, although the name Tynwald Hill is the name by which the mound is generally known, the Celtic name by which it is still known locally is *Cronk y Keeillown*, i.e. the Hill of St. John's Chapel, or Keeill.

Nowadays the lieutenant-governor takes the central seat on Tynwald Hill, the seat once occupied by the Norse king. With him, in the one-time seat of Odin's chief priest, is the Lord Bishop. In front are the deemsters and the members of the legislative council, who were formerly the lord's principal officers. On the next platform are the twenty-four members of the Keys; below these are the vicars and the captains of the parishes, and outside the mount are the freemen or commons.

The deemsters

The position which the deemsters hold in the Tynwald ceremony is historically the most important part of their office. It has already been explained why there are two; they represented the two original main divisions of the Island, the north and south. It has also been seen how

1. Such a fair was known in ancient Ireland as an *oenach* and either at it or at an assembly known as an *airecht* all the business typical of a Norse *thing* was transacted and games were also held. These fairs took place at regular intervals and lasted for some days, those visiting them living meanwhile in a regular encampment. Some are thought to have been the gathering-places which Ptolemy names as towns in his account of Ireland since no permanent urban settlements existed. There is perhaps sufficient similarity here between Gaelic and Norse custom to make assimilation easy. On the Irish assemblies see D. A. Binchy, *Crith Gablach* (Dublin, 1941), pp. 73 and 102.

their name has changed from the Manx *briw*, meaning judge, and the Norse *lagman*, meaning man of the law, to the English *deemster*.[1]

For a long time the laws were not written and were supposed to be locked in the memories, or the 'breasts', of the men appointed for that purpose. It was the duty of the lawmen to declare to the king what the laws were. Such declarations were called 'breast-laws', and they were, of course, based on the general customs of the Island. These form the basis of the existing Manx customary or common law, but they remained oral until about 1690 despite various attempts to have them committed to writing. It was then that Deemster Parr wrote his *Abstract of the Laws, Customs and Ordinances of the Isle of Man*, which did a great deal towards making Manx common law more stable and reliable and less dependent on the memories or caprices of the deemsters.

The Keys

The Manx House of Keys, which now corresponds to the English House of Commons, owes some of its characteristic features to the Norse period, including the fixing of its number which still remains at twenty-four. The earliest Keys were those chosen from the chief land-owners as being the 'worthiest men in the land' to represent the free-men of the Island, whose duty it was to assist at Tynwald in deciding what the law was. It was not until a later period that their function came to include the making of new laws.

Meanwhile how did such a number arise? A very likely explanation is to be found in a consideration of the system created by Godred Crovan—the King Orry of Manx tradition—to govern his maritime kingdom of Man and the Isles. As pointed out in the previous chapter, it was assumed that the area consisted of thirty-two islands, and it was decided that the common parliament should comprise the same number of chosen representatives. Of these thirty-two members, Man, being

1. The English term *deemster* represents a northern English and Scottish derivative from *deem* 'judge', also found in the surname Dempster. If the Norse term *lagman* ever existed in Man it has left no trace, and *deemster* seems to be a direct English translation of *briw*. The term *briw* is found anglicized in Lewis as *breve* and in Ireland as *brehon*, the first two representing the Irish nom. sing. *breitheamh*, while the third is the full stem *breitheamhan*. The Irish customary law was accordingly known as brehon law. In the formative period both Irish and Norse law would be transmitted orally and learnt by heart, hence the term 'breast-law'. The recording of the Manx version of the customary law is too late to enable us confidently to isolate the Irish or Norse elements in it and to decide which is the more important.

the wealthiest island and the capital, was to appoint one-half. The other sixteen came from the Hebrides, which were divided into the four groups of isles already described, each group sending four representatives to the Tynwald.

The next stage came after the partition of the Isles dating from Somerled's defeat of Godred II in 1156, as a result of which only the two northern groups, or Out Isles, maintained their connection with Man. This reduced the Hebridean membership to eight, and gave a total of twenty-four Keys, a number which was destined to remain permanent.

In 1266, at the time of the break-up of the kingdom and the cession of all the Western Isles to the crown of Scotland, only the sixteen Manxmen were left in the Keys. But the Manx refused to accept their defeat as final, and they continued to fill the places formerly occupied by the men from the Out Isles by appointing eight additional representatives from Man itself—thus preserving the total which has persisted to the present day.

Keeping these points in mind, it is not difficult to interpret the statement made by the Keys themselves in their famous declaration regarding the Manx constitution in 1422. Explaining the origin of the number to Sir John Stanley, they said that the Keys 'were twenty-four freeholders, namely eight in the Out Isles and sixteen in your land of Mann —and that was in King Orry's days'. Until recently the term Out Isles in this statement was taken to mean the whole of the Hebridean group, but such an interpretation is now seen to be incorrect.[1]

A striking feature concerning the original representation in Man is that it was probably on a parish basis, for there is no doubt that there were sixteen ancient parishes in early days when Marown was joined to Santan, and not seventeen as at present. When, in the end, the additional eight members had to be chosen from within the Island the parochial basis of the Keys was upset, and the sheadings came to be adopted as the units of representation.

The origin of the name Keys has given rise to a good deal of discussion and it cannot be said that the problem is finally solved. The suggested derivation from a Scandinavian word *kjósa* meaning 'choose' cannot be accepted on linguistic grounds,[2] but the most likely explanation is that it is an English word which owes its introduction to the

1. For a fuller discussion see W. Cubbon, *Island Heritage*, pp. 82–90.
2. The connection with *kjósa* would probably never have been suggested if the participle 'chosen', i.e. sing. *kosinn*, pl. *kosnir*, had been taken as the starting-point.

following combination of circumstances. In the first place the Manx name for the Keys has long been *Yn Kiare-as-feed*, literally meaning 'The Four and twenty'. Such a title would, no doubt, be more or less unintelligible to the earliest English officials who came to the Island, but they probably detected some resemblance in pronunciation between the first words 'kiare-as' and 'keys'. Then, since the essential function of the body in its original form was to 'unlock' or solve the difficulties of the law, it seemed quite apt and convenient for the English to use the term 'keys' in its figurative sense to describe its members. This word is, indeed, used in its Latin form of *claves* in the earliest document in the Statute Book dated 1418, in which the Keys are described as *Claves Manniae et Claves Legis* (i.e. 'Keys of Man and Keys of the Law'). The term Key is not found in documents between 1418 and 1585, but between 1585 and 1734 the title 'the 24 Keys' is used, and from 1734 onwards the phrase is 'the Keys'.

Before the Tynwald ceremony begins the Court is 'fenced'. That is to say, the chief coroner, the coroner of Glenfaba sheading, reads out a notice in which all are warned not to 'quarrel, brawl or make any disturbance'. We read in accounts of Norse assemblies of an actual fence made of sacred cords or ropes being drawn around the place where the Court sat. 'Fencing the court' is thus a Norse institution. But the practice of strewing the pathway from St. John's Church to Tynwald Hill with rushes (see Pl. 56), goes back to pagan days in the Island when Manannan, the Celtic sea-god, received rushes as his annual tribute.[1]

Some Tynwald promulgation ceremonies have been held at places other than St. John's. It is recorded that a Tynwald was held at Cronk Urleigh, Kirk Michael, in 1422, and at Cronk Keeill Abban, Kirk Braddan, a few years later.[2]

It has already been shown that the original division into sheadings, parishes, treens, and quarterlands was not the work of the Norse, but that the Norsemen caused them to be better defined and more fully organized. Each sheading is believed to have had the duty of supplying one war-galley for the Island's defence, while each of the treens had to supply four men to serve in this ship. Later on the obligation of the landholders to supply ships and men was altered to an obligation to pay

1. For the annual tribute of rushes to Manannán see the Traditionary Ballard, stanza 7, in *Etudes celtiques*, ix (1960–1), 529–30.

2. It seems probable that, as in Scandinavia, there were local as well as national assembly points, and that these may have been among them.

taxes to the king. A charter dating to the year 1313, by which the king of Scotland handed over the Isle of Man to the Earl of Moray, made it a condition that the earl should annually place six ships, each with twenty-six oars, at the disposal of the Scottish king, and this may possibly be a revival of what the Norse kings of Man had demanded from the Island.

RELIGION

With the coming of the pagan Norsemen the development of Christianity was seriously checked for a time. It was not until towards the middle of the tenth century that there was a marked revival of Christianity and the Norse began to give up their pagan beliefs. Their full conversion appears to have been a slow process, and even after they had adopted some forms of the Christian religion they still loved to think of the stories connected with their old gods and heroes, since many of these are depicted, as will be seen later, on what were intended as Christian memorial crosses.

When first converted to Christianity the Manx Vikings adopted the Celtic mode of organization in which there were no such institutions as dioceses or bishops with territorial jurisdiction. But in all likelihood during the early half of the eleventh century they began to break their links with the Irish Church at about the time when Iceland and Orkney also came under Roman influence direct from continental Europe, and the first Bishop of Man, who bore the ancient Norse name Roolwer (i.e., Norse *Hrólfr*, anglicized Ralph), dates to the middle of the eleventh century. Doubtless he owed allegiance to the English Primate, the Archbishop of Canterbury, and it is very likely that Roolwer's successor, Bishop William, was a Norman monk.

No definite information about the further development of the Christian Church is available until the time of King Olaf (1113–53), who, having been educated at the English court, must have been familiar with the English religious system. In all probability it was during his reign that the Island was organized into parishes, each with its recognized parish church or Kirk, and it is definitely known that in 1134 Olaf invited the monks of Furness to come and found Rushen Abbey.

The monks of Furness at first belonged to an order known as the Savignian, but in 1147 this was changed to the Cistercian, which stressed

the importance of doing manual work as well as performing the ordinary religious duties. They took a great interest in the improvement of
agriculture and the breeding of animals, and no doubt the brethren at
Rushen Abbey helped to improve methods of farming amongst the
Manx people. The neighbourhood of Rushen Abbey must have been
very marshy in those days, and it certainly involved a great deal of hard
labour to lay firm foundations for the group of stone buildings whose
ruins still remain there.

The abbey became a centre of great importance and many roads led
to it. It was in close touch with the chief landing-place at Ronaldsway
(now called Derbyhaven), while routes connected it through Foxdale
with St. John's and Peel. A very important road led by way of St.
Mark's and the Braaid, on by the old church of Marown, across the
central valley, thence following the mountain road to Ramsey, another
very important landing-place. The growing significance of the abbey
may be judged from the fact that a number of the Norse kings were
buried there, including Olaf II, Reginald II, and Magnus, the last king of
Man and the Isles.

At the outset Rushen Abbey was granted considerable tracts of land
in Malew, and as time went on it became still more wealthy. Olaf I's
son, Godred, gave lands in Lezayre for the building of another abbey
there, but these soon passed into the hands of Rushen Abbey. In 1246,
under King Harald, the monks obtained the use of 'all kinds of mines' in
Man, as well as some land near St. Trinian's, and they were granted
exemption from all tolls and taxes. Thus the power of the abbey became
very great indeed, and with it grew the influence of the Pope in the
affairs of the Island.

King Olaf I strengthened the links between Man and the Isles and
organized its religious activities by spreading Roman forms of ritual and
administration against the opposition of Irish monks, who continued
to assert their authority at Iona as late as 1203. This work was actually
entrusted to the monks of Furness Abbey to whom was granted, in
1134, the right of electing the bishop of the Isles. The correct title of the
diocese is *Ecclesia Insularum* (i.e. the Episcopal See of the Isles) or
Ecclesia Sodorensis—the latter being the Latin form of the Norse name
for Man and the Hebrides, the *Sudreyjar* (Sudreys) or 'Southern Isles'.
They were so called to distinguish them from the Nordreys, or Northern Isles, including the Shetlands and Orkneys.

Although the political connections between Man and the Isles ceased after 1266, the ecclesiastical link persisted until about the fifteenth century.[1] At the present day there is no connection at all, but the title of the Manx bishop serves as a reminder of Norse days. Strictly the actual title now used—Sodor and Man—is rather unduly inclusive, but it came into use during the seventeenth century when the original meaning of the term Sodorensis was not fully appreciated. From 1152 until the fifteenth century the bishopric was under the control of the Archbishop of Trondhjem or Nidaros in Norway, but now it forms part of the English province of York, an act of 1542 having confirmed the transfer which had been made almost a century earlier.

Bishop Simon

The best-known bishop of Sodor and Man during the Norse period was Simon, who held office from 1227 until about 1247. According to the *Chronicle of Man* he was a man 'of great prudence, and learned in the Holy Scriptures'. It was he, who, according to the *Chronicle*, began to build St. German's on Peel islet as the cathedral church of the Sudreys about the year 1230. When he became bishop there were very likely two churches on that small island, a spot of very special sacredness. One of the churches was St. Patrick's (an eleventh- or early twelfth-century building, now in ruins but originally the parish church of Kirk Patrick)[2] while the other was presumably the ancient parish church of Kirk German on the site now occupied by the ruins of the cathedral. Simon selected St. German's not only because of its association with the traditional first bishop of the Celtic Church in Man, but possibly because it had a larger endowment of land. He proceeded to rebuild it, but did not complete the work, being able to finish only the chancel and the tower and transepts, while the nave was built some years later by Bishop Richard. Simon was buried in his own cathedral, which continued to be used until the middle of the eighteenth century, but has since become dilapidated (Pl. 21). He is said to have had his palace in Kirk Michael on the site of the existing Bishopscourt, but the present building belongs to a later date.

1. Only in 1498 do the Scots seem to have despaired of recovering Man and applied to the Pope for permission to create a new diocese based on Iona. The suggestion appears to have come from the Earl of Argyll.
2. The lowest courses of this building seem to be pre-Norse, and some believe it was the Celtic cathedral.

SCANDINAVIAN STONE CROSSES

It has been seen in Chapter 3 that the art of carving in stone had already made great strides amongst the Manx before the Norsemen arrived, and that the form of memorial known as the Celtic cross had been developed by them. Native Celtic sculptors still went on with their art after the Norse conquest, thus indicating that they must have retained their Christian beliefs; indeed, they then produced very refined examples of Celtic crosses which do not show any traces of Scandinavian influence. When the Norse settlers adopted Christianity and began to erect monuments to their dead they naturally copied the models with which they were familiar, either in Man or in the Hebrides. Thus a new series of crosses—the Scandinavian—began from at least the middle of the tenth century, and these reveal certain differences from those previously made in Man.

In the first place the language of the inscriptions is Norse and the lettering is a special script known as runic. These runes represent the oldest form of writing amongst the Teutonic peoples, including the Scandinavian, and appear to be based mainly on the Roman letters, simplified so that they could be carved more easily on stone or on wood. It will be seen by the illustration (Pl. 16) that they consist almost entirely of straight lines because curves are much more difficult to cut.

The inscriptions are not very long, but say something like this: 'Joalf son of Thorolf the Red erected this cross to the memory of Fritha his mother.' Some of the inscriptions are nevertheless very significant as they give actual proof of the mixing of Norse with Celtic people. For example, on one stone a man with a Norse name, Thorleif, refers to his son who had a Celtic name, Fiac, and no doubt the mother was also Celtic. Other people named on the stones had purely Celtic names (e.g. Mael Brigde, and Druian, son of Dugald), yet their memorials were written in Norse!

The makers of the Scandinavian crosses added fresh details to the decorations and also depicted new subjects. Outstanding examples of some of the new designs are to be found in the work of the earliest and best known of Scandinavian sculptors named Gaut who was respon-

---

Plate 16. GAUT'S CROSS-SLAB, MICHAEL. Part of the memorial inscription (centre), running up the side of the cross records that 'Gaut made this and all in Man'. The interlacing is in a distinctive Scandinavian style which was much copied and developed by later craftsmen.

Plate 17. THORWALD'S CROSS, illustrating the end of the world of heathen gods and the coming of Christ to rule in Odin's stead. In the last great battle of pagan mythology, Odin is slain by the Fenris wolf, who in turn is slain in common with everything else; on the opposite side of the cross, a saint carrying a cross and Bible is trampling on the serpent of Evil.

sible for the ring-chain pattern, so well shown on the Kirk Michael cross, which is named after its designer, as well as on many others. This became such a favourite that it is met with at least eighteen times on various crosses, and it might indeed be considered a characteristic of Manx art of the period. Gaut also developed other interlacing designs culminating in the graceful tendril pattern to be seen in the Ballaugh cross, for example, while it was he who, according to Kermode, invented the peculiar Manx decorative treatment at the head of the cross which gave it such a distinctive character.

The origins of certain of these designs are to be found, in the view of some authorities, amongst the Anglo-Norse settlers of north-west England, and some of these patterns are to be seen in crosses at Gosforth and Muncaster in Cumberland. It was in this area that Gaut is thought to have spent his early life. The sculptor then settled in the Isle of Man, and, according to the inscription on the cross at Andreas, was known as Gaut Björnson (so that he was, in other words, the son of a Viking) who lived at Kuli, which is now identified by some writers with a farm at Ballacooley in the parish of Kirk Michael. Thus it was that he produced his crosses in the Island between the years 930 and 950.

The oldest group of Manx Viking crosses is best represented by the one already referred to at Kirk Michael which records, in Scandinavian runes, that it was erected by 'Melbrigdi son of Adakan the smith for his soul', and then goes on to make the claim that 'Gaut made this and all in Man'. This proud boast of Gaut can only refer to the first Scandinavian crosses to be erected on the Island, and no doubt it is literally true that he was responsible for all of these. It was left to his younger successors to introduce the pictorial element which was absent from Gaut's own work, while it was only in the later crosses that the more elaborate animal ornament was developed, including the typical dragons. In this connection it is important to keep in mind the fact that the Island continued for so long to have direct links with Scandinavia, and thus it is not surprising that the Manx crosses reflect Viking influences rather strongly both in their general content and in certain details. This is shown, for example, in the fact that the story of Sigurd is especially popular in the Manx series, while many of the human figures are based on Scandinavian rather than English prototypes (as, for example, in the case of the figure of a woman with a long pigtail and trailing dress shown on the Heimdall cross from Jurby). Taken as a whole the Manx Viking crosses belong to the Scandinavian art phases known as the Jellinge and the

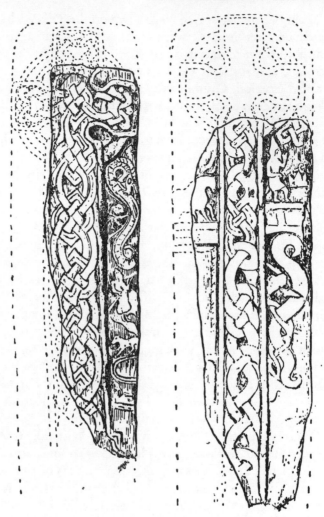

11. Crosses from Jurby and Malew.

Mammen, the former (and earlier) including the designs of the famous Gaut, while the later style is represented in such stones as the Thorleif and Odd crosses from Kirk Braddan and the Joalf slab at Kirk Michael.

The crosses from Jurby and Malew date from about the end of the tenth century. Although by different artists, and only fragments, both record portions of the famous Sigurd story telling how the hero slew the dragon Fafnir and carried off his hoard of gold. Sigurd had been advised by Odin to dig a pit in which to conceal himself so that he might pierce the dragon Fafnir with his famous sword as the monster passed over. Both crosses illustrate this incident on their right-hand panels, and the monster is seen writhing in its death-agony. Above this on the Malew cross Sigurd is shown roasting ring-shaped portions of the dragon's heart held on a spit over a fire, which is depicted by three triangular tongues of flame. Having scalded his fingers with boiling blood he cools them in his mouth, and once the blood touches his tongue he understands the language of the birds (one of which is shown near the bottom of the Jurby stone), who tell him of the treachery being planned by a dwarf, Regin. The same part of the story is represented on the Jurby cross below the dragon, but the picture is much less clear. Sigurd's horse Grani is also shown on the upper left-hand panel of the Malew cross (only the fore-portion of the animal having been preserved), while the horse also figures on the Jurby cross. Other incidents of the Sigurd story are recorded on crosses from Maughold, Andreas, and Michael, and so it is clear that this legend must have been a special favourite amongst the Norse settlers in Man. They must have taken a keen delight in reciting such stirring deeds during the long winter nights, and these stories remained vividly in their memories long after their adoption of Christianity. They could not resist carving many scenes from such exploits on their stone memorials along with symbols and stories derived from Christian sources. Thus the Scandinavian crosses represent a striking mixture of pagan and Christian beliefs.

Another famous example of the Scandinavian crosses is the handsome Thor Cross, from Bride, which Kermode describes as 'the richest example anywhere known of such illustrations of the old Norse mythology'. It is crowded with figures of all kinds—men, giants, birds, animals, and dragons. On one side Thor is shown attacking a serpent or dragon. There are also scenes from the mighty combat between Thor and the giant Rungnir. The god slew the giant but fell underneath him; and after all the other gods had failed to lift Thor up, his own son Magni, though only three nights old, had the strength to do so, whereupon he received the giant's horse as a gift. On the other side is a scene from Thor's fishing adventure with the giant Hymi. Thor had been staying with the giant overnight, and when in the morning Hymi wished to go fishing he would not help Thor to get any bait so that he could accompany him. The god therefore went to the giant's oxen and

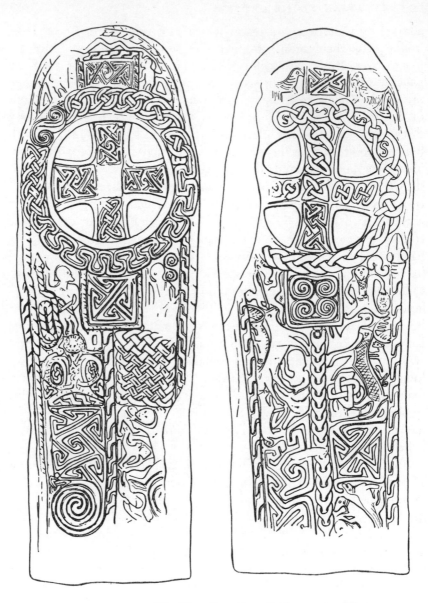

12. The Thor Cross from Bride.

wrung the head off the largest of them. The picture on the right-hand side of the cross, below the circle, shows Thor as a bearded man hurrying along and carrying the ox-head to be used as bait!

Thorwald's Cross, Andreas, symbolizes the passing of these heathen beliefs and the coming of the Christian ideas. One side tells how 'Swart shall cast fire over the earth and burn the whole world ... and the Powers shall perish'. The other side shows a saint holding the Cross in one hand and the Holy Book in the other. He is treading on the serpent and thus overcoming the powers of evil. The cross also has a figure of a fish, which was one of the earliest symbols of Christianity.

Of the 140 and more stone crosses so far discovered in Man only about 48 belong to the Scandinavian period. Most of them have been found in the northern parishes, including 9 from Michael, and 7 from each of Jurby and Andreas, while only 2 have been found in the shead-ing of Rushen. The distribution of the Celtic crosses is quite different, and the parish in which most have been found is Maughold, which has produced about 30 crosses of the earlier period but only 7 of Scandi-navian age.

The art of carving these stone crosses reached its height during the reign of Olaf I, but with the establishment and growth of Rushen Abbey, and the increasing influence of Rome, this type of monument came into disfavour. Latin was the language of the Church, and the Norse runes as well as the whole art accompanying them came to be regarded as pagan. Hence in the early twelfth century that great art which had been practised in the Island for almost six centuries died away.

CHAPTER SIX

From the Norse Kings to the Stanleys, 1266-1405

A PROFOUND CHANGE TOOK PLACE IN THE CHARACTER OF Manx history in the years following 1266. It will be recalled that in that year, after the death of Magnus, the Island was handed over to Alexander III of Scotland. This marked the beginning of a troubled era in the history of Man, since it was to fall a victim to the long struggle for supremacy between England and Scotland. So significant was the strategic position of the Island that both sides were anxious to gain possession of it. Hence it was tossed about like a shuttlecock between Scotland and England, with neither side caring anything about its unfortunate inhabitants.

The Manx clearly showed their unwillingness to accept Scottish rule by rebelling under the leadership of Godred, son of King Magnus. A force led by John de Vesci arrived from Scotland to quell the revolt, and the Manx were outnumbered and heavily defeated in the battle on St. Michael's Island close to the landing-place at Ronaldsway. Probably Godred himself fell in the battle and if so, the encounter marked the end of the male descendants of the famous Godred Crovan, or King Orry.

Still more troubles were to come. Scotland was plunged into confusion in 1290 on the death of her very young queen, Margaret—called the Maid of Norway—who had succeeded her grandfather, Alexander III. There was a host of claimants for the Scottish crown, and there were also at least two ladies who claimed the Manx crown as being descendants of the former kings of Man. The strong man of the period was then King Edward I of England, and he regarded the Island, which was said to be 'desolate and defenceless', as an English possession, so he took control of it. Meanwhile he had been invited to decide between the various claimants to the Scottish throne and, as is well known, he gave the crown to Balliol.

Being now king of Scotland, Balliol also took possession of the Isle of Man; but Edward I made it clear that the Scottish ruler was to pay homage to him for both Scotland and Man. Since Balliol refused to do this warfare between England and Scotland followed in which Edward was victorious, Balliol was dethroned, and the Island once more came into English hands. The person appointed to govern Man was Antony Beck, the ambitious and warlike Bishop of Durham who had helped Edward in his battles against the Scots. Having once gained control over the Island, Beck quarrelled with Edward, but the latter died before anything was settled. Since the bishop was a favourite of the weak Edward II, who succeeded his father, he was allowed to retain Man until his death in 1310. In the following year the Island was granted by Edward II to his favourite, Piers Gaveston. But Gaveston only enjoyed a brief period of power, for the nobles drove him from his position and had him beheaded.

The unhappy Island was now to be the scene of still more strife and bloodshed. Bruce had become king of Scotland in 1313, and in the same year he came in person to take possession of Man. The Scottish force landed at Ramsey and proceeded via Douglas, where Bruce stayed at the Nunnery, to Castle Rushen which had become the great stronghold of the Island. After a month's siege the garrison surrendered and the castle was largely destroyed. Bruce granted Man to Thomas Randolph, Earl of Moray.

Before returning to Scotland Bruce had made an expedition against Ireland, and in 1316, perhaps by way of revenge, a body of Irish free-booters under Richard de Mandeville appeared at Ronaldsway to pillage the land. The invaders scattered a Manx force on the slopes of South Barrule (then called Wardfell) and proceeded to ravage the surrounding countryside. Rushen Abbey must have formed an excellent prize for these raiders and, according to the Manx *Chronicle*, it lost not only its furniture but also its flocks and herds. When the Irish ultimately returned home after a month's raiding they were able to do so with their ships laden with choice plunder.

What a wretched period it all was for the Island! Who actually ruled the country between 1313 and 1333 it is well-nigh impossible to say; Scots and English appeared in succession, neither staying long. But after 1346 conditions became more stable, since the English, now under

Edward III, dealt the Scots a decisive blow at the battle of Neville's Cross, near Durham. The English were the effective masters of Man from that time onwards.

In 1333 Edward III had granted the Island to William de Montacute, first Earl of Salisbury, in full possession, so that he became King of Man without having to pay homage to the English monarch. Montacute's son in 1392 sold the Island, including the crown, to William le Scrope, Earl of Wiltshire, who was beheaded by Henry IV. Man was next granted to the Earl of Northumberland, who was in turn deprived of it on being accused of treason. Finally, in 1405, it went to Sir John Stanley on condition of his doing homage and giving two falcons at the coronation of each king of England. Stanley's descendants were destined to be rulers of Man, under the title of 'king' or 'lord', for over three hundred years.

THE CHURCH GROWS IN POWER

The condition of the people must have been quite terrible during this unhappy period, and there is little wonder that the Island was described as being poor and full of misery. Even the best rulers could do little since they stayed so short a time, and most of those who got possession of it regarded Man merely as a place from which they might take all they could to forward their own purposes.

While the civil power was weak and uncertain the Church was constantly gathering strength. The abbey of Rushen and the bishopric had received many grants of land and many valuable privileges from the Norse kings. Rushen was under the control of the Abbot of Furness; there was the nunnery at Douglas with its prioress; while lands in the Island were held by the abbey of Bangor and Sabhal in northern Ireland, by the priory of St. Bees in Cumberland, and the priory of Whithorn in southern Scotland. The heads of these religious houses ranked as barons and had their own officers and manorial courts.

As the power of the religious houses grew, so did that of the Pope as the head of the Christian Church, and the popes of those days were constantly striving for more and more power. Even in England papal interference was increasing. Powerful monarchs like Edward III found it difficult to resist papal claims, although many acts were passed to check them, but the Isle of Man had no strong ruler who could assist in curbing the power of the church.

The Abbot of Rushen alone held 99 quarterlands or farms and 77

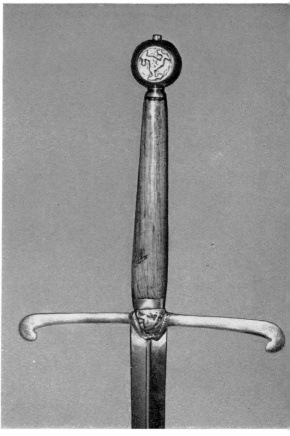

Plate 18. THE THREE LEGS OF MAN. Two early representations on the standing-cross in Maughold churchyard and on the Manx Sword of State.

OVERLEAF

Plate 19. CASTLETOWN HARBOUR in the early nineteenth century, with Castle Rushen towering over the quayside. Because the harbour has a rocky and exposed entrance, Castletown never became one of the island's main ports, although it was the island's capital until 1869.

Plate 20. CASTLE RUSHEN. Despite its immense strength, a weak-spirited defence of the castle during the Civil War allowed it to fall into the hands of the Parliamentarians who governed the island until the Restoration.

Plate 21. RUINS OF ST. GERMAN'S CATHEDRAL, begun by Bishop Simon in about 1230. His successor completed the work, and the church was used until the middle of the eighteenth century.

Plate 22. ST. PATRICK'S ISLE, PEEL, for long a place of refuge and sanctity. Apart from the ruins of the parish church of St. Patrick, and St. German's cathedral, its features include the Round Tower, built by the Celtic clergy to protect themselves from Viking raids. The much later massive fortifications encircling the island were erected in the second half of the fifteenth century.

Insula Mona

Customes of Outgates and Ingates laid down in alphabeticall manor.

A

		£	s	d
Ale the Barrell for the Countryman		00	00	0
for the Stranger		00	00	0
Allom the hundred		00	00	0
Anchorages of Barques with a cockboate		00	00	0
and without a Cockboate		00	00	0
Apples the thousand		00	00	0
Aules the hundred		00	00	0
Axes or hatchetts the dozen		00	00	0
Augers the dozen		00	00	0

note the Countryman to pay halfe anchorage

B

		£	s	d
Barley the boule. By the Stranger		00	00	0
By the Countryman		00	00	0
Bread the Batch containinge 36 Loafes		00	00	0
Beefe the carkass of Countryman		00	00	0
By the Stranger		00	0j	0
Beefe the Barrell vide H.				

cottages, and in connection with these holdings he had his own courts over which his steward presided. The bishop wielded a power almost equal to that of a king. He had his own courts and judges (called vicars-general), and his own prison on Peel Island. Moreover, the church passed its own laws, and had an advantage over the state because its laws were put into writing. There were no written laws of the Island itself before 1422, but the written laws of the Manx Church go back to 1229 when Bishop Simon held a diocesan synod at Kirk Braddan. At this synod tithes for the clergy had been levied on livestock, grain, beer, and woven cloths. In 1291 another synod was held under Bishop Mark and fresh tithes were also imposed on merchants and craftsmen.

In 1299 Mark was expelled from Man by Edward I, and the Pope replied by placing the Island under an interdict for three years. This was a punishment very much dreaded in those days since it meant that all church services ceased, except baptism and the last rites. When Bishop Mark returned to the Island in 1302, to show his authority, as well as to exact further punishment, he imposed a tax of one penny a year on every house with a fireplace. This tax lasted for centuries and was known as 'the smoke penny'.

The tithes which had to be paid to the Church covered all produce—grain, beer, animals, geese, poultry, eggs, butter, cheese, and fish—and the collection of these dues was carried out by the parson or his agent, called the proctor, while there were officers called sumners for enforcing payment. In the case of grain, which was the most important crop, the farmer was forbidden to stack his corn without notice to the proctor. If he did so, then the sumner and two neighbours took the stack down and seized the tithe. Certain tithes such as butter, cheese, and eggs had to be brought to the church on Sunday and handed to the parson at the altar; and the time came when the priest stopped people from receiving the sacrament because they had not paid these duties.

Of all the tithes paid in Man nearly half went to the bishop, who thus had the chief power. Of the remaining portion about half went to the religious houses, chiefly Rushen Abbey, and the rest was divided amongst the parish clergy.[1]

1. The appropriation of tithes, i.e. the assigning of part of them for a variety of purposes such as the maintenance of the bishop, of monasteries, and students, was a widespread medieval practice, but one which severely impoverished the parochial clergy from whose parishes the tithes were paid. The term 'vicars of thirds', applicable to most of the Manx incumbents, meant that they received only a third of the tithes payable by the parish. See D. Craine, *Manannan's Isle* (Douglas, 1955), pp. 104–6.

Offenders against the church could be sent to the bishop's prison. For more serious offences against Church discipline the punishment was excommunication, which meant that the guilty person was excluded from the Church and its privileges. Like the interdict this was regarded as a dreadful penalty, but in addition the offender had to pay a money fine which went to the bishop.

As proof of the increasing power of the Pope throughout this period it is significant that the Bishop of Sodor and Man had now to go to Rome for consecration—a thing which the kings of England would not allow in the case of English bishops. Formerly the Manx bishops had been consecrated by the Archbishop of Trondhjem, in Norway, but with Bishop Russell, who was elected in 1348, this practice ceased and he was consecrated at Avignon, where the Pope resided at the time.

During Bishop Russell's term of office the Franciscan friars came to the Island, for in 1373 they acquired a site in the parish of Arbory where they built an oratory. The Franciscans were sometimes called the Grey Friars, because of their clothing, or Begging Friars, since they were not allowed to own property. They were rivals of the Cistercian order to which the monks of Rushen Abbey belonged, and it may be supposed that they were encouraged in order to counteract the influence of the abbey. Little is known of the doings of the Franciscans, but the remains of one of their buildings may be still seen at the Friary farm in Ballabeg, Arbory.

Bishop Russell was succeeded in 1374 by Bishop Donkan, who was consecrated in Rome. For reasons that are rather obscure he got into trouble with the Pope. It is probable that he made a stand in resisting papal greed and aggression, and in this he was playing the part of a patriot. He was transferred to another bishopric, possibly in Ireland, in 1392. Soon after this date, as already seen, a new era was to begin in Man, when, with the accession of the Stanleys, the power of the State was to increase and that of the Church to decline.

THE THREE LEGS OF MAN

This was the period which saw the final establishment of the emblem as the official armorial bearing of the Island. The three legs is, in some ways, one of the most ancient of symbols for it is seen on a Greek vase of the sixth century B.C. Like the more widespread swastika or fylfot it is ultimately derived from a design showing the spokes of a wheel, which in turn represent the rays of the sun; and thus it was associated, no doubt, with sun worship. The design was taken to Sicily where it was adopted owing to the appropriateness of the three legs to the shape of that island, and it was used by the rulers of Syracuse on their coins of the fourth century B.C. as an emblem of dominion over that three-cornered island.

A similar device has figured on the arms of the Isle of Man since at least the thirteenth century A.D., and to explain this apparent coincidence, links between Man and Sicily have been searched for, but it is now felt that such a search is in vain for two reasons. Firstly, there is no evidence that the three legs device was used at all for Sicily in medieval times, so that the direct derivation formerly envisaged can no longer be regarded as possible, even although there may be some remote link with the much earlier Sicilian device. Secondly, a more likely immediate origin for the Manx arms can be found much nearer home on coins of the Norse-Irish kings of northern England in the tenth century. Thus a silver coin of Anlaf Cuaran, king of Dublin and York, who died at Iona in 981, bears the triquetra or triple knot, and this design suggests a possible ancestry for the Manx three legs, especially when it is realized that the Manx-Norse kings seem to have been a branch of this dynasty.

There is unfortunately a rather wide gap between the tenth and the thirteenth centuries during which there is a tantalizing lack of real information, but in the Rolls of Arms of the later thirteenth century which are the oldest heraldic manuscripts, there are definite references to the 'three mailed legs' or 'three legs in armour' which are consistently attributed to the king of Man. There is indeed much to be said for the view that the Manx-Norse kings had definitely adopted the Three Legs before the death of King Magnus in 1265. On the other hand it must be appreciated that in surviving references to the seals used by some of these kings, including Godred II, Reginald I, and Harald I, the device shown was not that of the three legs but a ship. This was of the 'Viking' type common to atlantic Europe, such being the emblem generally adopted in the maritime trading communities of western and northern Europe at that period. Quite possibly both devices were borne by these monarchs.

During the fourteenth century there are two representations of the three legs as the emblem of the Manx monarchs, one being that shown on the pillar cross now in Maughold churchyard. This cross was most likely erected during the rule of the Montague earls of Salisbury, (1333-93), who controlled the Island during that period. The other example is from the seal used by Sir William le Scrope, Lord of Man in 1395, and in this the legs are depicted in plate armour, this having by then superseded the chain armour formerly in use. In both of these cases the legs are 'spurred', the spurs in the Maughold cross being particularly prominent. The Latin motto, *Quocunque Jeceris Stabit*, i.e. 'Whichever way you throw, it will stand' was added later, being first seen on the earliest Manx coinage dating to 1668.

CASTLE RUSHEN AND PEEL CASTLE

The fortress of Castle Rushen existed in Norse times, because it is recorded that the last Norse king, Magnus, died there in 1265. It is therefore in origin a Norse castle, although many of its features belong to the fourteenth century.

It has been pointed out that the Southside portion of Man contains a rich lowland area; the mouth of the Silverburn river was a natural converging centre and an obvious site for a fortification around which a town would grow. Castletown harbour was, nevertheless, always difficult for shipping, partly because the entrance is obstructed with limestone rocks, and partly because it is very exposed to south and south-west winds. The important harbour during Norse times was Ronaldsway, which was sheltered from the prevailing winds and would provide good beaching for the war-galleys. On the other hand, Ronaldsway had not a satisfactory supply of drinking-water for the garrison of a castle, and vessels which landed there could be taken round when the weather became fine—or they might be dragged across the narrow peninsula—and could then lie safely under the protection of the castle walls. The earthwork at Hango Hill was very likely a half-way fort defending the road between Ronaldsway and Castletown.

Defensive works of some kind, perhaps an earth-mound surrounded by wooden palisades, have certainly existed at Castletown for many centuries. In Magnus's time the castle was built of stone and was a square keep in the late Norman style, probably constructed during the reign of Godred II (1153-87). This was captured by Bruce, but portions can be seen in the present keep. The first additions were the lower parts of the south and west towers, which were probably made during the reign of Reginald I (1187–1226). Next followed some sections which are regarded as being in the finest style of the castle, including the heightening of the original keep and its two added towers (south and west), an entirely new tower to the east side of the keep, and a twin-turreted gate-tower built on the north side of the keep. These date to between about 1340 and 1350 during the reigns of the first and second Earls of Salisbury. Some of the architectural features in the sandstone doorways and windows closely resemble those used in later parts of the Edwardian castles of North Wales, particularly Beaumaris and Caer-narvon, and there is reason to believe that craftsmen from Wales were brought over to help in strengthening Castle Rushen. In 1377 the French attacked it but failed to take it since the castle was now well able to withstand a siege. To the later years of the reign of the second Earl of Salisbury (1344–92) belong the curtain wall with its parapet walk as well as the uppermost third or quarter of the keep, the latter having had to be raised in order to enable the defenders to fire over the wall-walk of the curtain.

During the Stanley regime the castle with its garrison was the main centre of the Island's administration, and one of the most famous of the Stanleys, James, seventh Earl of Derby, lived in it for several years.

The actual Derby House was originally constructed during the later sixteenth century, but it was heightened and perhaps almost rebuilt in 1644 at the time of the Great Earl. In the eighteenth and nineteenth centuries, when the keep came to be used as a prison, the building was very much altered although at the same time it was preserved from falling into ruin. Nowadays it is used for holding the fortnightly courts, while new governors also continue to be installed there; otherwise the castle is essentially a show place.

The Island's other fortress and administrative centre was Peel Castle, and the islet on which it is erected, standing at the entrance to a good natural harbour, made it an admirable defensive site.[1] It lacked the richer economic basis available to the southern capital, and, facing west, it is more exposed to bad weather.

This islet, so famous under the name of St. Patrick's Isle, is the centre of much of the Island's early religious and civil history, and it well merits the description of 'The Tara of the Isle of Man' bestowed upon

1. It is to this location that it owes its alternative name Holme—a Norse word for 'an islet in a bay, creek, lake, or river' (J. J. Kneen).

it by a thirteenth-century Irish writer.[1] Unlike Castle Rushen its history, which has by no means yet been entirely unravelled, is complicated by the existence of both ecclesiastical as well as military buildings, and only the more significant features can be mentioned here.

Of the existing masonry the earliest is the Round Tower, dating to the tenth or the early eleventh century and occupying a prominent position on the islet. Built of well-jointed and squared blocks of local red sandstone it forms a splendid example of the refuge towers erected by the Celtic clergy to protect themselves and the treasures of their churches from the ravages of the Vikings. The tower has all the characteristic features of the Irish structures apart from their conical stone roof; no doubt the original one collapsed, to be replaced in medieval times by a battlemented top. The ancient parish church of St. Patrick and the cathedral church of St. German, both now in ruins, have already been noted (see p. 79 and Pls. 21 and 22).

On the military side the details of the earlier history of the island are still obscure, and further excavation is necessary before anything definite is said. But in any case it is clear that the actual name Peel, which early provided an alternative name for St. Patrick's Isle, and also gave its name to the settlement which ultimately grew up on the other side of the harbour mouth, originally meant 'a moated and palisaded enclosure, or a fort built of massive baulks of timber'. The earliest timber fort to which the title was applied was presumably the one erected by King Magnus Barefoot on the occasion of his visit to Man between 1098 and 1103 (see p. 62), and which was still, according to the Manx *Chronicle*, known by his name in 1260. Just what part of the islet was occupied by the fort is a matter for speculation. It has been suggested that the earthwork in the middle of St. Patrick's Isle was the site, but this was proved by excavation in 1947 to belong to the Derby period. On the other hand, it may be observed that for the greater part of its length there is a bank of earth on the inner side of the great ring line of fortification around the islet, and this no doubt formed part of the defences of earth and timber in the eleventh or twelfth century.

Of the masonry in the existing curtain wall enclosing the islet the

1. The phrase occurs in an Irish poem of about 1190–1200, edited by Brian Ó Cuív in *Eigse*, viii (1957), 283–301, stanza 8. Although the editor translates *Tara* as here, it is worth remembering that Irish *teamhair* is also a common noun meaning 'height' or 'eminence' and occurring in a number of other place-names besides the famous Tara. Furthermore, while Eamhain Abhlach is sometimes, as in this poem, used to refer to Man, there seems no ground for restricting it to St. Patrick's Isle at Peel.

earliest dates to about A.D. 1300 and is situated to the south-east of the chancel of the cathedral. Further work in this section as well as the rectangular tower overlooking the causeway linking the islet to the mainland are probably to be ascribed to Sir William le Scrope (Earl of Wiltshire) soon after 1392. The rest of the massive fortifications encircling the island, consisting of very large blocks of quarried slate, were probably erected by Thomas, first Earl of Derby, in the period between 1460 and 1504. Such defences may have been partly justified by the fear of Scottish raids, but they may also be regarded as another example of that grandiose expression of feudal pride which is rather characteristic of the period in question. Unlike Castle Rushen, Peel Castle has become a ruin since the disbanding of its garrison in the eighteenth century.

CHAPTER SEVEN

The First Stanleys

THE GIFT OF THE ISLAND TO SIR JOHN STANLEY BY HENRY IV marked the beginning of a new era in Manx history. Stable government replaced the wars and anarchy of the preceding period. The Stanleys, who became the earls of Derby after helping Henry Tudor defeat Richard III at Bosworth in 1485, were a powerful and highly placed English family and, though they rarely visited the Island themselves, they appointed responsible governors who, in the main, seem to have aimed at carrying out their tasks with justice. The new rulers retained the title of King of Man, but this was changed to Lord of Man in 1504.

The first ruler of the Stanley line never came to Man, but the second Stanley took a great interest in his kingdom and visited it with very beneficial results for the Island. With him, indeed, began the first systematic record in writing of the history of Man, for it was he who introduced written laws, curbed the power of the Church, and restored the ancient constitution of the country. It has been shown that the most striking feature of the preceding period had been the immense growth in the power of the Church and the weakening of the civil power. The Church was dominated by the great barons, of whom the chief were the Bishop and the Abbot of Rushen, and it was obvious to Sir John Stanley that he could never be the real ruler of the Island until the barons' power was checked. A beginning was made by forbidding them to give shelter —sanctuary as it was called—to wrongdoers who tried to escape from justice by fleeing on to land held by the Church and claiming its protection. Next, the Bishop and other barons were ordered to attend at a Tynwald held at Reneurling (now Cronk Urley) to give obedience to the new king. When three of them, namely the Prior of Whithorn, the

Abbot of Furness, and the Prior of St. Bees, failed to do so they were punished by being deprived of their lands in the Island.

Sir John Stanley then proceeded to codify the laws, and in this code, which was drawn up by the deemsters and Keys, the relative rights and duties of the king, Church, and the people were defined for the first time. Of the Keys it was stated that their existence had been uncertain since the Scandinavian period (or, as it was expressed, 'since King Orry's days'), during which they had consisted of twenty-four free-holders. It was also laid down that the king, or lord, had the right to veto the appointment of any member of the body. By the same code the council and deemsters were to aid the governor in all cases of difficulty, and the clerk of the rolls, in order to settle the law, was ordered to write all proceedings plainly so that a record of cases could be kept. Hitherto, as previously explained, the law had depended on the memory of the deemsters and the Keys. Trial by combat, or prowess, was abolished, and trial by jury (or, as it was then called, by God and the country) was adopted in its place. Although the second Sir John Stanley was a despotic ruler he was also a wise and bold one, and what he did left an enduring mark on the Island.

For almost a hundred years after the death of the second Stanley Man saw nothing of its rulers. The second Earl of Derby (1504–21), who was the first to give up the title of King and become Lord of Man, visited the Island in 1507 to put an end to some 'public tumult' that had taken place. Nothing is known of the origin or nature of this 'tumult', but it is mentioned in an old Manx ballad.[1] The earl, who had been raiding the Scottish coast of Kirkcudbright, possibly in revenge for a previous attack by the Scots on Man, landed at Ronaldsway and soon quelled the rising. It was on the occasion of this visit that the port of Derby-haven received the name it still holds.

The third earl (1521–72) never came to the Island, but during the course of his long reign certain grievances of the people against demands of the Church were settled. This was in 1532 when it was agreed that the tithe on ale and on all marriage presents, which had been paid to the Church, should be abolished, while the death dues were reduced.

During the period of the third Earl of Derby's lordship in Man the

1. The edition of the Traditionary Ballad in *Etudes celtiques*, x. 77–8, suggests that 'boirey'n theay' in stanza 54 means 'the troubling of the people' by incursions such as that which had been avenged by the burning of Kirkcudbright in 1457, rather than 'the raging of the people' in any riotous sense.

important religious changes known as the Reformation were taking place in England. The great break with Rome occurred and Henry VIII became the supreme head of the Church of England in 1534, while shortly afterwards the monasteries were suppressed. The Act of 1539, by which the lands of the English religious houses were confiscated, did not mention the Island, and consequently did not extend to it, nor was any statute dealing with the matter passed in Man. Nevertheless, the Manx monasteries were suppressed soon after those in England, and all the property belonging to Rushen Abbey, the Nunnery of Douglas, and the Friary of Bemaken (Ballabeg, Arbory), was seized by the Crown, while the buildings gradually fell into ruin.

It took some time for the new religious ideas to be accepted in the Island, since, in 1594, orders were issued to the vicars-general to bring to trial all persons carrying bells or banners before the dead or praying for the dead. It was not until 1610 that the Manx clergy were free to marry, whereas the English clergy had been allowed to do so since 1549. This slowness of the Manx Reformation was partly due no doubt to the fact that its ruler, the third earl, was a strong Roman Catholic, but the main reasons were probably the isolation of Man together with the ignorance of the English language and the lack of any books in the Manx tongue.[1]

After the death of the fifth Earl of Derby, in 1594, a dispute arose as to who should be the new Lord of Man. While the dispute was proceeding Queen Elizabeth I took control of the Island, and she and her successor, James I, continued to appoint its governors until 1610. It is said that during her period of control Queen Elizabeth presented to Castle Rushen the ancient clock which still adorns its walls and does duty as the town clock of Castletown.

In 1612 the rule of the Derbys was restored when the sixth earl and his countess, Elizabeth, began to rule jointly. The government of the Island was entirely in the hands of the countess, but neither of them visited Man. On the death of the countess, in 1627, the control of the Island was taken over by their son Lord Strange, who was to become the seventh Earl of Derby in 1642. His period of rule is the most memor-

---

1. The first book in Manx, a translation of the Book of Common Prayer, was finished by Bishop John Phillips (1605–33) early in 1611 but his attempts to print it then, and possibly again about 1630, when the surviving copy was written, were frustrated, probably in part by the expense of producing a very limited edition of a large book. It was eventually printed by the Manx Society in 1893–4.

able in the whole of the Stanley regime, as will be seen in the next chapter, and he came to be known as 'the Great Stanley'.

SOCIAL AND ECONOMIC CONDITIONS

Almost the only information we have about the life of the farmers, fishermen, farm labourers, and artisans during these two centuries is contained in the book of the Statutes, and it suggests that the Island's rulers were more anxious for the Lord's privileges and his revenues than for the people's welfare. Many of these 'statutes' are mere records of old customs in the State and the Church, while others are decrees made by the lord or his officers. The Keys at that time were not really the makers of laws; their duties were those of a supreme jury rather than those of a parliament. They were not called together regularly or even frequently. Thus no laws were passed between 1430 and 1504; indeed, the whole record of the laws, customs, and ordinances up to the end of the sixteenth century covers only some seventy pages in the statute book.

The lord had the right to receive the 'royal fish' of porpoise, sturgeon, and whale, and to take the better sort of game such as hawk, heron, hart, or hind, all wrecks and treasure trove, and the goods of persons condemned to death. He was also entitled to a very large quantity of free food for his castles at Rushen and Peel, each quarterland having to supply one beef per annum, which amounted to six hundred beeves a year, while there were 'customs' of corn and herring. Turf and ling had to be brought to the castles free. Not only did the lord claim toll on the produce of his subjects, but he also claimed to control their personal freedom. Thus no tenant could leave the Island without special licence, and if he did so he was to be treated as a felon and his goods forfeited. The reason for this was, no doubt, that tenants were not easy to find. Tenants had to labour on certain fixed days in repairing the lord's forts and houses. Taxes had to be paid for the liberty of fishing for herrings, for importing and exporting goods (Pl. 23), and for grinding at the lord's mills. To avoid going to the latter many people used hand-mills, or querns, which were seized and destroyed by the lord's order whenever they could be found.

There was compulsory military service in those days, and all men between twenty and sixty years had to train as militiamen under the captains of the parishes. The weapons used were bows and arrows, the sword, and buckler, and every man had to provide himself with them. Moreover, practically every man was obliged to take his turn in keeping 'watch and ward' at the various watch-stations, both by day and night, for an enemy that might approach. Great stress was laid on this duty, and very severe penalties were imposed for any neglect in carrying it out. The only men exempted from watch and ward were some of the chief officials together with 'one head smith, the head or chief miller in every parish', and even they had 'to be ready to encounter the enemy'. It was, significantly, laid down that only those should be sent on watch who were 'of discretion and able to discern and to be careful'. The means of summoning in turn the men required for this service has never been described in detail, but it is known from various records that there were recognized watch tokens, in the form of a cross, which passed from house to house within the parish and were accepted as a stern summons.

Strict rules were laid down for the hiring of farm labourers and servant-maids. The usual form of hiring was by the year, menservants being hired in November and women in May. Deemsters and other officers had the right of forcibly hiring or 'yarding' one male and one female servant 'or more if it be needful for them' from each sheading. As some return for this enforced service such servants were entitled to have their porridge made so thick that the pot-stick would stand upright in the middle of the pot. Tenants who had difficulty in obtaining servants could appeal for the help of the deemster through the coroner; and if no 'vagrant' servants were available, then the tenants paying a lower rent had to serve those paying a higher rent, 'rather than that the lord's land should fall into decay'.

Parents who were old, disabled, or sick were allowed to retain one of their children, called a 'choice-child', at home, but only if they gave public notice at the parish church at least a month before hiring day. Servants who refused to carry out their duties were liable to whipping and being sent to gaol. Though whipping has long been out of use, imprisonment of farm labourers who broke their contracts was common until quite recently; but while the law permitting imprisonment is still unrepealed, it has become a dead letter.

CHAPTER EIGHT

Man during the English Civil War

THE MIDDLE YEARS OF THE SEVENTEENTH CENTURY WERE very memorable for the Isle of Man, no less than for England. Stirring events were taking place 'across the water', where the vital struggle between King and Parliament was in progress, leading ultimately to the Civil War, the execution of Charles I (1649), and the establishment of the English Commonwealth, which lasted until 1660. Whatever its own wishes might have been, the Island was bound to be involved in the English struggle, since its ruler, the seventh Earl of Derby, was the head of a great Royalist family who felt in honour bound to give active support to the King. On the other hand, the sympathies of a great many of the Manx must have been with Parliament, since they had many grievances against their own rulers. This feeling of discontent found expression in the rebellion of William Christian (Illiam Dhone), which led to the execution of this Manx patriot in 1663.

James, the seventh Earl of Derby, was a remarkable man, as may be judged from the title he earned for himself in the Island as the Great Stanley, or Yn Stanlagh Mooar. He was barely twenty-one when his father gave him the government of Man, and he began by doing something which had not been done by any of his predecessors—choosing a Manxman as his lieutenant-governor. The person chosen was Edward Christian of Maughold, a man of great ability who had lived a life of adventure. He had been a captain in the service of the East India Company, a courtier in the suite of the Duke of Buckingham, and a commander of a naval frigate. Finally, he had retired to his native Island with a considerable fortune and had acquired the mine workings at Bradda Head.

This is how the earl, in writing to his son years later, described him:

'I was newly got acquainted with Captain Christian, whom I soon observed to have abilities enough to do me service . . . but which took most with me, when he offered his service it was on these terms, that he would be content to hold the staff until I chose another. For the pay, he so little valued that, as he would be content to do service without any or as little of it as it pleased me. He is excellent company, as rude as a sea captain should be, but refined as one that hath civilised himself half a year at court.' But these professions of caring nothing about the pay were too good to be true. Christian was dismissed in 1639, and the reason given by the earl was that 'the more I gave, the more he asked'.

THE GREAT STANLEY

On the outbreak of the Civil War in England, Lord Strange, as his title then was, raised an army of 5,000 men to fight for Charles and equipped them at his own expense. He also gave the King large sums of money and rendered many important services in the field. In spite of all this he was distrusted by Charles, whose advisers seemed to look on him as a rival for the throne.

The troubles in England were, in a smaller way, being repeated in Man. Edward Christian had been partly restored to favour, and had been given command of the Manx forces. He formed a training camp at the Lhen, Jurby, and, if we may trust the evidence given against him afterwards at his trial, stirred up the soldiers to rebel against the earl. But the trouble was not confined to the armed forces; the feeling of discontent about paying tithes had again become acute, and the governor, fearing an insurrection, invited each parish to send representatives to state their grievances. Instead of this the whole population was summoned by the sending round of the muster cross, or *Crosh Vusta*, and they came bearing arms, to the terror of the court. The governor tried to put them off by promising to give them a hearing another day, but they answered that they desired no other day, and a man named William Garett, of Sulby, declared that the country would pay no more tithes but would fight and die first. The governor appeased them by promising to send for Lord Derby.

When the earl came he brought with him a small troop of English cavalry. This, in his own words, is how he dealt with the threatened revolt: 'When first I came among the people, I seemed affable and kind to all, so I offended none. For taking off your hat, a good word, a smile

or the like, will cost you nothing, but may gain you much.' The meeting of parish representatives was then held and the earl was told of the
people's grievances. He next summoned the officers, the twenty-four
Keys, and four men from every parish to Peel Castle to aid him in
settling the complaints. Edward Christian and the ringleaders of the
disturbances were present at this meeting, which threatened to be a
stormy one. Lord Derby was equal to the occasion. 'There were some',
he wrote, 'who saucily behaved themselves, and of those I put some out
of countenance with austere looking on them; troubling their discourse
in seeming not to hear well what they said and asking them to repeat
the same; which astonished them so, that oft they did forget the matter
they were about, and sometimes feared to speak more of it. . . . Another
sort were more dangerous, who said nothing openly but instructed
others and whispered behind the company. Some of these I espied my-
self; others were pointed to me by such as I had set in several places
about the bench, to observe them and give me some private beck, which
I took notice of as I saw occasion. These I called nearer to the bar, who
it may be, would speak so as not to offend, or hold their peace; at least
there they could not incite others so conveniently.'

In the end the meeting agreed to leave the settlement of their grievances to the earl himself. Christian, who saw himself being outwitted,
rose to call attention to some questions which had been overlooked, but
Lord Derby promptly ruled him out of order and declared the meeting
at an end. Shortly after this Christian was arrested and cast into prison
to await trial on a charge of treason. He was charged with attempting
to overthrow the government, to make the House of Keys an elected
body, to have the deemsters chosen every three years from amongst the
Keys, and to impose a new oath on both Keys and deemsters to repeal
all laws not in the interests of the people.

Christian had no doubt counted upon winning power by a sudden
stroke, and then declaring openly for Cromwell and the Parliament. He
had failed, and the penalty was a fine of 1,000 marks and imprisonment for life. He remained in gaol until 1651 when the Parliament
forces entered the Island. In 1659 he was concerned in a plot against
Governor Chaloner and was again sent to prison in Peel Castle, where
he died in 1661.

To some extent the earl satisfied the people by securing a reduction
of tithes and other payments to the clergy. But he created another and
even more serious grievance which was destined to be a sore in the

Island's life for the next sixty years. Though the lord had always claimed the full ownership of the soil and had endeavoured to treat the Island as a feudal manor, there was an ancient system by which the 'tenants' had been able to pass on the farms to their children or to dispose of them to other people. Lord Derby now planned to establish a system of leases by which no family could claim to hold a piece of land for longer than three lives.

The full effects of this policy were not yet realized, however, and the tithe trouble having been settled for the time being, Lord Derby was free to give his full attention to increasing the military forces and strengthening the defences of the Island. He raised a troop of cavalry consisting in all of 288 men, the foot-soldiers were constantly drilled, and the garrisons of Castle Rushen and Peel Castle were strengthened. Seven camps were formed, three in the north and four in the south of the Island. New forts were also erected, one at Fort Island, called Derby Fort, another at Ramsey, called Fort Loyal, and a third at the Point of Ayre. There was also a large earthwork at Ballachurry in the parish of Andreas.

At sea Lord Derby raised and equipped a small fleet which from time to time came into conflict with opposing ships. On one occasion they defeated five men-of-war and on another defended the Calf of Man from an attack by three Parliamentary ships. The burden of these increased armaments by land and by sea bore heavily on the people, who grew more and more discontented, and this feeling was no doubt aggravated by the disasters which befell the Royalist cause.

After the execution of Charles I in 1649 the earl was offered the return of his English estates if he would surrender the Island to Parliament. He indignantly refused. 'If you trouble me with any more such messages,' he said, 'I will burn the paper and hang the bearer.' So when in 1651 an attempt was made to regain the crown for Charles II, the earl hastened to join the royal standard. The small Manx force of 300 foot-soldiers which he took with him was attacked near Wigan and overwhelmed by superior numbers. The earl made good his escape, succeeded in joining the King's army, and shared in the rout of Worcester. He was taken prisoner, and although his life had been promised him by his captors, he was tried by court martial and executed at Bolton in 1651.

Whatever his faults the Great Stanley was a man of 'loyal nature and of noble mind'. In spite of great discouragement he adhered to the cause

JAMES STANLEY, 7ᵗʰ EARL of DERBY K.G. Royalist, B. 1607, M.P. for LIVERPOOL, RAISED SIEGE of LATHOM HOUSE, PROTECTED the ISLE of MAN, EXECUTED at BOLTON, 1651.

Plate 24. JAMES STANLEY, 7TH EARL OF DERBY, called 'The Great Stanley'. His defence of Man against the Parliamentary Forces during the Civil War drained the island's resources, and his autocratic style of government was strongly resented. Taken prisoner at the battle of Worcester in 1651, he was later executed at Bolton.

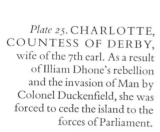

Plate 25. CHARLOTTE, COUNTESS OF DERBY, wife of the 7th earl. As a result of Illiam Dhone's rebellion and the invasion of Man by Colonel Duckenfield, she was forced to cede the island to the forces of Parliament.

Plate 28. THOMAS WILSON, Bishop of Sodor and Man, 1698–1755.

Plate 29. BALLAUGH OLD CHURCH, one of many churches repaired and extended by Bishop Wilson, often out of his own limited means. On 19 June 1717, he wrote in his Memorandum Book: 'Then laid the foundation of an addition of twenty-one feet to the church of Ballaugh. The worthy Rector, Mr. Walker and I engaged to finish it, the Parish contributing only twelve pounds.'

Plate 26. WILLIAM CHRISTIAN, called Illiam Dhone, 'brown-haired William'. Brought to trial ten years later for his part in the rebellion of 1651, he was shot on Hango Hill before news of his successful appeal to Charles II reached the island.

Plate 27. ILLIAM DHONE'S DEATH-WARRANT, accusing him of 'notorious treason'. The sentence to 'a most heinous and ignominious death by being hanged and quartered and his head smitten off' was commuted to shooting on account of his wife's 'inconsolable condition'.

YN
VIBLE
CASHERICK:

N Y,

Yn Chenn Chonaant.

VEIH

Ny Chied Ghlaaraghyn,

Dy kiaralagh chyndait ayns

GAILCK;

Ta shen dy ghra,

Chengey ny Mayrey Ellan Vannin.

AYNS DAA LIOAR.

LIOAR I.

Pointit dy ve lhaiht ayns KIALTEENYN.

WHITEHAVEN:

PRENTIT LIORISH JUAN WARE AS E VAC.

M, DCC, LXXI.

of his king, and was not afraid to die for it. Yet the Stuart period was not one in which we might expect to find the perfect ruler. The earl was masterful and grasping. Like his royal master he tried to quell opposition by force, and he was not above that kind of diplomacy which could more bluntly be called artfulness. His land laws left a legacy of hate, but in imposing them he was acting in the manner of other great English noblemen. What he has written about the Isle of Man shows that once the people had recognized his position as not only their lord but their landlord, he was anxious to do what he could for their welfare. Though a most devout churchman, he tried to remedy the exactions of the Church. His loyalty to the King, natural as it was, placed the Island under great burdens and in great danger for the sake of a cause which was not really its own.

THE REBELLION OF ILLIAM DHONE

When Lord Derby had set sail on that fatal expedition in 1651 he had left the Island under the care of his countess, Charlotte. She was a woman of great courage and constancy, as she had proved by her heroic defence of Lathom House for over two years against the forces of the Parliament. One of her principal officers was William Christian, who held the offices of receiver of the revenues and major-general. There were other officers in command of the castles, but Christian trained the unpaid native soldiers, the militia. This William Christian, or Illiam Dhone (brown-haired William) as his countrymen familiarly called him, was a son of Deemster Ewan Christian and a distant relative of Edward Christian, the former governor.

When the news of the earl's defeat and capture came the Manx seized the opportunity to try and get their grievances regarding the land leases and the free quartering of troops remedied. On 19 October some eight hundred of them, including the leading men in the various parishes, met at Illiam Dhone's residence at Ronaldsway and took an oath 'that the people should withstand the Lady of Derby until she had

---

Plate 30. TITLE PAGE of the 1771 edition of the Old Testament in Manx. The page reads as follows: The / Bible / Holy: / or / The Old Testament, / from / the original tongues / carefully translated into / Manx; / that is to say, / the mother tongue of the Isle of Man. / In two parts. / Book I. / Appointed to be read in churches. / Whitehaven: / Printed by John Ware and Son. / 1771.

yielded to their aggreavances'. They were told that the countess, without their knowledge, had sent to make conditions of peace, and that she 'would sell them for twopence apiece'. It was true that she had written to Colonel Duckenfield, the commander of the force which Parliament had now sent to capture the Island. Duckenfield's expedition set out from Chester the day before the Ronaldsway meeting, but owing to bad weather it did not reach Ramsey for a week. Christian and the militia had in the meantime obtained full possession of all the forts except Rushen and Peel and had sent a message to Duckenfield offering to surrender Man on condition that the islanders 'might enjoy their lives and liberties as formerly they had'. He and his associates did not trust the countess to think about the Island's constitution and customs!

Duckenfield sent one section of his forces to take Peel, while he him-self prepared to besiege Castle Rushen. He first summoned the countess to surrender and in the letter referred to 'the *late* earl of Derby'. This was the first news Lady Derby had heard of her husband's death, and she was 'extremely affected'. She sent a message offering to surrender, but on terms more suited to a victor than to one in her hopeless situation. Duckenfield's reply was to bring up his cannon and make ready for the attack. Part of the garrison attempted flight by leaping from the battlements, while others made a breach in the walls and admitted the attackers to the outer ramparts. Seeing that the end had come, Lady Derby surrendered on the sole condition that the lives of the defenders should be spared, and that she and her family should have liberty to go to England to seek terms from the Parliament. The resistance might have been much prolonged if only the garrison had had any heart in the defence, because Castle Rushen was immensely strong and was well provided with arms and munitions. This was well known to the be-siegers, who were greatly relieved when the place fell so easily into their hands.

Illiam Dhone has sometimes been called a patriot, and sometimes a rebel and traitor. That he was disloyal to the countess and betrayed a great trust reposed in him cannot be denied. But he considered that he owed a greater duty to his own Manx countrymen, and that if the countess had been allowed to make resistance, the Island would have been conquered by bloodshed and its ancient liberties taken away. At the same time it seems clear that he and those who joined in the Ronaldsway plot intended in any case to change or to coerce their rulers. If they hoped to secure their old ownership of the land they were, however, to be disappointed, for under the Commonwealth government nothing of this nature was changed.

In anticipation of final victory, Parliament had already granted the Island to Lord Fairfax, under whom governors continued to administer Man in accordance with its old constitution. The best known of these governors was James Chaloner, who wrote a short history of the Island which has been reprinted in the Manx Society's publications. He acted as head of the Manx Church, since the bishops were abolished in Man as well as in England, and used the bishop's salary partly in founding schools in the four towns. During Chaloner's governorship William Christian was accused of being short in his accounts, and he retired to his estates in Lancashire early in 1659, some months after Oliver Cromwell's death. The army was in disagreement with Parliament, and the commander of Peel Castle seized Chaloner and imprisoned him. In this the commander had the assistance of Edward Christian and also, it is alleged, of William Christian. Parliament recovered its power and ordered Chaloner's release. He was in office at the time of the Restoration, but died shortly afterwards.

The restoration of Charles II to the throne of England was announced in Peel, Castletown, Douglas, and Ramsey with great rejoicings, and Manxmen appear to have accepted the change back from the Commonwealth to the monarchy as readily as they had adopted the previous change-over. The rule of the Parliament had brought none of those benefits for which they had so fondly hoped. The land leases imposed by the seventh earl were still continued, and the condition of the people in general was, according to Chaloner, one of great poverty.

With the restoration of Charles Stuart came also the restoration of Charles Stanley, the eighth Earl of Derby, as Lord of Man. He restored the bishopric and set about punishing the ringleaders in the rebellion against his mother and, above all, William Christian. Christian was then in London, a prisoner for a debt; but on his release he came back to the Island, believing that the general pardon granted by Charles II extended to the Island. Despite this he was immediately arrested and brought to trial.

Whether or not Christian was justified in his actions in 1651, there could be no doubt that he had broken the law and, but for the King's pardon, had incurred the penalty of death. The argument of the earl and his officers was that the pardon covered offences against the King of England, but not offences committed against the Lord of Man. Christian denied the right of the court to try him and refused to plead, so that he was virtually condemned without trial. Several members of the House of Keys were unwilling to condemn him and were removed, their places being filled by others. Before his trial Illiam Dhone had sent an appeal to the King in Council, but the appeal did not reach London until after he had been shot on Hango Hill. He made a fine end: he delivered an eloquent speech claiming that he had acted in the best interests both of the countess and of the country.[1] The soldiers offered to blindfold him so that he should not see the shots being fired, but he declined. It is said that most of the firing squad deliberately shot in the air and that only one aimed true and killed him. He was mourned by the Manx as a martyr for his country, and a ballad *Baase Illiam Dhone* was written to commemorate him.[2]

In the end the appeal to the King was upheld, William Christian's name was cleared, and his estates were restored to his family. Three other ringleaders of the rising, who had been imprisoned, were released and their lands returned to them.

1. A version of Christian's speech, together with an investigation of the whole episode, is to be found in Sir Walter Scott's introduction to his novel *Peveril of the Peak*.

2. The ballad was printed only in 1781, probably, like the first printing of the Traditionary Ballad in 1778, in connection with a contemporary political agitation; the final verse may have been added during the Atholl period. It was no doubt much older though hardly so old as the death it laments, for it is able to refer to the fate of some of William Christian's opponents. For the text see *Manx Ballads*, pp. 134–6.

CHAPTER NINE

The Last Stanleys and the coming
of British Rule

THE RESTORATION OF THE DERBY RULE IN 1660 HAS ALREADY
been described in the previous chapter, and it will be recalled that the
first great event after the arrival of the eighth earl was the trial of Illiam
Dhone. Apart from this his period of rule was marked by the efforts of
Bishop Isaac Barrow (1663–71) to improve the position and education
of the Manx people and clergy. The bishop was much shocked on his
appointment to find that many of the people were, in his own words,
'loose and vicious in their lives, rude and barbarous in their behaviour
and without any true sense of religion', while the clergy were, for the
most part, ignorant and underpaid. He said that their livings did not
amount to above £5 or £6 per annum, which forced them to engage
in other occupations, even to the keeping of alehouses, to procure a livelihood. It should be added that his severe criticisms are not supported by
other contemporary observers, and much of the trouble arose from the
fact that he did not understand Manx which was to him a 'barbarian'
tongue.

Their congregations understood only Manx, and as there were no
books printed in this language the clergy had to translate from the
English Bible and Prayer Book as they went along, and many of them
did not properly understand English. In order to help to remedy this
the bishop seized the estates of Hango Hill and Ballagilley,[1] in Malew,
and gave them to trustees with the intention of founding a school. This
object was not fully accomplished until 1833, when King William's

---

1. As far as Hango Hill farm was concerned its acquisition has been described as an act
of 'blatant confiscation'. The details of this discreditable episode in Manx legal and
ecclesiastical history can be studied in E. H. Stenning, 'The original lands of Bishop
Barrow's trustees', *I.M. Nat. Hist. and Antiq. Soc.* v (1942–56), 122–45.

College was built on the site thus provided, and the principal endowment of that college is still called the Bishop Barrow Charity. In the meantime young men intended for the Church received scholarships at the 'academic' school in Castletown.

On the death of Earl Charles the succession fell upon William, the ninth earl (1672–1702). Until his time there had been no official coinage in the Island, and most of the coins in use were of Irish origin, being known by such names as 'St. Patrick's halfpence', or 'Limerick' tokens. In 1668 John Murrey, a farmer and merchant who lived at Ronaldsway, had issued a copper coinage bearing his own name. These 'John Murrey' pence were the first coins minted in the Island and they were made legal by an Act of Tynwald in 1679 (see Pl. 39).

Throughout the ninth earl's period of rule the quarrel regarding the method of holding the land, which had become critical under the Great Earl, was continued with increasing bitterness. Farms were becoming empty, not only as a result of the uncertainty of the rights of landholders, but also because a succession of bad harvests and poor fishing seasons had caused much emigration. Attempts to find new tenants met with scant success and at last the earl determined to deal with the matter in person. He crossed to the Island in 1699 and appointed Bishop Wilson, then in his second year of office, to receive proposals from the tenants for a settlement. Although nothing final was accomplished before the earl's death, it was the first business to be taken in hand by his brother and successor, James, tenth earl, the last of the Stanley rulers. Bishop Wilson, in consultation with the Keys, had drawn up proposals to which the earl's consent was obtained. These were embodied in the famous Act of Settlement of 1704, known as the Manx Magna Carta, by which the land question was finally settled.

THE MANX SYSTEM OF LAND-HOLDING

In order to appreciate the significance of this Manx Act it is necessary to look back a little to see what changes had taken place in the methods of holding land in the Island. It is believed that at the beginning of the Stanley rule the land was regarded as the property of the King, and that the land-holders, or tenants, simply held it from year to year without any right of inheritance.[1] As time passed on it became customary for

1. The nature of land tenure *before* the Stanley regime is a disputed and complicated one. The view adopted by Deemster Farrant in *Mann, Its Land Tenure*, etc. (1937), is that prior to the Scandinavian period the tenure was Odal (or Udal), and that the land was

the lease to be renewed automatically, until in the end the estates came to be regarded by the farmers as essentially their own possessions, from which they could not be turned out, but which they could sell, if they wished, or hand on to their descendants. When land was sold the seller gave the buyer a straw grown on the land, and the new owner was said to hold by the straw. This system of land tenure—known as the 'straw tenure'—became well established, and was recognized in the Island courts. It should, however, be pointed out that the sale was carried out in the presence of the lord or his steward; from the legal point of view, the straw was a symbol which really meant that one tenant was surrendering his holding to the lord, and that the latter was granting it to the incoming tenant or purchaser. Land-holders had to pay the lord a fixed annual rent (known as lord's rent), and when the ownership changed there was a kind of succession tax called an alienation fine.

This system of land-holding was confirmed by James I of England in 1607 when he was in charge of Man; but when the seventh Earl of Derby came to live in the Island, like an English lord of the manor settled in the midst of his tenantry, he determined to put an end to all this. He ordered that all lands were to be held on lease, and that the leases lasted either for three lives or for twenty-one years. This meant that the rents could be altered from time to time, and that, moreover, a tenant could not be certain that his son would possess the land after him. Most of the inhabitants lived by farming, and so everyone felt insecure and discontented. This, more than anything else, was the real grievance which Illiam Dhone and his eight hundred fellow-conspirators wished to redress when they deserted the countess and threw in their lot with the Commonwealth.

By the Act of Settlement of 1704, the so-called 'tenants' became in reality the owners of the land, possessing the rights of inheritance and of sale and paying only the fixed 'lord's rent'. The alienation fine was retained, but the irritating services which had grown up, such as supplying food and carrying turf to the castles, were abolished. In recent years, as the result of an Act passed in 1913, the lord's rent has been bought out

held in hereditary right and not from the King. He further argues that this tenure remained essentially the same throughout the Scandinavian period, despite the legend of Godred Crovan who, according to the *Chronicle of Mann*, after the battle of Skyhill divided the Island between his own followers and the surviving Manxmen on condition that 'none should ever presume to claim any of the land by hereditary right'. Thus the period when the Udal tenure fell into disregard was the dismal one between 1266 and 1405, when chaos prevailed for considerable intervals.

by the payment of a lump sum. Until 1949 the British Crown, which had the rights of the former lords, owned the minerals under the soil, the slate and stone (subject to the landowner being allowed to take stone for the use of himself and his neighbour), and charged a royalty to those who worked the mines and quarries. It also owned part of the mountain pastures, which are let off for the rearing of large numbers of sheep.

BISHOP WILSON

Bishop Wilson, the most remarkable of all the rulers of the Church in Man, was thirty-four years of age on his appointment and died in office fifty-seven years later at the advanced age of ninety-one.

He was a man of saintly life; he took an active part in spreading Christianity in distant corners of the world; he was selfless and fearless, and his kindly acts brought him the love of the mass of the people. He devoted at least one-fifth of his income to pious uses, and when a great famine occurred in 1739, and many people were in danger of dying from starvation, he not only gave away large quantities of grain from his own farms but purchased cargoes for distribution to those in need. From the outset he refused to hold more than one Church living at once because he could not personally attend to the duties involved. He did this at a time when pluralism, as it was called, was very common, and he did it although the income from the bishopric was only £400 a year. Late in life he was offered a richer see but nobly refused, saying, 'I will not leave my wife in her old age because she is poor.'

He rebuilt the bishop's palace, Bishopscourt, and took steps to repair the residences of the poorer clergy and to improve their stipends. He also had several churches rebuilt. He reformed the Church in many ways, one of which was by summoning the clergy to their convocation, or annual parliament, and preparing for their consideration a fresh code of ecclesiastical laws. Parents were compelled to send their children to school until they could read English distinctly, and thus the bishop may be considered the pioneer of universal education in the British Isles. It

---

Plate 31. CASTLE MONA, DOUGLAS, in the middle of the nineteenth century. It was built by the Duke of Atholl in the early 1800s as his Manx residence, at a cost of over £30,000. Following the duke's death, the mansion was opened as a hotel in 1832.

Plate 32. COURT HOUSE AT RAMSEY, built in about 1790. It was the first administrative building constructed after the island was ceded to the Crown by the Duke of Atholl. The architect, George Steuart, also built Castle Mona.

was he, too, who began the printing of the Bible in the Manx language.

There was, unhappily, another side to Bishop Wilson's character which showed itself in his desire to revive the ancient power of the Church and of the ecclesiastical courts. A conflict between the Church and the State arose when the governor refused to allow the soldiers, who in those days performed the duties of policemen, to arrest persons sentenced by the vicars-general and take them to the bishop's prison in the damp crypt beneath St. German's Cathedral. It was carried further when the governor denied the right of the ecclesiastical courts to punish members of the castle households and garrisons, and when he allowed persons sentenced by the Church to appeal to a civil court. The climax was reached in 1722 when the bishop passed a sentence upon the governor's wife, Mrs. Horne, who was held guilty of slander against another lady and was ordered to make a public acknowledgement of her offence.

This was too much for Governor Horne. He had already drawn up a series of charges against the bishop and his two vicars-general, and he now ordered them to cancel these and other recent proceedings as illegal. They refused and were each heavily fined, and on failing to pay the fine were committed to prison in Castle Rushen. The bishop appealed to the King in Council and, after having been in prison for nine weeks, was released until the appeal could be heard. The decision did not arrive until two years later, and although partly in the bishop's favour, it did nothing to uphold the ecclesiastical rights for which he had fought. The governors who succeeded Horne were even more hostile to the claims of the Church, and the bishop lived to see his cherished Church discipline falling gradually into disuse.

The Revd. John Keble, in a biography of Bishop Wilson, has compared the bishop's conflict against the Lord of Man with the conflict between Archbishop Thomas Becket and King Henry II of England, and it may be said that in many ways, as a bishop, Wilson lived some centuries too late. It is very difficult for us today to understand how an infinitely kind man like Bishop Wilson could have committed acts

---

Plate 33. KING WILLIAM'S COLLEGE, CASTLETOWN, founded in 1668 after Bishop Barrow had seized the estates of Hango Hill and Ballagilly. The school's present buildings date from 1833.

Plate 34. FARMERS' COTTAGES AT CREGNEASH. Now carefully restored, they form part of the Folk Museum administered by the Manx Museum and National Trust.

which seem to us tyrannical and barbarous. For offences which nowa-days would not be punished at all, or at all events not punished severely, people were obliged to stand in church clothed in a white sheet and to acknowledge their repentance before the congregation, or to stand in the market-place with a horse's bit in the mouth and a bridle over the head. Wicked, but half-witted, women were dragged behind a boat through the sea, and the owners of the boats were sent to prison if they refused to carry out this sentence. Yet the bishop cared passionately for the souls of his people, and believed that punishment of this kind was a way of leading them into right ways of life.

No doubt to some extent he was helped in carrying out his policy by the fact that many of the Manx of those days were very superstitious and ignorant; but certainly many of his own ideas were out of date, and the task which he set himself was doomed to failure. At the end of his life the Church discipline which he had fought so hard to revive and maintain was decidedly weaker than he had found it, and the same causes which had led to its earlier abandonment elsewhere were soon to bring about its final disappearance from the Island.

THE SALE OF THE ISLAND

The tenth Earl of Derby left no children and he was succeeded in the earldom by a distant cousin, Edward Stanley. On the other hand, under the terms of the grant made by James I the Lordship of Man passed (in 1736) to the second Duke of Atholl, James Murray, who was descended from a daughter of the seventh Earl of Derby. The Atholl dynasty in Man lasted less than thirty years, for the third duke sold the lordship to the British Crown in 1765. Yet the Atholl family maintained its association with the Island for sixty years longer, since the fourth duke possessed extensive rights as a landowner, and he was appointed governor-general in 1793.

James, second Duke of Atholl, who succeeded to the lordship in 1736, signalized his accession by coming to the Island in person and presiding at the annual Tynwald. He was given an official welcome, for the people had grown very weary of the rule of the Derbys. Crowds of spectators cheered and waved their hats in the air, while the soldiers and militia saluted by firing a volley.[1]

There was more than pageantry in this visit, for the duke played a personal part in the passing of some much-needed reforms. The chief of

1. For a description of Tynwald Day, 1736, see *J. Manx Museum*, v (1945–6), 171.

these were embodied in an Act of Tynwald, passed in 1737, and chris-
tened the Manx 'Bill of Rights', which assured to everyone the right of
trial by jury. It also declared that the customs duties, which had hitherto
been levied on the sole authority of the lord, should in future be fixed
only with the consent of the Keys and of the council and deemsters.

The duke died in 1764 and was succeeded by his son-in-law John, the
third duke, whose reign was destined to be very short. The British
authorities had for some time been considering how best to stop the
illicit trade which had become so serious in the Island. The growth of
smuggling will be dealt with more fully in the next chapter, and for the
moment it is sufficient to say that Man had become the centre of a vast
network, as a result of which the British government was being deprived of large sums that should have been paid as customs duties. The
traffic had reached such enormous proportions that it was estimated to
be worth as much as a third of a million pounds annually. The remedy
which finally suggested itself was that the King of England should
again become the sovereign of the Island, with the right to appoint
officers to collect Manx customs duties. To effect this it was necessary to
buy the sovereign rights from the lord. Thus the Manx people would be
taxed without having the right to decide what the taxes should be, but
exactly the same thing was being done with the American colonies.
This was the period which saw the outbreak of rebellion in North
America and the foundation of the United States; and the great orator,
Edmund Burke, in one of his famous speeches, compares the results of
the British government's conduct in the Isle of Man and in America.

Shortly after his accession the third Duke of Atholl was asked to state
the sum for which he would sell his rights. He demanded time to consider the question, but was told plainly that steps would be taken to
compel him to sell. The sum of £70,000 was decided on, and the agreement was put into effect by a measure of the British Parliament called
the Isle of Man Revesting Act. This meant that the sovereignty of the
Island, which the King of England had granted to Sir John Stanley in
1405, was now vested in the King once more. The bargain did not cover
the duke's rights as lord of the manor, the most important of these being
the ownership of the minerals, the 'boon' services from the tenants,
and the appointment of the bishop and many of the clergy. The sum
of £70,000 did, on the other hand, include the customs duties of the
Island, which were henceforth transferred to the British government.

Just before this Parliament passed a measure, usually called the

Mischief Act, whose object was to stamp out the 'mischief of smuggling'. It gave power to the English customs officers to come into Manx ports and search suspected vessels, and decreed that any offence against the revenue which had been committed in Man could be tried in the courts of Britain and Ireland. Manx merchants were prohibited from obtaining dutiable goods from foreign countries until they had been imported into England; and later, the British government only allowed such goods to reach the Isle of Man in limited quantities, with the result that the few persons who received the licences to import were able to charge what prices they chose. By another act of the same year actual Manx produce was allowed, with certain exceptions, to be imported into Great Britain free of duty.

These drastic changes in their constitution came upon the Manx people as a humiliation and a disaster. Their ancient kingdom was destroyed by a bargain made over their heads. Although the House of Keys and the legislative council remained, the only power they had concerned things which did not cost money. The British government paid the expenses of administration and kept any surplus taxation under its own control. At first this surplus was paid into a separate account, and there was an undertaking that it would be spent for the Island's benefit; but after a while it went straight into the revenue of the United Kingdom and the government denied that the Isle of Man had any claim upon it. The officials sent to collect the customs duties regarded the Island as a nest of smugglers, and accordingly they treated the Manx with suspicion and disdain.

The smuggling trade had been so extraordinarily profitable that Manxmen had largely lost interest in fishing and farming. They had to rebuild these and other native industries, and in the meantime they suffered great loss. There was a panic amongst the owners of houses and warehouses, which could not be let or sold for as much as previously; merchants from Liverpool and Glasgow hastily left the Island, and the bold seafaring men who had earned their living by 'running' cargoes from Douglas to the adjoining coasts had to look for other occupations.

In one respect the Island was almost immediately the better for the Act of Revestment. Its leading men came into closer contact with the British government officials and realized that some of the Manx laws were out of date. In 1777 Tynwald repealed the oppressive statutes which forced workmen to take employment in certain places and at certain rates of wages, and which enabled deemsters and other officials to obtain labourers and maidservants compulsorily by 'yarding'.

THE FOURTH DUKE OF ATHOLL AS GOVERNOR-GENERAL

The third Duke of Atholl died in 1774, and his son, who had had, of course, no share in making the bargain with the government, immediately began to claim that the sum paid was not enough. The Keys vigorously resisted the duke's demands, and also passed laws obstructing the duke in the collection of his manorial dues such as the custom on herrings, and denying the right of free labour on the duke's houses. The British government repeatedly refused to increase the sum paid for the duke's rights, but in 1793 they gratified him by appointing him the Island's governor-general. This gave him the power to superintend the administration of the Island, and he came over from time to time and built as his Manx residence the splendid mansion overlooking Douglas Bay which is now the Castle Mona Hotel (Pl. 31). But there were still lieutenant-governors who carried out the work in detail.

The duke's office enabled him to appoint some of the lesser officials himself, while his closer contact with the Manx people enabled him to win a measure of support amongst them. He continued to press his claims in London, and he had as 'friend at court' no less a person than the great William Pitt. Although the government's legal advisers had reported that the duke's claims were unjustified, Pitt's authority was great enough to enable him, in 1805, to persuade a reluctant Parliament to pass an Act granting the duke £3,000 a year, to come out of the Island's revenues. This grant was opposed by the House of Keys, and John Christian Curwen, a member both of the Keys and the House of Commons, made an eloquent speech in the latter chamber. In opposing the grant in the House of Lords, Lord Ellenborough, the Chief Justice of England at the time, condemned the whole transaction as 'one of the most corrupt jobs ever witnessed in parliament'.

Although always opposed by the Keys, the duke was for a time a favourite with the people. The Keys were all men of property, and as farmers their interest was to keep the price of corn high, so they tried to prevent its import even when it was scarce in the Island. On one occasion the duke promised the people that they would not starve while he had a loaf. As to the Keys, he once told them that 'they were no more representatives of the people of Man than of the people of Peru'.

There was a certain element of truth in this description when it is considered that the Keys were at the time a self-elected body. The duke also used his influence with the government to stop the press-gangs from taking Manx fishermen to serve in the Navy; and in various ways, despite his restless ambition, the Island's interests were better looked after by him than by the British officials.

What Manxmen could not endure was the increasing presence of the duke's Scottish dependants in various paid offices, and the limit was reached when he appointed his nephew George Murray as bishop. In 1825 Bishop Murray announced that a tithe of 12s. per acre would be levied on potatoes and this naturally led to serious trouble. Even under normal conditions such a rate would have been considered excessive since the charge in Ireland was then 3s. and in the north of England only half a crown, while in actual fact tithes on potatoes had lapsed in the Isle of Man during the later eighteenth century. To make matters still worse the crop that year was bad; farmers therefore refused to pay and riots broke out in many parts of the Island. The bishop was confronted in his own palace at Bishopscourt by a mob which called upon him to give up his claim, and he believed he was in danger of his life. It was in a bitter mood that he admitted surrender and gave up his proposed potato tithe. Shortly afterwards he was translated to another bishopric at Rochester and he left the Island finally in 1827.

By this time the duke was tired of the Isle of Man, and everyone was tired of the agitation over his claims. The British government offered to buy out the remainder of his rights, and in 1828 they were purchased for £417,000. He continued to be governor-general until his death in 1830, but his last visit to the Island was in 1826.

In all, Great Britain paid about half a million pounds for the financial control of the Isle of Man, and, judged by the values of those times, the sum was most excessive. Yet in the hundred years during which they collected the Island's revenues, the British government gained a surplus greater than the total paid to the duke, and in addition they earned good interest on the price of the crown lands and the royalties on the mines. The real sufferers from the deal were the Manx people, whose money was taken from them in taxation while public works, such as harbours, were for most of the period sadly neglected. An era of progress was to come, but it was not until a considerable time after the Atholls had left the Island.

CHAPTER TEN

Society and Religion in the Eighteenth Century

'THIS ISLE WILL NEVER FLOURISH UNTIL SOME TRADING BE.' This remark in a letter of the seventh Earl of Derby, written about 1643, gives some indication that in his time Manx trade was very small, and this is not surprising in view of the prevailing economic and political attitudes.

Ever since the arrival of the Stanleys trade had been regulated in the primitive and thorough manner which was possible in so small an island. No goods could be taken out and none brought in and distributed without the permission of the lord. Customs duties were levied on all imports and exports.[1] Various officers were appointed to see that these rules were enforced, and the most interesting were the 'four merchants' whose business it was to bargain with the merchant stranger on behalf of the lord and the country.

The system of watch and ward enabled the authorities to know whenever a ship was about to reach land. On the ship's arrival in port its master had to go in person before the governor to declare the nature of his cargo, and also to tell him the latest news. After this he was taken in hand by the four merchants, whose duty it was to make the best bargain they could with him. The receivers of Castle Rushen and Peel Castle had the first choice in securing what they needed for those places, and afterwards the four merchants disposed of the remainder in the various parts of the Island. In one of the early orders it is directed that if the cargo consisted of wine, the clerk of the ships was allowed to bargain for one choice hogshead for himself, but, with this exception, no one was to have choice of wine 'but my lord, the captain [i.e. the governor], bishop, abbot, or archdeacon and to drink it free of cost'.

1. Export duties were cancelled in 1737.

No one was allowed to send goods out of the country until the governor had decided with the council what could be spared. The stranger buying commodities for export was forbidden to obtain them except in the public markets; laws were enacted in the time of the seventh earl against what we should call middlemen. It will be evident that such restrictions would not tend to encourage trade, but rather to stifle it. There was very little money in circulation, and for a long time most of the trade, both internal and external, had to be carried on by barter. The Island was badly in need of salt, iron, timber, tar, coal (though it produced its own fuel in the form of turf), besides all of the luxuries. Until the development of lead and silver mining the Manx had nothing to export except the products of agriculture and the fisheries. Indeed, the external trade between 1660 and 1700 was so little that the customs duties on exports and imports combined produced less than £100 annually. During the eighteenth century the amount increased very considerably, so that by 1750 the annual value was £3,500 or more.[1]

Conditions improved after the defeat of King Charles I, when many royalist refugees sought refuge in Man and brought with them a quantity of new money. Later, as has been stated, copper coins were minted in the Island, replacing the base currency in which traders could have no confidence. Instead of being confined to the Manx coast, fishermen ventured to Scotland and England to market their goods abroad, and trading vessels also began to disregard the old restrictions.

TRADE AND SMUGGLING

Manxmen have a well-marked aptitude for a life of seafaring and maritime commerce, but unfortunately during the greater part of this period they were hampered by many restrictions imposed not only by their own government but also by the governments of surrounding lands. Normal trade with England was practically impossible, since it was laid down in the Navigation Acts that goods could only be brought into that country by English-built and English-manned ships. Moreover, the English tariff was so heavy, especially after 1689, that any trading intercourse between the two countries became prohibitive.

1. According to inquiries made by British Treasury officials in 1759, the income from the Insular customs was £6,000. See C. R. Jarvis, 'Illicit trade with the Isle of Man, 1671–1765', Trans. Lancs. and Ches. Antiq. Soc. lviii (1945–6), 58.

Tynwald complained of this in a petition to Lord Derby in 1705 in which they pointed out that it was impossible for them to get the chief articles they required, including those indicated above, unless they were able to export such articles as they could spare, and that they were prevented from doing this by the high English tariff. This appeal produced no result.

Under such conditions it is not surprising that towards the end of the seventeenth century smuggling, or, as it was called, the 'running trade', became a tempting enterprise and a thrilling adventure. Wines and spirits, tea, tobacco, and other commodities could be brought from abroad, particularly France, Spain, Portugal, Norway, and Sweden, landed at the Manx ports on payment of the comparatively small local duty, and run across to creeks and small bays on the coasts of England, Scotland, or Ireland. Smaller boats were specially built in such a style as to give them speed when dodging or flying from the revenue cutters, and also to enable them to run in to the Lancashire and other coasts, preferably at dusk, at a state of tide when deeper-draught vessels could not follow.

The prevailing economic conditions were, of course, such as to encourage similar activities round most of the English coasts, particularly in the south and east where investigations in the second half of the eighteenth century disclosed an amazing and bewildering state of affairs. But the Island's position, both strategically and constitutionally, helped to make it 'the very citadel of smuggling', as Edmund Burke described it in his speech on American taxation in 1774. Merchants from surrounding countries, particularly England and Scotland, came to invest their capital in this new and promising business.[1] Gone were the old ideas of keeping 'strangers' at arm's length; the law was altered so as to place them in almost as good a position for trading as the native Manxmen. Manx ports, especially Douglas, were busy with fine ships carrying cargoes of the most desired goods in the world. The more the

---

1. It should, indeed, be stressed that amongst the chief 'smugglers' were not merely those who carried the goods across the seas, but also the merchants who traded in them in Man and in England; most of these traders were of English or Scottish origin. On purely legal grounds it could be argued from the Manx standpoint that the trade was legitimate in so far as it did not violate Insular laws. The British authorities, on the other hand, condemned the trade as 'illicit and clandestine'. See *Abstract of the Laws . . . of the Isle of Man*, Manx Soc. 12, p. 105. For some indications of conditions all round the coast of England see A. L. Cross, *Eighteenth Century Documents relating to the Royal Forests and Smuggling* (Ann Arbor, 1928), and G. Bernard Wood, *Smugglers' Britain* (London, 1966).

trade grew, the greater were the customs duties paid in the Island, and the lord and his officials made only a pretence of discouraging such trade.

The British government officials had no desire to be defrauded. They autocratically threatened to take steps for raising the Manx duties to the same level as those in Britain; they stationed their own officers in the Island to watch over their interests; they passed a law prohibiting the importation of foreign goods into Man for the purpose of being re-exported into Britain. An agreement was made whereby the Island was to pass that legislation for itself, provided that England withdrew the duties upon goods which were the home-grown products of the Island. Parliament did not keep its promise, and Tynwald did not consider itself bound either. Thereupon Parliament passed the Act over the head of Tynwald and, later on, as described in the previous chapter, it regained by force the sovereignty of the Island. So, by limiting the quantities of Manx imports, fixing the amounts of the duties, and policing the Manx waters it gained control of what was called the 'smuggling mischief'.

HOW THE PEOPLE LIVED

Little is known of the domestic and social life of the Manx before the period of the Commonwealth. In the year 1648 a Lancashire gentleman named William Blundell, 'wearied', as he says, 'with being so often wakened at midnight to fly from the king's and parliament's troops (both equally feared because equally plundering)', sought rest and refuge in Man. Other writers about the Island were Governor Chaloner, a late seventeenth-century governor named William Sacheverell, and George Waldron, one of those English customs officers who had the 'mortification', as he himself puts it, of seeing a 'stately cargo of indigo, mastic, raisins of the sun and other very rich goods, sold to the traders of Douglas without the least duty being paid to His Majesty!'

Then, as now, there were four principal towns; Castletown, Douglas, Ramsey, and Peel. Castletown was the capital and the place of the lord's residence; Douglas had more trade and a rather larger population because of its better harbour. In Blundell's day Ramsey and Peel were scarcely bigger than villages, and Ramsey port had been washed away not long before by a great storm.

The gentry and well-to-do folk lived in the country, and their houses

were substantial and well built. They generally spoke English, and Blundell says they were very like the people of Lancashire and Cheshire, both
in manner of speech and way of life. The houses of farmers and tradesmen usually had only one storey, and were thatched with straw. In
Douglas and Castletown there were houses of two storeys, and even
three, and a few were roofed with slate. In such houses there was a
stone stairway outside, such as may still be seen in old-fashioned barns.
The poorer people lived in small cottages built of stones bound with
mud or of turf sods alone, sometimes thatched with straw, broom, or
bent, but often covered simply with sods of turf. The thatch was held
in position by twisted ropes made of straw, called *suggane*.

These cottages very often consisted of a single room with a loft over
one end of it. If a second room existed it was called a *cuillee*, or parlour.
The floor was generally of earth, with an open fireplace or hearth
called a *chiollagh*, where there was a long chain, called a *slouree*, which
suspended the big pot over the fire. Turf, ling, and gorse were used as
fuel, though the better-class houses used a mixture of turf and coal.
In these cottages, small as they were, large families were often reared.

Blundell says that in many places, besides the man and his wife and
children, there were geese and ducks under the bed, cocks and hens
overhead, and the cow and calf at the bed's foot. This, of course, is an
overstatement, but it must not be forgotten that T. E. Brown, more than
two centuries later, could write in *Betsy Lee*:

> You know the way them houses is fixed
> With the pigs and the hens and the childher mixed.

The food of the poorer classes consisted chiefly of herrings and oat-
cakes, while their drink was water or buttermilk, with beer (*jough*)
on feast-days and market-days. When potatoes were introduced they
joined the herrings to form the principal articles of Manx diet. These
two are linked in the Christmas greeting of good wishes, *Palchey
phuddase as skeddan dy liooar* (potatoes in plenty and herring enough).
The Island was not short of mutton, beef, bacon, poultry, eggs, honey,
or butter, but these were produced chiefly for sale.

Clothing was made from the wool of the native or *loaghtan* sheep,
and from native-grown flax. *Loaghtan* wool, the natural colour of
which is light brown, has practically died out, but formerly it was
much valued. Shoes and stockings were seldom worn either by men or
women, except on Sundays. For work in the fields *carranes* were worn.

They were untanned strips of cow-hide bound to the feet by thongs of the same material.

The native Manx horse was a small hardy beast with long black hair. Blundell says that a reasonably sized man needed no stirrup to mount one; but once mounted, the little animal would trot along all day and all night, needing very little to eat or drink. The cows are described as being small and poor. They lived in the open, summer and winter. When fodder became scarce they were often fed on bruised gorse shoots, and most upland farms had a gorse mill for this purpose. When near the seashore they would feed on dulse and other seaweeds. According to Blundell cattle got to like this diet better than hay or grass, and thrived better and gave more milk on it; but, with all respect to that writer, this is hard to believe, and he was probably trying to impress his English readers with the wonders of what was then a little-known Island.

Down to the second half of the eighteenth century there were no wheeled carriages, sleds being used, and the roads were little better than bridle paths. Travel was mostly on foot or horseback; goods were conveyed on panniers on the backs of horses or donkeys. Prices generally were very low. A goose could be bought for fourpence, and eggs ten or twelve for a penny.

Fairs were held very frequently throughout the parishes, and the writers tell of two great national fairs—Midsummer, when the laws were proclaimed at St. John's, and Michaelmas, held near the church of Kirk Michael. Allhallowtide (or Hollantide), when the farm servants entered their new employment, was also an occasion of importance and a fair was held on that day at Douglas. Women servants were hired on Lady Day, and until fairly recently a 'Ladies' Fair' was held in Sulby Claddagh, though no longer on Lady Day.

Though the Manx impressed their outside observers as being serious and even melancholy, they could amuse themselves on occasion. The young men had skill with bows and arrows, and archery matches were frequent. They also played a kind of hockey called *cammag*, which was exceedingly popular, and was played until very recently. Dancing to the music of the fiddle and bass viol was their favourite pastime, and they practised it in the fields in summer and in the barns in winter.

Except for the upper classes and the shopkeepers in the towns, Manx was the common speech. There were no books in that language until Bishop Wilson published a Catechism in 1707, and started the translation of the Scriptures. When people were taught to read they could only learn to read English; any other teaching must have been by word of mouth. Most of the schools were carried on by the clergymen, though there were a few licensed schoolmasters; in the early part of the nineteenth century, as may be gathered from the poems of T. E. Brown, the schoolmaster was often a tailor who went on sewing after he had set the children their tasks. Teaching was also considered an occupation suitable for a cripple.

Manxmen are always interested to learn what other people think of them. English writers say that they were shy and reserved with strangers, though friendly enough on a longer acquaintance, and that they were extremely frugal. The men were tall and 'of strenuous bulk', and though full of mettle they were patient and law-abiding and loath to resist when oppressed. The women were active and lively, and much more industrious than the men. While the men were fishing it was the women who performed much of the agricultural labour.

The people were at the same time deeply religious and highly superstitious. Unconscious of any inconsistency, they would offer prayers to Christ and St. Patrick but would leave gifts to keep themselves on good terms with the fairies. The 'fairy doctor', the 'wise woman', and the seller of charms were often resorted to.

The national character was greatly injured by the advent of smuggling, and the consequent cheapness and abundance of intoxicating liquors. Drunkenness became the Island's besetting sin. Colonel Richard Townley, who visited Douglas at the end of the eighteenth century, gives the Manx fishermen a bad character, and says that after a good period of fishing they would neglect their industry while they spent their profits on drinking. Seventy years earlier Waldron wrote that the only diversion of the better sort of people was drinking. When people settled down to a quieter but more honest form of livelihood, when liquor became less plentiful, and when the legislature took steps to regulate the number of alehouses, the Manx gradually returned to sobriety. They were helped in this by the reforming influence of the Methodists and a fine group of clergymen, and by the Rechabite and other temperance societies.

THE MANX CHURCH

Bishop Wilson was followed by the equally good, though not equally great, Bishop Mark Hildesley (1755–72). Hildesley's lovable disposition is shown in numerous letters to friends in the Island and in England, which are delightful in their wit, their wisdom, and their kindliness. If Bishop Wilson was born to command, then Hildesley was born to be an elder brother.

He plunged with enthusiasm into the work involved in the publication of the Manx Bible.[1] Most of this was printed in his time, besides the Prayer Book and some religious works; and before he died he had the happiness of seeing the last printed pages of the translation of the Bible. The task was divided amongst the parish clergymen, their work being revised by the Revd. Philip Moore, headmaster of the Douglas Grammar School, and his pupil John Kelly. Once when Kelly was bringing a batch of the manuscripts to Whitehaven to be printed, his ship was wrecked and the precious papers were saved through Kelly holding them out of reach of the water for five hours. In some passages the Manx Bible differs from the English, since Philip Moore made use of the results of the learning which had been made available since the English translation of 1611. The Manx translation is thought to be of a very high standard, but this naturally varies from book to book according to the command of grammar, vocabulary, and idiom possessed by the individual translators.[2]

Bishop Hildesley was less successful in his endeavour to keep alive his predecessor's system of ecclesiastical discipline. He found that the churches were not large enough to hold the population, so he caused some to be rebuilt and added one or two new ones. St. Mark's church, Malew, is the work of Bishop Hildesley, and St. George's, Douglas, was begun in his time.

Another great church-builder was Bishop Ward, who held the see from 1828 to 1838. He raised large sums of money in England for the replacement and increase of churches in the Island. St. Barnabas's, Douglas, and St. Luke's, Baldwin, were founded by him. By the same

1. The first portion of the Bible translation and the only one produced under Bishop Wilson, was a version of St. Matthew's Gospel in 1748. Under Bishop Hildesley, who was unable to share in the work of translating but exerted himself to great effect in the no less essential work of fund-raising in England to make the publication possible, there appeared the Gospels and Acts in 1763 (with a revised text of Matthew), the Epistles and Revelation in 1767, and the old Testament and major Apocrypha in two volumes, 1770 (reprinted 1771), and 1772. The Book of Common Prayer appeared in 1765.

2. See the Rhŷs Memorial Lecture for 1969 (*Proceedings of the British Academy*, lv, 1971). An illustration of the attention given by the translators and revisers to advances in scholarship is their rendering of Song of Solomon 6 : 4, 10, not adopted again until the New English Bible in 1970.

appeal to English friends and sympathizers, mainly through the efforts of the Revd. Hugh Stowell, Rector of Ballaugh, he greatly increased the funds of the Bishop Barrow Charity, and a dream of over two centuries was made real by the opening of King William's College in 1833. The education given there is similar to that in the important English public schools, and it is provided for boys living both within and outside the Island. In recent years, especially since the legislature helped to find money for modernizing the school buildings, King William's College has been linked more closely with the whole Manx educational system. Other educational activities during this period included the establishment of a new school in Peel (as a result of the efforts of Bishop Hildesley), and also what was called the Lancasterian school in Athol Street, Douglas. Bishop Ward played a major role in resisting a strong attempt to abolish the independent bishopric of Sodor and Man and to unite it to that of Carlisle. In 1836 an Act was actually passed at Westminster whereby the see of Sodor and Man was to be suppressed on the death or translation of Bishop Ward. In favour of such a step it had been argued that the see was very small and the money so saved could be used to increase the stipends of the parish clergy. The bishop, who loved the Island and had worked hard for the improvement of his diocese, led a very successful protest against its absorption into that of Carlisle, so that in 1838 a special Act of Parliament restored the Manx bishopric after a bargain had been struck with the Island's legislature, whereby Tynwald was to pass a law for the commutation of tithes.

By the Act of Tynwald of 1839 for the commutation of tithes the church ended the long quarrel which had particularly embittered Island life for the last quarter of a century or more. Tithes on herrings and other fish about which there had been a long controversy had ceased to be paid by the end of the eighteenth century, but then storms had raged once again following Bishop Murray's ill-fated attempt to collect the tithe on potatoes. Moreover, the method of collecting tithes had also given rise to disturbances, and it became clear that the payment of a definite money charge, rising or falling each year according to the English market price of grain, was much preferable to that of paying in kind. The Tithe Commutation Act of 1839, which made the money payment possible, not only improved the position of the Manx clergy, but made less likely any friction between them and the tithe-payers.

THE APOSTLES OF METHODISM

The first Methodist preacher in the Island was John Murlin, sometimes nicknamed 'the weeping prophet'. He visited Ramsey in 1758 and declared that the Isle of Man was such a nest of smugglers that he could do no good there. Eighteen years later John Crook came from Liverpool and ultimately met with success. At first he had to face opposition and even violence, for in Douglas he was attacked by a mob who thought they had the support of the minister of St. Matthew's. Bishop Richmond, a haughty overbearing man, issued a letter to his clergy violently condemning the Methodists, but the governor was very friendly, and some of the clergymen gave the movement their approval.

John Wesley himself visited Man in 1777 and 1781 sailing on each occasion from Whitehaven and landing at Douglas which was, of course, largely located around the harbour at that period. On his first visit the latter port reminded him of Newlyn in Cornwall 'in its situation, form, and buildings'. He was greatly surprised at the country as he travelled to Castletown where he preached near the castle 'to all the inhabitants of the town'. The people were 'deeply serious' apart from 'two or three gay young women' who 'showed they knew nothing about religion'. He then went on to Peel where he met with official opposition, although the local clergyman was sympathetic to him with the result that he preached two sermons, one during the afternoon and the other at five in the morning! In recording his visit Wesley noted in his Journal: 'a more loving simple-hearted people than this I never saw. And no wonder; for they have but six papists, and no dissenters in the Island. It is supposed to contain near thirty thousand people, remarkably courteous and humane.' This reference to dissenters emphasizes the fact that John Wesley did not intend his Methodism to disrupt the Church but to stimulate it and to give its followers more zeal. That something of this kind was necessary can be judged by a comment of Bishop Hildesley to the effect that 'if the parochial clergy had some of his (i.e. Wesley's) zeal the Christian Church would not be the worse. I verily believe he has set some of us upon being more active in our duty.'

Plates 35, 36. TYNWALD DAY AT ST. JOHN'S, in about 1800 and 1860. To the left is Tynwald Hill, where the Court is seated during the formal proclamation of the island's laws. A great Midsummer fair is taking place on the same day.

1788 *The* CÆSAR *Captain* William Stowell

On his second visit, in 1781, Wesley first preached in the Douglas market-place near the site of old St. Matthew's church, being well received. The next day he had a large congregation in Castletown market-place in the morning; then about four in the afternoon he preached at South Barrule 'on the mountains to a larger congregation than that in the morning'. That same evening he preached on the shore at Peel 'to the largest congregation I have seen in the Island'. The next day found him preaching at Ballaugh during the morning before moving to Kirk Andreas and to Ramsey where he preached twice, apparently with success.

The island was made a separate circuit in 1778 when the number of Methodists was some 600; by 1781 the number had reached 1,597, and later Wesley recorded about 2,100 members of the Methodist societies out of a total adult population of some 15,000. He was very enthusiastic about the progress made. 'What a fair proportion is this! [he wrote] What has been seen like this, in any part either of Great Britain or Ireland?' He was also delighted with the earnestness of the local preachers and the singing of the congregations. 'The local preachers are men of faith and love, knit together in one mind and one judgment ... I have never heard better singing either in Bristol or London', he wrote in his Journal.

His general impressions of the Isle of Man and its inhabitants are revealing. He regarded the Island as 'shut up from the world; and having little trade ... visited by scarce any strangers'. 'The natives are a plain, artless, simple people; unpolished, that is, unpolluted; few of them are rich or genteel; the far greater part moderately poor; and most of the strangers that settle among them are men that have seen affliction.' It is, however, something of a shock to hear his views on the Manx language as expressed in his reply to a wish of George Holder, one of Wesley's preachers in the Island, to publish a Manx hymn-book. Wesley wrote to him in 1789: 'I exceedingly disapprove of your publishing anything in the Manx language. On the contrary, we should do

---

Plate 37. THE BRIG *CAESAR* in the Bay of Naples, 1788. Built at Douglas in 1783, the ship travelled to Mediterranean ports with red herrings, returning with wines and silks; and to the West Indies, bringing back rum and sugar.

Plate 38. MONA'S ISLE I, the first steamer of the Isle of Man Steam Packet Company. Built in 1830 to transport the increasing number of visitors to the island, she could carry two hundred passengers at more than 8 knots.

everything in our power to abolish it from the earth, and persuade every member of our Society to learn and talk English.'[1]

The Wesleyan Methodists were followed by the Primitive Methodists who established themselves in the Island in 1823 after the arrival of John Butcher, a preacher from Bolton, who landed from a fishing-boat at Derbyhaven.

The Manx Bible was succeeded at no great interval by a Manx hymn-book (1795), published for the Methodists. About the same period there was being composed a mass of religious verse, under the general title of *carvals* or carols, which is almost the only kind of original literature in the Manx language.[2]

Manx Methodism

There is much evidence that in the eighteenth century England was sinking into irreligion and looseness of life, and that it was helped in raising itself by the virtue and zeal of the Methodists. In the Island similar evils were calling for a similar remedy. The smuggling trade had made a number of the people somewhat reckless and drunken. Methodism, happily, with its strong personal appeal together with its insistence on temperance proved an immense power for good in winning the people back to better ways of life. An emotional form of worship like early Methodism may have its dangers, but it filled men and women first with fear and then with a glowing hope. Moreover it reached those who had been unaffected by the orderliness and the serene beauty in the Book of Common Prayer.

Methodism has a great hold on the Manx people today, but it has caused little serious disagreement with the established Church. The Island has indeed been fortunate in having been spared not only the mutual persecution of Protestants and Roman Catholics during the period of the Reformation, but also the repression of Dissenters which was practised in England particularly during the seventeenth century. On the contrary, for long after the coming of Methodism people would go to the church in the morning and the chapel at night, and the parish clerk might

---

1. For a similar attitude noted by a writer in the following century, see Matthew Arnold's *Study of Celtic Literature* for quotations illustrating the then prevailing English attitude to Welsh. Bishop Hildesley's letters show that such views were held also by some in Man; for quotations see the lecture referred to in the previous note.

2. A collection of these carvals was published by A. W. Moore, with translations by various hands, as *Carvallyn Gailckagh* (Douglas, 1891). The collection contains versions of about half the *carvals* known from manuscript sources.

be a local preacher. To this day some of the church-wardens are active Methodists. Legislation has been obtained which enables Nonconformists to have baptisms, marriages, and funerals performed in their own churches; but a good many Methodists have such an attachment to the parish church that they do not think of exercising their liberty. Religious differences sometimes have an influence in elections to the House of Keys. As a rule, however, churchmen and Methodists live happily together; and a notable feature of the present day, at any rate in one parish, are the united services held, for example, in support of the Island's hospitals.

Wesleyan Methodists and Primitive Methodists have been known to be suspicious of each other, with separate chapels in some districts, but the union of the Methodist churches which came into effect some years ago is expected, in Man as in other places, to cause these disagreements to pass away. Under modern conditions the process is going a stage further and amalgamation is taking place between the various Methodist churches. Thus Douglas in 1967 witnessed the first stage of a rationalization programme by the union of Buck's Road and Rosemount Methodist churches into a new church which, although housed in Rosemount church, has the name of Trinity; and it is anticipated that the process will continue until the former six Methodist churches in the town are reduced to three.

CHAPTER ELEVEN

Fiscal and Political Reform in the Nineteenth Century

THERE IS NO DOUBT THAT IN ADDITION TO THE IMMEDIATE turmoil caused by the abolition of the smuggling traffic, the passing of the Mischief and Revesting Acts by the British parliament had various depressing effects on the economy of the Island, so that poverty was widespread, prices increased rapidly, and many people were forced to emigrate to obtain a livelihood. Naturally the difficulties were heightened by particular events such as the tithe disputes and potato riots of the 1820s as already described.

There were, it is true, some relieving features during this period, including some seasons of prosperity amongst the fishermen. Considerable quantities of red and white herrings were exported to British as well as to French, Spanish, and Italian ports, and even to America. The customs duties were considerably lower than those in England, and people who lived on comparatively small fixed incomes found that a sum which would barely maintain them in England or Ireland would, in the Island, enable them to live comfortably. Their number was increased at the end of the Napoleonic wars, when many army and navy officers were retired upon half-pay.

There was another, and much less respectable, class of immigrant into the Island. People who owed money in England, and were under the laws of that period liable to be imprisoned until they had paid their debt, could not be pursued by their creditors into Man. Some of them were dishonest and brought with them considerable sums of money with which they usually paid their way. Their purchases were of benefit to the Manx tradesmen, and laws were passed for their protection. The tradesmen were in turn protected against them by laws which allowed them, if they suspected the people were about to leave the Island, to have them arrested and detained until they paid or gave security for what they owed. The presence of such absconding debtors tended to give the Island a bad reputation; but after a while the laws were modified and Man ceased to be regarded as a refuge for the dishonest.

Residents in England began to visit the Island in the summer for the sake of what was then called the 'sea bathing', and communications became easier, quicker, and more regular after the establishment of a passenger steamer service between Douglas and Liverpool in 1829. The political union of the Island with Britain entitled Manx ships to be regarded as British ships, and therefore obtain their share of the British carrying trade.

THE HOUSE OF KEYS

From the financial and political viewpoints the conduct of the British parliament in passing the 1765 legislation was, in the words of Deemster G. E. Moore, 'high handed and aggressive whether one looks at the position through the eyes of the duke of Atholl or the eyes of the Manx people'. This sharp reaction is more easily understood against the background of the earlier history of the House of Keys.

It has already been seen that in Norse times the Keys were a kind of jury, assisting the deemsters when any question of doubt or difficulty arose to declare the ancient customary or 'breast' law. This was also their function at the beginning of the Stanley period, when records of the Keys really begin; but their meetings were by no means regular, nor were they regarded as a permanent body. This judicial aspect of their work persisted, and the Keys continued to act as the supreme Court of Appeal in the Island until the Act of 1866 finally abolished that side of their duties. It is not definitely known how the Keys were appointed in the early days of the Stanleys, except that in 1430 it is vaguely suggested that the 'twenty-four' were selected from thirty-six men, six being from each sheading in which they had been chosen by the whole commons.

From declaring the old laws the function of the Keys passed in time to the making of new laws; but this development did not take place quickly, nor was it accomplished without a long struggle.

The first occasion on which the Keys are referred to as meeting with the two deemsters to enact certain laws was in 1585. During the early seventeenth century laws were made more frequently, and the Keys took part in making them, but the seventh earl, the Great Stanley, did not wish this to be regarded as a definite right to do so.

After the Restoration, in 1660, the Keys lost much of their authority, for the high-handed eighth earl removed seven members in 1662 because they were suspected of being favourable to Illiam Dhone who was then on trial; and he threatened a number of them in 1668 because they returned a verdict which challenged his ownership of the land. In 1677 he altered the customs rates without consulting them and apparently dismissed nine members who had protested. This may be gathered from the fact that in a list of members of the House of Keys from the earliest times, which has been drawn up by Mr. Ramsey B. Moore, a former attorney-general, nine new names appeared in 1677. The customs duties were again altered without the Keys' consent in 1692. Promises were made that they would be consulted in the future, and they did take part in legislation connected with the customs in 1711 and 1714; but the principle that taxation could not be altered without the consent of the Keys was not definitely stated until 1737 in that great measure which has already been referred to as the Manx Bill of Rights.

At what date the Keys came to be self-elected it is very difficult to say, although it is known that it was such a body in 1610 and that it had been so for at least a generation before then. When a member died or ceased to hold office the remainder nominated two persons of whom the governor selected one as the successor. It is, however, an interesting fact that in 1643 (and also in 1608) there is reference to 'four men of every parish' chosen by the people, who were consulted along with the Keys when any special matter was under discussion. Apparently they had no power, but their existence reveals that the idea of popular election had to some extent survived.

AFTERMATH OF THE REVESTMENT

Since 1737 the rulers of Man had not possessed the right to impose taxation without Tynwald's consent, but in an Act of 1767 Parliament for the first time imposed taxation on the people of the Island and ordered that the proceeds should be paid into a separate account in the United Kingdom exchequer. It was further stipulated that after the necessary expenses incurred in the government of the Island and the administration of justice there had been defrayed, whatever balance remained should be 'reserved for the disposition of Parliament'.

Such conditions persisted until 1866, except that although the separate account in the 1767 Act was kept for some years, later on no such distinction was made, so the revenue from the island became merged into the revenue of the United Kingdom government. From time to time Tynwald tried to ascertain what surplus out of the Manx revenue was retained by the United Kingdom exchequer, but without success. This surplus has been estimated at over £1 million, and despite the Manx claim to have an unquestionable right to this money the Island never received it. Meanwhile, from 1765 onwards the Island was 'without an insular revenue, without an annual budget, and without resources for development', and if Tynwald desired to raise revenue internally for insular purposes, as, for example, the care of persons of unsound mind and the upkeep of the highways, a separate board had to be established and given the power to raise revenue by rates. Incidentally, it is an interesting fact that the present system of administration by boards, which began under these circumstances, continued to develop throughout the years so as to become an established feature of the constitution.

After 1796 the receipts from Manx customs duties so increased that they exceeded the amount spent on the Island's government and left the British government with substantial surpluses for several years. On the other hand, the British authorities paid little attention to the growth of the Island's population, or to the need for better harbours which followed from the increase in trade. For another half-century the Manx were agitating for the right to handle their own revenues, so that they could provide harbours and other national necessities, instead of having to wait until the British government could be made interested in the subject.

Side by side with this nationalist movement for self-government there was a democratic movement for government by the people. As early as 1780 a petition signed by 800 inhabitants was prepared for submission to Parliament, urging that the House of Keys might be dissolved and replaced by a body chosen at regular periods by popular election. The Keys declared that this petition was organized on behalf of the Duke of Atholl in order to undermine their influence when fighting for what were the people's rights.

In 1832 Parliament passed the celebrated Reform Bill, which went a long way towards making the choice of government the genuine privilege of the mass of the people in England. A reform party newspaper, the *Mona's Herald*, was established in the Island in the following year, and the battle for popular government became increasingly keen. At first the British authorities told the agitators that if any reform was decided upon, it might consist of giving the Manx one elected representative in the House of Commons and bringing the Island's separate government to an end. Later they told Tynwald that they could not hand the control of taxes paid by the people to a body whom the people had not chosen.

LORD LOCH AND THE REFORMS OF 1866

Such was the state of affairs when Henry Brougham Loch (later Lord Loch) became governor in 1863. Soon after his appointment he came to the conclusion that the Island's future prosperity depended upon developing trade and the holiday traffic, and that the Manx government must obtain power to raise and spend money on harbours, in particular the construction of a low-water landing pier at Douglas and the protection of Douglas harbour. As that power, he declared, could only be obtained on condition that the House of Keys was reformed, the self-elected House must vote itself out of existence. The House was ill-advised in the meantime to imprison James Brown, the editor of a Douglas newspaper, for criticisms passed upon it, with the result that an English tribunal, the Privy Council, quashed the sentence and the Isle of Man Common Law Court ordered the House to pay the editor compensation. The two problems, namely, the reform of the Keys and the question of financial control, were settled together after lengthy negotiations in 1866, when an Isle of Man Customs and Harbours Act

---

Plate 39. MANX COINS. The obverse and reverse of five coins are shown in pairs down the page. The earliest known coin to have circulated in the Island, a penny (top), was issued by John Murrey in Douglas in 1668. The Earl of Derby penny of 1709 carried the family motto and crest. The banker George Quayle issued his own token coinage in 1811, at a time when regal coins were in short supply. The Queen Victoria penny of 1839 was one of the first Manx coins to have equivalent exchange rates with British coins; prior to 1840 the rates had been fourteen Manx pence to twelve English pence. The King William's College halfpenny (bottom), issued from 1937 to 1952, was intended to prevent the boys spending their money other than at the school shop.

OVERLEAF

Plate 40. MAP OF THE ISLE OF MAN, from James Chaloner's *Short Treatise of the Isle of Man*, published as the Appendix to Daniel King's *Vale Royal of England* in 1656.

Prospect of Castel Rushon from E.N.E.

The Prospect of Castel Rushon from E.N.E.

St. Michaels Iland or Derbie Fort from S.W. b S

Balesale Bridge.   from the South.

This Scale as to be meafured from the Compaffe in the midst of the Ifland vnto the feuerall Coafts of England Scotland Ireland, and Kildar.

| 5 | 10 | 20 | 50 |

MAN by Cafar Called Mona, by Pliny Monabia by Ptolom. Monoeda, and by Gildas Eubonia, is an Iland featel in the Ocean betwixt England, Scotland and Ireland. it formerly bare the name of a Kingdom & hath bene populous & well inhabited. very plentifull of Cattell foule and fiſh. at is now deuided into 17 Pariſhes, many Villages & defended by two Caſtells.

SCOTLAND

Salful
Coſwell   GALLOWAY

Iorby point

Rughlines

The Sound

Kirk Mighhill

Clanboy
Knokfergus
Tharde
Melnay
Son

Olderfleet hauen
The Maidens

Knokfergus
North rock
Rockes
South rocke
Strangford hauen

Peel ioune
S. Johns
W

Peel castle
Kirk Iarman
Kirk Patrick

Patrik
Donne
Clan Bofel

Kilbart point

Glanfala fhad
ing

Clanmay

Sheape hauen

Newry
Carlingsford hauen

Dauby point

Dauby pitt

Dundalle hauen

Watch hill
Kirk Krcho

St Katherins chap

Old:
towne

Kirk Mali
Balafhe

Bremore
Island
patrik
Cobeti

Fleshik

Kirk Chrest
Kirk Kugh
Portwik

Pole bash
feacthlat

Popes
fild

Port Erau

Cifterch
Chapell

Portell Morrey

Dublin

The Mull heils

The
Spalarck

Deleay

The Chicken

The Calfe of Man

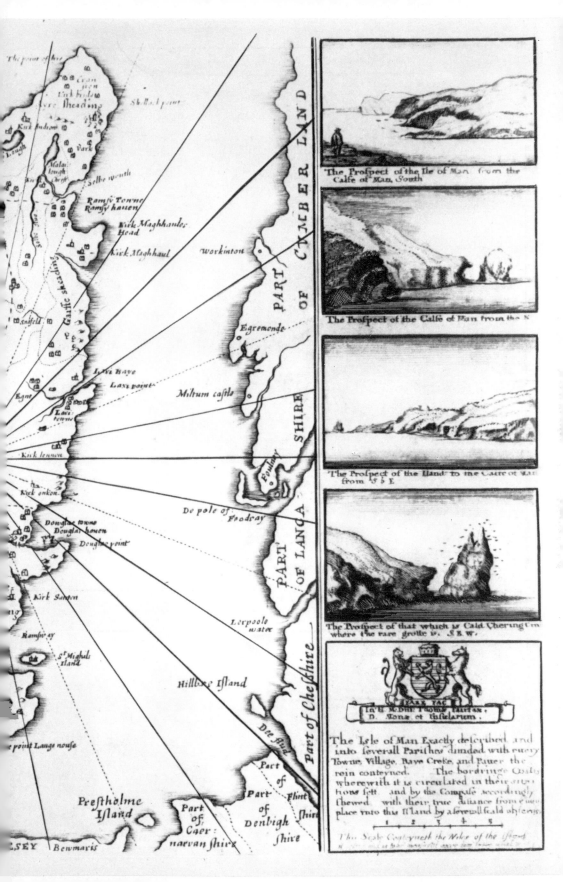

was passed by Parliament, and a House of Keys Election Act was passed by Tynwald.

As a result of this legislation in 1866, (1) the Keys were to be elected and (2) various financial and other proposals were agreed upon which can be summarized in this way:

(a) The Isle of Man harbours were to remain under imperial control.

(b) One-ninth of the Manx customs revenue was to be set aside for harbour improvements and other public works. Tynwald was to determine what these improvements and public works should be, the governor having a veto in such matters.

(c) The revenue from the Crown lands, properties, and rights was to be retained for the benefit of the English exchequer.

(d) After the payment for government and the administration of justice and police (these constituting what were called the 'reserved services') and the payment of £10,000 per annum, surplus customs revenue was to be applied by the English exchequer as Tynwald determined, the governor having a veto. Expenditure sanctioned by Tynwald under such conditions came to be known as the 'voted services' (as distinct from the 'reserved services') and the distinction continued until 1958 when an Act giving effect to an agreement between the United Kingdom and Isle of Man governments gave the Island complete control of its internal expenditure.

The amount to be paid to the English exchequer each year was ultimately fixed at £10,000 after a much larger sum had been asked for, and it represented 4½ per cent on the sum of £220,000 alleged to have been paid to the Duke of Atholl for the customs of the Island. The English government considered the payment to be 'a very moderate return to ask from the Island' since 'the military and naval defence is entirely at the expense of the United Kingdom and its inhabitants enjoy the privileges of British citizenship without its burdens'. Some have

---

Plate 41. MANX BANK-NOTES. Dumbell's Bank (top) financed many Manx industries, but its sudden collapse in February 1900 caused great financial loss to many Manx people. The Isle of Man Bank still functions, and was allowed to issue its own one pound and five pound notes until 1961. The Onchan Internment Camp note was issued to detainees during the Second World War, and could be spent only inside the camp. The Isle of Man fifty pence note (bottom) is one of the few notes of this denomination issued by any currency authority.

argued that the Manx people ought not to be called upon to pay such a sum, and it might be added that many have considered that the sum paid to the Duke of Atholl was, in the words of Governor Spencer Walpole, 'absurdly extravagant'. On the other hand, it must be pointed out that since the First World War the contribution made by Man to the British government has been considerably increased, as will be seen in the final chapter.

CHAPTER TWELVE

The Structure of the Manx Economy

DURING ITS HISTORY THE ISLAND HAS HAD FIVE PRINCIPAL industries: agriculture, fishing, mining, tourism, and manufacturing. The relative importance of these has naturally changed considerably in the last two centuries as the Island has developed away from the pre-industrial activities of agriculture and fishing to the broader-based economy of a modern community.

AGRICULTURE

Agriculture of some kind has been practised in Man for about four thousand years, since it is now known that a form of wheat was being cultivated by the builders of the Meayl Circle, Cregneash, about the second millennium B.C. Knowledge of Manx agriculture is, nevertheless, very scanty indeed until the seventeenth and eighteenth centuries; and it is not until the beginning of the nineteenth century that a systematic account of farming conditions over the Island is available in a survey made by Thomas Quayle for the English Board of Agriculture in 1812.

From descriptions given by Quayle as well as by other writers, conditions appear to have been very primitive in many parts. Quayle speaks of Manx agriculture as being 'a recent art', and complains that many farmers gave it little serious attention. There was not much attempt at a proper rotation of crops, the prevailing practice being to plough and raise corn crops, chiefly oats and barley, until the land became exhausted when it would be allowed to lie in grass until it had recovered some of its fertility. Clover had been introduced about 1770, while turnips were first cultivated about 1780, so that it was only after that date that the

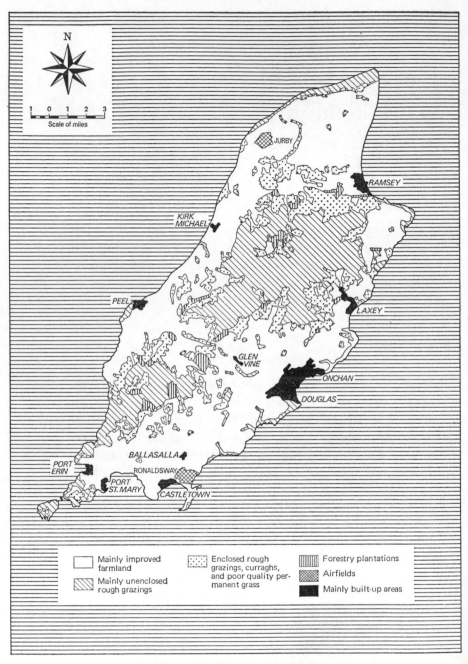

N

1 0 1 2 3
Scale of miles

JURBY

RAMSEY

KIRK
MICHAEL

PEEL

LAXEY

GLEN
VINE

ONCHAN

DOUGLAS

BALLASALLA

PORT
ERIN

RONALDSWAY

PORT
ST. MARY

CASTLETOWN

Mainly improved
farmland

Mainly unenclosed
rough grazings

Enclosed rough
grazings, curraghs,
and poor quality per-
manent grass

Forestry plantations

Airfields

Mainly built-up areas

13. Generalized land use distribution.

existing 5- or 6-course rotation became possible. Many of the cattle and sheep at that period were of the original Manx breeds, and were small if hardy animals. They were being replaced by imported breeds, a process that has gone on steadily ever since. It is difficult to say how many cattle existed at that time, but in 1806 it was estimated that there were about 18,600 sheep in the whole Island, a small total compared with about 95,200 which existed in 1938, and 107,615 in 1972.

The implements used by Manx farmers during the late eighteenth century were very primitive. Though threshing machines had just come into use, farm carts were almost unknown, the usual method of carriage being by creels on horses' backs or by sleds, which were carts without wheels. Their ploughs, which were of a very rude make, and required two men to manage them, were drawn by teams of oxen or horses, the latter being preferred on the lowlands; their harrows had teeth made of wood hardened over the fire and they had to be sharpened every morning before being used.

The farms containing the cultivated land are found on the lowlands of the south-east and the north, as well as on the coastal plateaux on both sides of the Island, and now extend up the slopes of the hills to a height of about 600 ft. At the beginning of the nineteenth century cultivation extended for another 100 ft. or so above its present limit; and while some of the higher land belonged to lower-lying farms, some of it was *intack* (or *intake*) land, held by manorial tenants and smallholders, or crofters who also engaged in fishing or mining. With the decline of the other industries came the decay of these little homesteads, and the many *tholtans* or ruined cottages now remain as mute witnesses of the change that has taken place. Some of the most striking instances of the abandoned cultivation of these marginal lands, and the consequent downhill movement of population, are to be found in the higher parts of the parishes of Rushen, Arbory, and Malew. Whereas, for example, in the area surrounding Ronague chapel (*c*. 590 ft. above sea level) in the parish of Arbory the tithe maps of about 1840 show at least forty houses, there are now only four which are inhabited, but there are many *tholtans*, or ruined cottages, to be seen.

Manx agriculture has undergone many changes in recent years. Table 1 shows that whereas there has been little change in the United Kingdom pattern of agricultural land use since the war, the acreage of grazing land in the Island has increased at the expense of arable.

The high proportion of arable land to total cultivated land has been

TABLE I

Comparative use of farmland, 1939–71

Shown as percentage of total cultivated land

	Isle of Man			United Kingdom		
	Arable	Permanent grassland	Rough grazing	Arable	Permanent grassland	Rough grazing
1939	53	20	27	27	38	35
1948	52	11	37	39	26	35
1965	51	14	35	39	25	36
1966	47	16	37	39	25	36
1971	43	21	36	38	26	36

Sources: United Kingdom, *Annual Abstract of Statistics*; Man, *Report on Agricultural Returns, 1971.*

falling consistently as knowledge of grassland management has spread and the suitability of grass to the soil and climate of the Island has been accepted.

An inspection of acreage figures for non-grassland arable since the last war (Table 2) shows that, as elsewhere in the United Kingdom, the acreage of oats planted has fallen very sharply. This is due in the main to the virtual disuse of the horse, the acceptance of barley as a suitable food for cattle and to the greater yield of barley and wheat as cereal crops. The increase in the acreage of barley is welcome, for this crop is suitable for moist grain storage, which makes the farmer more self-sufficient and therefore less reliant on bought-in foodstuffs.

TABLE 2

Summary of acreage under cereal and green crops, 1945–71

	1945	1966	1969	1971
Oats	14,637	6,450	5,106	3,924
Wheat	676	397	476	1,029
Barley	531	4,642	4,808	5,130
Other cereal crops	1,903	457	483	456
Potatoes	2,586	1,522	1,347	1,199
Turnips and swedes	4,698	3,081	2,658	2,139
Other green crops	2,122	1,847	1,595	1,789
Totals	27,153	18,396	16,473	15,666

Source: *Report on Agricultural Returns, 1971.*

Although modern potato varieties produce higher yields, the fall in the potato acreage also reflects some lack of confidence in the United Kingdom market for this product, while silage has taken the place of labour-intensive root crops. Market-gardening products and fruit crops are not well developed in the Island, perhaps largely because of the usually cold and very boisterous weather during the early spring.

Fairly small farms have always been characteristic of the Island, and this was noticed by Quayle in his report of 1812. Amalgamations of smaller properties has been taking place for some years as high capital investment costs and a shortage of labour have made themselves felt.

TABLE 3

Trends in the size and number of Manx farmholdings

	1964	1966	1969	1971
Under 20 acres	252	237	216	198
21–50 „	142	119	112	111
51–100 „	263	241	222	232
101–150 „	162	160	159	144
151–200 „	90	100	107	101
201–300 „	70	73	79	76
Over 300 „	56	57	70	73
Totals	1,035	987	965	935

Source: *Report on Agricultural Returns, 1971.*

The sharp fall in the number of agricultural workers since the last war, from 1596 in 1945 to 510 in 1971, means that a small farmer will usually have no help apart from members of his own family. It is not surprising therefore that he depends heavily on his farm machinery, and there are indications that Manx agriculture is highly capitalized in this respect.

The relative importance of agriculture in the Manx economy is small, for together with forestry and fishing it produces only about 3 per cent of the gross national product. Income per person engaged in agriculture is considerably lower than in the United Kingdom or for example in the State of Jersey, and declared profits from most farming enterprises are very small. But the climate of the Island is particularly suitable to the mixed farming now being energetically encouraged. With some further farm amalgamations and an increase in productivity, Manx agriculture should enjoy some prosperity in the years ahead.

HERRING FISHING

This industry goes back many centuries, and herrings have formed a staple article of diet for Manx people until quite recent times. Definite records exist as early as the thirteenth century, when the Church claimed a tithe of all fish caught, while the lord of the Island also claimed one-fifth of all the herrings landed, for his own use as well as for the use of the garrisons at Castle Rushen and Peel castle (the Castle Mazes, as these supplies were called). All quarterland holders were compelled to provide themselves with nets, and the people were warned to keep their boats and nets in readiness for the fishing. After 1610 a water-bailiff was appointed to supervise the herring fleet and to see that all the various regulations were carried out. Herring fishing was not allowed to begin until the early part of July, a rule that was kept until the early nineteenth century when boats from other parts of the British Isles came to take part in the fisheries, and regulations were relaxed so that fishing began earlier.

Herring fishing was not a whole-time occupation for Manxmen since it only lasted normally during the four months July to October; during the remainder of the year the men usually did farm-work. Fishing operations were conducted off the western coast, beginning north of Peel, always the chief fishing port, and working south as the season advanced, so that in August, the principal month, the chief grounds were to the south-west of the Calf of Man. At one time it was customary for the boats to move to the eastwards during the later part of the season to fish off Douglas in September and October, but this area was very uncertain, and no serious fishing has been conducted there since 1918.

During the second half of the nineteenth century, it became the regular practice for many fishing-boats to go to the mackerel fishery at Kinsale, in the south-east of Ireland, before the local herring fishing began. The boats went to Kinsale in March and returned in the middle of June. Then, with the close of the Manx fishing season, some boats

---

Plate 42. RUINED UPLAND FARMSTEAD OR *THOLTAN* at Earyglass, German. In the foreground, a horse-walk with a gear in the centre which would have been connected to a threshing machine in the barn beyond.

Plate 43. TRADITIONAL FARMHOUSE KITCHEN, erected as a permanent display in the Manx Museum. Poorer families would be born and grow up in a single room.

followed the herrings along the west and north of Scotland, using as their base ports Stornaway in the Island of Lewis and Lerwick in the Shetland Isles. The practice ceased during the early years of the present century.[1]

In 1826 the Manx fishing fleet consisted of 250 boats totalling 7,000 tons and employed 2,500 men, all natives of the Island. There were, in addition, about 300 vessels from Cornwall, Scotland, and Ireland which came to fish in Manx waters, while other boats were employed as carriers of fish for the English and Irish markets. After this there came a decline in the fishery, and the Manx fleet numbered only 200 in 1835. A revival came in the 1850s, after which there was an increase not only in the number of vessels but also in their size, while their equipment, particularly as regards nets, was much improved. In 1864 the herring fishery employed nearly 300 boats and 2,800 men, and earned about £70,000 in the year. It should also be remembered that the additional trades of net-making, sailcloth-making, and boat-building were maintained by the fishing industry. Since 1883 there has been a fairly steady decline, so that by 1914 the Manx herring fleet had dropped to 57, including 35 large boats, called *nickies*, about 50 ft. long, and 22 smaller *nobbies* between 30 and 35 ft. long. Most of these were owned by Peel men, the remainder belonging to Port St. Mary.

Despite financial help from Tynwald, the Manx fleet had gradually dwindled by 1939 to only 9 vessels, with crews totalling 47. These boats consisted of 4 motor-nobbies, 4 motor-boats built in 1937 for ring-net or drift-net, and one smaller motor-boat engaged in drifting for herrings and seine-netting for plaice. That this decline cannot be attributed, as is frequently suggested, to a falling off in the

1. Modern research has shown that basic problems affecting the Manx herring industry are more complex than was formerly realized; it has been established that existing stocks are composed of two races, one of which is local and one which spawns elsewhere, and that the relative ratios of these races may vary significantly from year to year, as well as the age-ranges within each race. The historic and economic implications of the mixed nature of the herring stocks have hardly been dealt with so far. See D. J. Symonds, 'Racial studies on Manx herring stocks', *Journal du Conseil permanent international pour l'exploration de la mer*, xxix (1964), 189–204.

Plate 44. QUAY AT PEEL, about 1900. Scottish women, who came over to the Island during the fishing season, are moving barrels of herrings. Alongside, a steamer is discharging salt.

Plate 45. FISHING BOATS IN PEEL HARBOUR. After a period of poor years, the total catch from the herring fishery has recovered recently, although few boats are Manx-owned.

abundance of fish on the grounds is proved by the fact that boats from other ports are still attracted to the fishing in good numbers. In 1939, for example, there were 163 vessels from other ports, principally Scottish, although some came from East Anglia and some from Ireland. Of these other vessels taking part in the Manx herring fishing 67 were motor-drifters, 64 steam-drifters, and 32 ring-net boats. Hence the Manx vessels were responsible for only 11 per cent of the herrings landed during the last pre-war fishing season. One important factor which has contributed to this unhappy decline of Manx fishing is the high capital cost of the very specialized modern fishing vessels. An additional reason is to be found in the fact that to the Manxman fishing has never really been the whole-time occupation it is to his English or Scottish competitor, while in recent times the tourist industry has proved a profitable alternative to fishing.

The returns for 1947 indicated that on the whole conditions were no worse than they were in 1939, but that there seemed to be distinct possibilities for development. Of the 10 Manx vessels engaged in 1947, with crews totalling 52, 8 were new-type motor-boats. In 1971 only three Manx vessels took part in the fishing, so that apart from harbour dues the large increase in the total catch of recent years has been of little direct benefit to the Island. Whereas in 1966 the total catch amounted to about 15,000 crans, of which 22 per cent were landed locally, over 89,000 crans were landed in 1971, 60 per cent of them in the Island. The size and power of the trawlers involved has increased, and the closure of the herring fishery in the North Sea throughout the summer of 1971 has resulted in more intensive fishing in Manx waters than ever before. Providing stock levels are not depleted by intensive trawling over the spawning grounds, there is every reason to expect that this revival of the Manx herring fishery will continue.

As regards the disposal of the catch, it is known that herrings were cured in the Island two hundred years ago, since it was recorded in 1754 that 'everybody at Douglas is busy curing herrings. . . . Upwards of 500 tons were salted in bulk at Douglas, and shipped to Ireland, etc., besides some thousands of barrels cured for the West Indies.' Pickled herrings were exported to England and Ireland, and formed a large part of the diet of the poorer people in many villages and inland towns.

The art of curing red herrings was introduced from Yarmouth in 1771, and the business increased in Man towards the end of the eighteenth century and continued to flourish until about 1830. Douglas was the main centre, having five large red-herring houses in operation in 1815, but curing houses also existed at Port St. Mary and Derbyhaven.

In those days the greater part of the catch was taken by buying boats which received the herrings direct from the fishermen at sea; the fish were then carried into the ports of the Island to be barrelled up or taken to such markets as Liverpool or Dublin. At Liverpool they were smoked for 'red' or packed for 'white' herrings according to the demand. This port was then actively engaged in the slave trade and exported large quantities of cured herrings to the West Indies, where they formed an important part of the diet of the negroes. With the abolition of slavery in 1834 the consumption of herrings in the West Indies rapidly declined, so that by 1840 the export trade both from Liverpool and the Isle of Man almost ceased.

From that date most of the Manx herring catch seems to have been disposed of mainly in a fresh state, and there are no records of curing operations of consequence until 1900 when the establishment of a curing station at Port St. Mary stimulated the herring fishery there. Further stations were opened at that port and also at Douglas and Peel, and in the period between 1925 and 1939 pickle-curers took about 67 per cent of the total catch. Kipperers have also taken a fair proportion of the Manx catch for fifty years or so, and during the fifteen years ending in 1939 they accounted for about 30 per cent on the average.

However, an even greater proportion of recent catches—nearly 90 per cent—has been bought by continental pickle-curers. The quantity bought for kippering has started to grow again, but the production of fish meal as a fertilizer has declined with such a high demand for herrings at the Manx market.

Escallop and other fisheries

Just as in other areas, with the decline in pelagic fishing, the demersal and shell fisheries have become very important, now contributing nearly half the value of all fish landed. The dredging of escallops and queenies from the sandy inshore areas has become especially significant, since the products are almost exclusively for export to France and the United States. An important feature is that, since the season extends from 1 October to 31 May, it provides employment during that period for men in Port Erin and Douglas, the two main ports involved, who during the summer are concerned with running pleasure trips for visitors or with tending their crab- and lobster-pots. Nearly forty

Manx-registered vessels are now engaged in escallop and queenie fishing, and in 1971 trade estimates stated that shellfish to the value of £500,000 were sent from the Island. There are some signs that this shellfish may be somewhat less profitable in future, due to over-fishing, and a number of fishermen have had their vessels converted for white fishing.

The chief demersal fish are cod, skate, and plaice, and although the first are taken throughout the year in Manx waters, the local fishery is mainly conducted in the winter months from Douglas, and the height of the season occurs in March. Fishing for skate was formerly almost confined to Ramsey where it was the principal summer fishing, but since about 1940 Douglas boats have taken part and this port has now become the chief one for landings. Plaice fishing is operated from Peel during the winter and spring months from November to May.

MINING

It is well known that ores of lead (also containing silver), zinc, iron, and copper occur in veins throughout many portions of the Manx slates, and mining operations have taken place in a number of centres in the past. Two areas have stood out as being of primary importance, namely Foxdale (producing lead and silver) and Laxey (producing lead, silver, and some copper), but old workings may be seen, for example, at Bradda Head, Ballacorkish, and Ballasherlogue (all for lead and silver) in the parish of Rushen, at Langness (for copper), and at Maughold Head (for haematite).

It is difficult to say how far back actual mining operations go, but there is documentary evidence that lead was obtained from Man in the thirteenth century for the roofing of castles built by Edward I in Wales. In the grant of the land to Sir John Stanley in 1405 'mines of lead and iron' are also mentioned. After the Restoration in 1660, it is known that the search for minerals was carried out more systematically, much attention being devoted to coal, which has never been found in Man.

The most prosperous period for mining came after the third and fourth decades of the nineteenth century, when Foxdale and Laxey came into the first rank as producers. As an indication of the prosperity of the Laxey Mining Company, its £80 shares were selling at £1,000 to £1,100 in 1852, while they reached £1,200 in 1854. In the latter year was erected the famous Laxey wheel (Pl. 51), one of the largest waterwheels in the world, for pumping water out of the mines.

Mining reached its heyday during the seventies and eighties of the last century when the production figures for lead, silver, and zinc reached their highest limits.

In 1876 the value of the ore shipped from Laxey alone was £90,915, while the annual value of the products of the Foxdale mines never was less than £40,000 during the period between 1858 and 1864. Taking the total output of Manx mines together, the figure for lead-ore in 1885 was 6,868 tons, while in 1878, 11,898 tons of zinc-ore were produced, and in 1877, 186,019 ozs. of silver. Even in regard to iron-ore, the Manx mines produced 2,256 tons in 1873, and in 1865 they produced 1,317 tons of copper. Precise figures of the number of people employed are not available, but in 1848 it was estimated there were 300 at Laxey and 350 at Foxdale. Later the numbers increased, and it may be estimated that during the period between 1855 and 1880 the mining industry in the Island as a whole absorbed well over 1,000 men. Since then there has been a steady decline owing to the competition from workings in other parts of the world, so that now even the richest mines—Laxey and Foxdale—have closed down. The decay of the mines caused an extensive emigration of Manx miners to the goldfields of South Africa and Australia, as well as to various parts of the United States and Canada, where their descendants may now be found in appreciable numbers.

In recent years the very high prices of lead and zinc have stimulated investigation into the reworking of waste heaps at Laxey and Foxdale, and a considerable amount of exploratory work has been carried out, using modern techniques, by Canadian and British, together with Manx interests. No practical developments have, however, so far been reported. The Manx government, which in 1949 acquired control of the mineral rights formerly held by the Crown, has given assistance in such developments through the Forestry, Mines, and Land Board to whom these rights were transferred in 1950, but the Island's extractive industries employ less than 1 per cent of the working male population.

As a result of the current interest in industrial archaeology, old mine workings are receiving a good deal of attention today. The mines at Foxdale and in particular at Laxey have been recently described,[1] and 'Lady Isabella', the great Laxey wheel, has been restored by

1. See L. S. Garrad and others, *The Industrial Archaeology of the Isle of Man* (Newton Abbot, 1972). The most comprehensive work on the engineering of the Laxey wheel is written and published by Anders Jespersen of Virun, Denmark.

enthusiasts to working order, though it would be a mammoth task to restore the fabric of the viaduct, and connect the crank to the rods which drive the drainage pump.

THE TOURIST INDUSTRY

The Isle of Man possesses a capital asset of great value in the magnificent scenery of her mountains, glens, and coasts, so that in modern times catering for summer visitors has come to be an important Manx industry. As in the case of most of the other British tourist centres, the main developments came during the later part of the nineteenth century. About 25,000 visitors came every year between 1830 and 1840. The number had increased to 90,000 by 1873, when the Victoria Pier was opened at Douglas. That number was doubled during the next ten years, and progress continued so rapidly that by 1901 the total had risen to 418,000. The highest recorded figure was in 1913, when there was a total of 634,512 summer passenger arrivals; and the nearest approach to that before the Second World War was in 1937, when there were 593,037. In the years just after the war, the number of Isle of Man visitors expanded again: in each of the three years 1947–9, it exceeded 600,000. During the 1950s the figure showed a slight decline to an average annual level of about 475,000, and since 1960 the number of visitors has remained near this mark.

TABLE 4

*Arrivals in the Isle of Man, May–September 1972,
including day-excursionists*

	Number	Percentage
England and Wales	393,618	78·8
Scotland	35,347	7·1
Northern Ireland	51,325	10·3
Irish Republic	19,005	3·8
Others	363	—
Total	499,658	100

Note: About 80 per cent of arrivals can be classified as tourists. The remainder were Island residents, visitors staying with friends, or were businessmen.

Sources: Tourist Board and Government Statistician.

During the peak period of the season, in early August, the great number of people who travel by boat used to present some problems. As many as 68,372 passengers have been embarked and disembarked at Douglas in one day, on 7 August 1937, and in order to transport them about fifty steamer sailings were arranged. To provide for the huge annual influx, many kinds of improvements have been necessary, such as the harbour works and promenades at Douglas, Ramsey, Peel, Port Erin, and elsewhere. Inland areas have been opened up by a network of roads, including the course of one of the world's most famous motor-cycling races, from Douglas via Ballacraine and Glen Helen to Ramsey, thence back again over the well-known mountain road, past Creg-ny-Baa.

There has been a slight decline in Manx tourist traffic during recent years, due to causes of a fundamental nature which have reduced the appeal of the Island to holiday-makers.[1] While there has been a dramatic increase in the number of British people taking annual holidays, rising standards of living and improvements in transport have made it possible for many go much further afield, within Britain or abroad. In addition, many people like to take the family car with them on holiday, and the cost of transporting a vehicle to the Island probably acts as a significant deterrent. Nevertheless, more than £11 million was spent on the Island by visitors in 1972.

Partly because of the cost of transport and partly because caravans are not permitted at all, the interior of the Island is largely unspoilt. This should soon be made more accessible to the visitor, thus relieving Douglas of the overwhelming numbers who concentrate there, and the major capital asset of tourism, the hotels and boarding-houses built before the First World War, must continue to be radically modernized.

Much is already being done to ensure that the Island continues to attract today's more mobile and demanding holiday-makers. A public casino was opened in 1963 which, after an uncertain start, has settled down to provide an exciting addition to the entertainment available to visitors. Realizing that the weather in the Island is not always reliable, Douglas Corporation more recently constructed near Derby Castle a very successful venture called 'Summerland', a huge indoor leisure centre completed at a cost of £1¼ million, which catered for a wide variety

1. The number of bed spaces available to tourists dropped from 42,100 in 1961 to 39,400 in 1971. This may be due, in part, to the closing of smaller businesses which were never profitable in any case.

of tastes. In August 1973 this building caught fire, and nearly fifty people died in the most terrible tragedy in the Island's history.

MANUFACTURING INDUSTRIES

In earlier days manufactures were on a modest scale and were concerned either with working up local materials such as wool or catering for the needs of local industries. Thus the herring fishery gave rise to the making of nets, first by hand in cottages and then in small factories in Peel and Port St. Mary. Sail-making was also important and a sail-cloth factory existed at Tromode near Douglas, while boat- and shipbuilding were active industries at Ramsey, Douglas, Peel, and Port St. Mary, where employment was provided for a number of shipwrights and other craftsmen in the building of schooners, sloops, and herring luggers. With changing conditions many of these industries disappeared or declined during the nineteenth century.

During the late 1950s increased attention was given to the urgent need for light industry to offset the decline of tourism and to ensure a growing economy to meet the rising costs of the social services. Active measures were taken both to stimulate older industries that had survived, and to attract new light industries, inducements being offered by the availability of suitable male and female labour, the advantages due to lower taxation, assistance in obtaining suitable sites, and the residential amenities provided by the Island.

Obviously there are obstacles, arising from the almost complete lack of raw materials and the expenses of transport. Of the traditional industries which have survived, however, knitting and cloth-garment factories established during the inter-war years still exist at Peel and Laxey. A modern enterprise which satisfies the special requirements of the Island is a textiles factory at Ramsey, set up in 1956 and employing about 100 people, most of them women, at the end of 1972. Until the revival of ship-repairing in Ramsey in 1963 and the opening of Jurby Trading Estate in 1967, this was the only major establishment in the agricultural north. It makes full use of local labour, while it also enjoys exceptionally low transport charges. Carpet manufacture has also been introduced since the war, through contact with Kidderminster, and a factory located at Douglas employs 50 workers. It is located in a building forming part of an industrial area known as Hill's Meadow, on the flood plain of the River Douglas, so that it enjoys the benefits of nearness to the harbour and availability of local labour. The factory produces carpets of medium price for export; but since labour costs represent only about 20 per cent of the total and bulky materials are used (so that shipping charges are high), the success of the ventures relies very much on such factors as skilful administration and low taxation.

Light engineering industries, which provide employment for the largest manufacturing group of nearly 1,100 people, are located on favourable sites, either on the Douglas Trading Estate or at Ronaldsway adjoining the airport. Engineering was established in Douglas as long ago as the 1820s by an iron foundry which continued its activity in various ways, such as the casting of ship's propellers and the making of crushing rollers for the mining industry. The concern is now engaged in general engineering for the Island market, while other factories have been introduced during the last fifteen years or so with direct government assistance. These are concerned, for example, with precision engineering of aircraft components involving the use of light-alloy castings and bars, with labour costing about 55 per cent of the total production. Indeed, in one Douglas factory producing minia-ture aero-engines the labour input is as high as 65 per cent, and for the dispatch of exports parcel-post is used.

Another successful firm, which took on its modern form in the early 1960s, is a shoe manufacturing company at Ronaldsway. The total production of the factory is marketed by a leading chain-store on the mainland, and most of the raw materials and final products are shipped in and out of Castletown by a container service from Glasson, near Lancaster.

The largest engineering concern on the Island is the Ronaldsway Aircraft Company occupying quite extensive modern premises adjoin-ing the airport and employing over 500 people of whom the majority are Manx. The company came to Man in 1951 to produce automatic ejector seats which are fitted to military aircraft, and these are estimated to have saved more than a thousand lives so far. Such seats require a very high standard of workmanship and they are exported to all the major countries including the United States.

Some progress has therefore been made in the introduction of suitable industries and by the end of 1972 the new factories established since 1954 were employing 1,550 men and women. But 80 per cent of these were already employed by 1961, and a large majority of job oppor-tunities since have arisen in firms already established by then, so manufacturing has grown much less quickly during the last decade. Among possible explanations for this are the almost exhausted supply of labour and the greater range of relocation incentives available in the United Kingdom. A recent survey has urged that future policy should aim at strengthening existing industries and developing natural resources, as well as increasing local production of goods which would otherwise have to be imported.

POPULATION

The first official census took place in 1821 when the total population was 40,081. Judging by the calculations that had been made by the clergy during the eighteenth century, this represented a big increase on the former population of the Island, since according to an estimate made in 1727 the total number of people was then only about 14,400. Not only was the population very small in those days but the conditions in which the people lived were very primitive. Sanitation was bad, various diseases such as smallpox and cholera were rampant, and the death-rate must have been very high.

The population rose consistently until 1891 despite the considerable emigration of the 1820s and 1830s, caused by bad conditions in agri-

TABLE 5

Growth of the Isle of Man Population, 1821–1971

Year	Population	Year	Population
1821	40,081	1911	52,016
1831	41,000	1921	60,284*
1841	47,975	1931	49,308
1851	52,387	1939	52,029†
1861	52,469	1951	55,253
1871	54,042	1961	48,133
1881	53,558	1966	50,423
1891	55,608	1971	56,289‡
1901	54,752		

Source: *Interim report, 1971 Census.*

* The 1921 census was taken in June, after the opening of the tourist season. Since 1961 the census has been taken towards the end of April, when far fewer visitors are on the Island. † Mid-year estimate. ‡ Provisional figures.

culture. Emigrants who went beyond Britain settled mainly in America, where the Manx colonies of Cleveland, Toronto, and San Francisco were established. Another cause of great distress was the failure of the potato crop in 1846 and many Manxmen went to California and other parts of America, or to Australia, attracted by the gold discoveries there. Without urban industry to make up for the fall of agricultural employment, the Isle of Man was largely saved by the highly successful tourist industry during the early part of the twentieth century. The population fell until 1931 but has grown regularly since then, apart from a fall in 1961 before the effects of new manufacturing schemes and fiscal incentives to new residents had made themselves felt.

New residents, many of whom are retired, continue to be attracted to the Island from the United Kingdom and elsewhere,[1] and the present population is biased towards the elderly and the retired. For example, in 1971 nearly 28 per cent of the Island population were over 60, against a figure of 18·7 per cent for the United Kingdom. Although retired members of the population do not use schools and transport as do young families, there is some evidence that the medical services and facilities of the Island are heavily burdened.

In addition to the changes that have occurred in the total population, there has been a profound alteration in the distribution as between the town and the country. In 1726 the total population of the four towns was only 2,530, representing about 17 per cent of the whole Island. Douglas had become slightly the most populous with 810, Castletown having 785, while Peel had 475 and Ramsey 460. By 1821 the town population had reached 11,500 or 28 per cent of the total; but although the country population (28,581) was then relatively less than previously, it was actually twice as much as the total for the whole Island a century before that. Since then there has been a steady movement away from the country districts, and if the village populations in Onchan, Laxey, Port St. Mary, Port Erin, and Michael be added to those for the large towns, then the total town population in 1971 is as high as 73 per cent for the whole Island. Douglas with a total of 20,389 in 1971 has far outstripped the others, being followed by Ramsey with 5,048, Peel with 3,081, and Castletown with 2,820.

---

1. The continuing arrival of new residents has led to a very large expansion of the construction industry. 560 new dwellings were completed in 1971, nearly a fivefold increase over the 1961 figures.

CHAPTER THIRTEEN

Modern Times

THE YEAR 1866 WAS A CRUCIAL TURNING-POINT IN MANX history and may well be regarded as the one that ushered in the modern phase of the nation's development, socially, politically, and economically. Not only did Man then regain to some extent the right to spend its own money but the people gained the power to choose their representatives in the House of Keys. At about the same time the Island set out upon a new economic path and resolved to draw a large part of its livelihood from the business of providing food, lodging, and recreation for summer visitors. The period that has elapsed since that date has witnessed profound changes in government, business, education, and in the standard of living that have given this phase of the national evolution a particular fascination and significance.

To an outside observer the system of internal government of the Isle of Man is almost as hard to understand as the nature of the constitutional relationship between the Island and the United Kingdom. In a recent statement it was admitted that no-one has ever answered satisfactorily the question—'What is the government of the Isle of Man?'[1] For a community the size of Man, which is no larger than a medium-sized English town, the government is unusually complex, and a review of its councils and boards may help us to an understanding of its historic development.

THE GOVERNMENT

At present the Government of Man consists of (1) the Lieutenant-Governor who represents the Crown, (2) the Legislative Council, or as

1. *Evidence submitted by Tynwald to The Royal Commission on the Constitution* (1970).

it is occasionally termed, the upper house, consisting of ten members, (3) the House of Keys, consisting of twenty-four members, which is the elected chamber, and (4) Tynwald, or the Tynwald Court, which consists of the governor and the two branches of the legislature sitting together.

If the Isle of Man had had the kind of constitution which exists in Great Britain, the governor would have been advised and assisted by a 'cabinet' of ministers whose duty it would have been to recommend to him and to Tynwald what laws should be passed, and to take charge of the various departments of government as they are carried on day by day. But in 1866 cabinet government was not considered suitable for a community of this size, and the lieutenant-governor, who is appointed by the Crown, remained supreme head of the government; part of his duty has been to make sure that the Island does not get into debt by spending more than it has received. Until recent years it could be said that he was his own chancellor of the exchequer with financial responsibility and a complete veto on any financial proposals Tynwald might make, and that he was his own home secretary, with direct control over the police. Now, however, he is assisted by a Finance Board and also by a Police Board, although he retains the ultimate authority. He presides over the Legislative Council, although he is unlikely to attend, and also over Tynwald, but he is not in charge of such departments as are entrusted to boards, although he has power to limit the amount of money these boards can spend. Hence over a vast range of subjects his authority is very considerable, and it is clear that the government of the Island depends for much of its smooth and harmonious working on the experience and the judgement of the governor.

Up to the time of Lord Raglan, who was appointed in 1902 and who left the Island in 1919, no time limit had been imposed on the appointment of governors. Since then the period of office has been limited to seven years, and the only exception has been Earl Granville, whose seven years of office expired during the Second World War, and who for special reasons was asked to remain for an additional year.

The Legislative Council

The consent of the Legislative Council as well as the consent of the Keys is necessary before any law can be passed. Although the functions of the council and of the British House of Lords are now very much the same in this respect, the history and composition of these two institutions are very different. The Legislative Council has developed from a body called 'the lord's council' which existed in the fifteenth century when it consisted of the lord's officers, those who collected the revenues and helped the governor (in former times styled the 'Lieutenant' or the 'Captain') to manage the lord's business and keep his records. In the course of time there have been added to this body the principal officers of the law, the deemsters and the lord's attorney (now termed the attorney-general), and the principal officers of the Church, the bishop, the archdeacon, and the vicar-general, the official who advises the bishop on points of law. Until quite recent days the council met in private and discussed any proposed legislation with the governor, advising him whether or not it was appropriate.

Prior to 1919 the Manx upper house was composed entirely of officials; it contained no representatives of the people, and most of its members were appointed by the British government. The remainder represented the religious aspect in the life of the nation, but they had obtained their places in the legislature at a time when there was only one organized religious group in the Island, namely the Anglican Church.

An agitation was begun for constitutional reform during the late nineteenth century, and in 1911 the British government set up a special committee presided over by Lord MacDonnell to investigate Manx problems. Some of this committee's recommendations were carried into effect by the Isle of Man Constitution Amendment Act, 1919, the delay that had occurred in carrying out the proposals having been due in part to the intervention of the First World War. The officials who remained as members of the council after its reform were the bishop, the attorney-general, and the two deemsters, while those who were removed comprised the archdeacon, the vicar-general, and the receiver-general. An entirely new element was introduced into the council by the addition of four members elected by the Keys and two appointed by the governor. Each of these elected and appointed members sat for eight years, but the eight-year period did not begin for them all at the same time; half of them retired and were eligible for re-election or re-appointment every fourth year. Further changes in 1960 replaced the second Deemster and the two appointed members by three further members elected by the Keys, and the attorney-general, although remaining a member, has no vote.

Besides the two deemsters there had been a senior judge styled the

Clerk of the Rolls. The latter office became vacant by death in 1918 and was never filled, but since then the First Deemster has performed the special duties which belonged to the other office, and the phrase 'Clerk of the Rolls' has been added to his title. While there were three judges two of them were always available for the hearing of appeals against a judgement given by a third. When the clerkship of the rolls was amalgamated with that of the First Deemster it was provided that some British barrister of eminence should be appointed to sit in the Manx Court of Appeal.

The Keys

For the popular elections to the House of Keys in 1866, the Island was divided into ten constituencies made up of the six sheadings with three members each, the town of Douglas with three members, and the towns of Ramsey, Peel, and Castletown with one member each. In time the population of Douglas increased while that of some of the sheadings became less, so in 1891 a Redistribution Act was passed, under which one member was taken from Michael and one from Garff, and Douglas was made into two electoral districts, of which the northern returned three members and the southern two.

Further changes were made in the constituencies in 1951 and the number of members are now as follows: Glenfaba 2, Michael 1, Ayre 2, Garff 2, Middle 3, Rushen 3, Peel 1, Ramsey 2, North Douglas 1, West Douglas 2, South Douglas 2, East Douglas 2, and Castletown 1. It has been claimed in recent years that the proportion of population has altered still more in favour of Douglas as against some of the sheadings, but there has not been any further change in the basis of representation.[1]

Nowadays, every man and woman above the age of eighteen has a vote in choosing the members of the House of Keys, who are elected for five years, and the members themselves are no longer bound to be owners of property. The only disqualifications are those of being a clergyman of the Church of England in actual charge of a parish, or of holding any office of profit under the British government or the government of the Isle of Man. The first woman member was elected

1. It may be noted that despite the existence of a Manx Labour Party and attempts from time to time to form other enduring political parties the majority of the members of the Keys remain formally Independents and the government is not conducted on party lines.

in 1933. Unmarried women and widows who owned property have had the right to vote since 1881, thirty-seven years before women were granted the franchise in England.

Tynwald

This body is unique in the British Isles since it consists of the two legislative bodies sitting together, and, as already seen, the governor presides over Tynwald. As expressed by the MacDermott Commission report in 1959, 'this historic body is firmly seated in the affections of the Manx people'. All bills passed in the branches must be signed in Tynwald before they are submitted for the royal assent. Tynwald is not a legislative body and could not alter any bill, but the signature to a bill must be given by the governor and six members of the council and by thirteen of the Keys, being the respective majorities in each house.[1]

The principal functions of Tynwald are to levy the taxes and, subject to the governor's right of veto, to decide how the national revenue shall be spent, also to appoint committees, or boards as many of them are called, to administer defined departments of government.

These committees of Tynwald represent another distinctive feature of the Manx political system as it has developed since 1866. They perform duties which in Great Britain are performed by ministers chosen by the Prime Minister and holding office so long as the House of Commons approves the policy of the Cabinet as a whole. At the present time boards of Tynwald, appointed from its members, and in some cases assisted by representatives of local authorities and of cultural organizations, and financed wholly or partly by votes from the Insular revenue, administer education, highways, harbours, airports, health and the various social services, fishing, agriculture, advertising, forestry, and town and country

---

1. It should be noted, however, that the First Deemster continues to sign bills separately in accordance with long-established custom.

Plate 46. DOUGLAS PIER IN 1900. Early in the 1840s, J. Quiggins wrote in his *Illustrated Guide to the Isle of Man* that Douglas was 'unsurpassed for the salubrity of the air . . . the numerous suitable residences and lodging houses erected along the shore and in the town for the accommodation of visitors, and the moderation in all charges, are strong inducements for genteel families to take up their summer residence here for sea bathing'.

Plate 47. MODERN SEA TERMINAL AT DOUGLAS, completed in 1965. Beyond is the beginning of the broad two-mile promenade, with its sunken gardens, hotels, and boarding houses.

planning. The total sum estimated for expenditure by these boards in 1973 is almost £11 million. In recent years other boards have been set up to administer the supply of electricity outside the Douglas area and to provide water supplies over the whole of the Island. As will be seen later, the chairmen of all these boards are now appointed by a special selection committee consisting of three members of the council and six members of the Keys.

The Speaker

Since the Keys not only meet in their own chamber but sit with the council in Tynwald, there is a considerable difference in function between the Speaker of the House of Keys and the Speaker of the House of Commons. It is sometimes remarked upon as curious that the holder of the office is called the speaker although he does not speak and confines himself to the duties of chairman. But if the rights and privileges of the House are challenged, the Speaker must defend them; and if something has to be said in the name of the whole House, he has the responsibility of saying it. The word speaker really means 'spokesman', one who speaks on behalf of others, and it may be remarked that in the days of arbitrary kingship the Speaker 'spoke for' the House against the King, as, for example, in the case of Speaker Lenthall and Charles I. The Speaker of the Keys occupies this position, particularly when facing the council and the governor. Since he is not chairman of Tynwald, he may then speak on ordinary subjects as a private member. But on occasions of crisis there is no leader of the House such as there would be under a ministry, and the Speaker himself must act as leader. The character and personality of the Speaker must, therefore, count for a great deal in guiding the Island's political life. In the Keys the Speaker has a vote like other members and also a casting vote. He can, however, abstain from voting there if he wishes, but he is still under an obligation to vote as a member of Tynwald.

Local government

By the Towns Act, 1852, commissioners had been appointed for the four towns of the Island, primarily to look after questions of sanitation.

Plate 48. INDUSTRIAL AREA on the river Neb at Peel. From top to bottom the photograph shows a power-station, oil-storage tanks, a brickworks, a light-engineering complex, a concrete block manufacturing plant, and a kipper-curing factory.

In 1886 the Local Government Act was passed, and under this measure, together with various acts amending it, commissioners have been established for every parish and for several village districts, and increasing powers have been given to them from time to time. The development of the towns and villages has been largely the work of the commissioners, who have established sewerage works, provided water, maintained roads, dealt with infectious disease, cleared slums, established fever hospitals, abattoirs, public baths, libraries, and recreation grounds, and in some areas provided workmen's houses. They have also controlled the erection of new buildings and generally provided the amenities of modern life. In 1896 Douglas was created a municipal borough with a mayor, six aldermen, and eighteen councillors.

EDUCATION

The period since 1886 has witnessed remarkable progress in the educational sphere. As a result of the great Manx Education Act of 1872, which laid the basis for the development of sound education for all, school boards were formed in every town and parish district, and free elementary education came into force in 1892. In one important respect the Manx Act differed from the English Act of 1870. Bible instruction was compulsory in every provided school, with the result that when all the old parochial schools carried on by the Church were handed over to the new school boards this change was achieved with little disturbance of the religious atmosphere. In 1894 the first higher-grade school was established, and this has ultimately led to the formation of the secondary schools at Douglas, Ramsey, and Castletown.

Despite what might seem to have been such promising beginnings, the position that had developed by 1911 had some very unsatisfactory features which were condemned in no uncertain manner in the report of the MacDonnell Committee. In the sphere of elementary education there were twenty-one separate school areas in the Island, and there were four higher education authorities, one in each High Bailiff's district. The result was that the management was excessively parochial, while the quality of the education and the housing and equipment left much to be desired. A more unified system was strongly advocated, and the Island was urged to provide more funds for education in general as well as greater facilities for higher education.

Since 1920 very substantial progress has been made. From that date there has been one elected Education Authority which administers primary and secondary education in the Island as a whole under the general supervision of the Board of Education, which is appointed by Tynwald. Even before the Second World War a number of new buildings were erected, for example at Rushen, Laxey, and Pulrose, although many of the older buildings still survive. Since the War new primary schools have been built at Ballasalla, Peel, and in Douglas. Additional secondary education accommodation has been provided by the erection of Ramsey Grammar School and Castle Rushen High School, in addition to the separate High Schools for Boys and Girls in Douglas. Moreover, with the establishment of the College of Further Education a beginning has been made in providing a limited number of courses for adults and for pupils who have left the secondary stage. In recent years, the number of children in the Island has shown a net increase of over 200 annually. New schools have to be built, older ones extended, and the numbers of staff increased. This accounts for the great rise in expenditure on education since the war, from £200,000 in 1948 to £810,000 in 1972-3.

The Education Act of 1949 brought the Manx educational system into complete line with the system established in England by the 'Butler' Act of 1944. In fact since 1946 the Island has operated a comprehensive system of secondary education as far as its maintained schools are concerned, and was the first authority in the British Isles to do so.

MAJOR POLITICAL AND ECONOMIC REFORMS

Although the arrangements made in 1866 marked a definite advance on the dismal conditions that had previously existed, the people of the Island were certainly not satisfied with the gains achieved; there was still much to be done both as regards the improvement of financial and constitutional relations with the United Kingdom and also in the extension of democratic representation within the Manx government itself.

On the financial side some difficulties regarding customs existed where Manx rates differed from those of the United Kingdom; these were partially resolved by a British act of 1874 which provided that no duty be paid on goods brought into the Isle of Man if duty had already been paid in the United Kingdom. The Isle of Man Customs Act of 1887 gave Tynwald power by resolution to impose, abolish, or alter Manx customs duties, subject to these resolutions being approved by the British Treasury and confirmed by a United Kingdom Act of Parliament. This legislation required the annual Isle of Man Customs Act which was necessary to legalize the Manx budget until 1958.

It is thus clear that the position was still quite unsatisfactory, since the governor alone prepared the Manx budget and Tynwald's role was a negative not a positive one; it could not propose financial matters but only vote against the governor's proposals, so the two parties tended to be in a state of continuous antagonism. Demands for reform became more insistent after 1903, and ultimately the MacDonnell Committee was appointed to deal with the Island's finances and their control as well as with various constitutional matters. One of the recommendations of that commission, issued in 1911, was that the Manx budget should be prepared for the governor by government officers and should include the income of the various boards as well as the general income of the government. As regards the £10,000 contribution then paid by the Island to the United Kingdom exchequer, it was considered that this was not an unreasonable charge in view of the 'manifold national advantages', including protection, which she enjoyed as the result of her connection with the United Kingdom. On the other hand, it was conceded that the Island could fairly claim more liberal treatment from the Department of Woods and Forests, which had taken control of the Manx Crown lands purchased in 1828 and treated them as part of the hereditary revenues of the Crown.

The intervention of the First World War inevitably delayed any solution of these problems, and conditions after the war served to intensify them. The fact that the Island's income after 1918 multiplied something like fourfold as compared with pre-war years, largely because of greater customs duties but also partly due to income tax imposed for the first time in 1918, naturally stiffened British pressure for a larger contribution to the United Kingdom exchequer. For its part the Manx government was willing to increase the amount, but the problem was to fix an equitable sum having regard to all the factors concerned. Actually in 1921 Tynwald assumed liability for British War Stock to the value of £250,000, to be paid off in twenty years, and this meant that an additional payment of £20,000 a year would be made to the British government over and above the statutory £10,000 already provided for. The British authorities considered this inadequate and suggested an enhanced figure of £100,000 a year for fifty years and £50,000 a year thereafter in place of the £10,000 fixed in 1866. These proposals raised a storm of protest in the Island since they attacked the whole principle of the Island's control of its finances, and in any case the amount was considered to be excessive. As to the former there was already deep resentment in the Island at the interference of the Home Office and the Treasury in Manx financial and other affairs. An example of this had occurred in 1921 when a dispute arose between the governor and the Home Office over an increase in official salaries in the Island. In the end the Keys obtained from the Home Secretary some concessions in their rights over finance when it was provided that in future before additions were made in the 'reserved services' the governor should ask the opinions of each of the branches. Hence, even if these opinions were not accepted, the possibility of salaries being increased without Tynwald's knowledge was ended. Negotiations continued, but it was clear that if any satisfactory solutions were to be found, it was essential that an atmosphere of mutual trust would have to be created between the Manx and British governments. As an indication of the greater feeling of harmony that developed it is significant that in 1938 Tynwald, without any suggestion or request from the British government, voted a sum of £100,000 towards the cost of re-armament which Parliament was then facing, and subsequently made further contributions to the cost of the Second World War amounting in all to £1,750,000 with an additional £500,000 on loan free of interest.

Prolonged negotiations between the Manx and United Kingdom governments resulted in two agreements being reached in 1957. The first of these provided that Manx customs duties would in general be kept in line with those of the United Kingdom, while the second agreed that the Island would pay to the United Kingdom each year a contribution towards defence and other common services. The precise amount of this contribution was based on an Act of Tynwald passed in 1956 which specified that the figure should be 5 per cent of the net Isle of Man receipts from the Common Purse (see p. 170). In 1970-1 this amounted to just over £$\frac{1}{4}$ million. These decisions cleared the way for far-reaching reforms in 1958 when the United Kingdom Parliament passed the Isle of Man Act which repealed certain previous Acts (including those of 1866 and 1887) as well as various other obsolete enactments affecting the Island, while Tynwald passed two acts which regulated the future control of finances and customs duties of the Island. The year 1958 thus initiated a new era in Manx affairs since it meant that the English Treasury's control of the Island's finances had been, in effect, removed, while the power of Tynwald to control revenue and expenditure was no longer restricted, although the necessity for the governor's concurrence in financial matters still remained.

The MacDermott Commission

During the discussions that had accompanied the reforms of 1957 and 1958, it was evident that differences of opinion existed in both branches of Tynwald on key topics such as the control of expenditure and the function and composition of the Executive Council. To help in ventilating these problems the Governor, Sir Ambrose Dundas, appointed a commission having as its chairman Lord MacDermott, a former Attorney-General and Lord Chief Justice of Northern Ireland, and containing four other members, including financial experts. Within a year this commission produced a report giving a comprehensive survey of the outstanding questions affecting the Manx constitution with suggestions for their solution. These have since been further debated and in 1961 two Acts of Tynwald were added to the Statute Book, one being the Isle of Man Constitution Act, dealing with a number of matters affecting both the Keys and the Legislative Council, while the other was the Finance Board Act which not only set up this special board but created a new post of Government Treasurer who would in future be adviser to the governor as well as to the board on all financial matters. This board, consisting of three members of Tynwald was, indeed, envisaged as a first step towards a more representative government by the members of the MacDermott Commission and it has become increasingly important since its creation.

Other changes in the constitution made by the 1961 Act affected the method of electing members to serve on any committee or board of Tynwald, and in future all such appointments will be determined by Tynwald voting as one body and not by council and Keys voting separately. The number of elected members to serve on the Legislative Council was raised from four to five so increasing the extent of democratic representation in that body. Moreover, in future, it will not be possible for the council to delay the passing of any bill already passed by the Keys for more than two sessions.

But the most important section of the Act was that setting up an

Executive Council consisting of seven members, namely, the chairman of the Finance Board, the chairmen of four of the boards of Tynwald to be elected by Tynwald, and two members of Tynwald not *ex-officio* members, to be appointed by the governor. The latter presides over meetings of this council which meets weekly or at such other intervals as directed by its president, and this body has the duty of advising the governor on all matters of principle, policy, and legislation. The composition of the Executive Council has now been changed by statute so that Keys and council representation is governed by the ratio of five to two.

There had, in fact, been an Executive Council in existence in the Island since 1946, when it was created after discussions with the Home Secretary. This council was in some ways based on the experience gained during the Second World War when an Advisory Committee representing Tynwald had been set up to have regular meetings with the governor for discussion of matters relating to the general government of the Island as well as those specifically related to the war. This experiment had been proved to be very useful, but after the war it was felt that a more permanent body somewhat in the nature of a 'cabinet' should be instituted to replace the wartime committee; and the initiative in the discussions that followed between Tynwald and the Home Office was taken by the then Speaker of the House of Keys, Sir Joseph Qualtrough.

The 1946 Executive Council was composed of seven members of Tynwald, the majority being persons who had already been elected as chairmen of the five principal spending boards, while the remaining two were recommended by Tynwald but were not necessarily chairmen of boards. The creation of this council was regarded as one of the greatest constitutional developments the Island had ever known, but it must be acknowledged that it did not have the success expected from it, and the MacDermott Commission refers to 'the failure of the Executive Council ... to provide a form of responsible government'. The Commission broadly accepted the view, often put forward, that such a failure was due to the fact that the council was composed mainly of chairmen of boards of Tynwald and that board loyalties in Tynwald 'were too strong to accept the authority of the new body or to give its members a chance of generating a sense of collective responsibility'. It was strongly urged that if the Island wished to move towards representative government it must 'expect and encourage a constructive effort to found and develop a sense of collective responsibility', and this is, no doubt, a somewhat difficult task in so small a community where local differences are apt to loom large.

Unfortunately trouble concerning the composition of the reconstituted Executive Council arose in 1967 when the Governor nominated the Speaker of the House of Keys as one of the two members to be appointed by him. This proved to be a very controversial issue and in 1967, an Act of Tynwald made it impossible henceforth for the Speaker to be nominated or elected as a member of the Executive Council or of any board.

As to the future, the MacDermott Commission believed that the essential features of the Island's constitutional relationship with the United Kingdom should remain unaltered, and it quoted with approval the definition of this relationship as expressed in a memorandum of the Home Office submitted to this Commission. This was to the effect that the Isle of Man is a dependency of the Crown, that the United Kingdom government is ultimately responsible for the good government of the Island, and that it controls its international relations and external defence, while, finally, Parliament at Westminster has power to legislate for the Island while all insular legislation requires the assent of Her Majesty in Council.[1] In other words the Isle of Man cannot be a dominion because a dominion is a completely independent state.

In the light of the foregoing summary it is of great interest to review the controversy that flared up during the summer of 1967 between the United Kingdom and the Island concerning the suppression of the pirate radio ship *Caroline*, which was anchored off Ramsey. There can be no doubt about the justification for the policy of getting rid of these

1. This view of 'ultimate responsibility' with its implication of 'ultimate authority' residing at Westminster and the consequent impossibility of independent action on any question of real importance has given rise to particular anxiety in connection with the United Kingdom's application to join the Common Market, and a Select Committee of Tynwald was set up in April 1970 to examine the probable consequences and explore possible alternatives for the Island.

Plate 49. SNAEFELL DISASTER RESCUE TEAM, 1897. Following an overnight underground fire, men descending on the morning shift were overcome by undetected carbon monoxide gas. Nineteen miners were killed, the worst disaster in the mining history of the island.

Plate 50. SNAEFELL MOUNTAIN RAILWAY which connects at Laxey with the Douglas-Ramsey electric railway. The route, which is a favourite ride with holiday-makers, climbs to 2,036 ft., the highest point on the island.

Plate 51. THE LAXEY WHEEL, LADY ISABELLA, one of the world's greatest water-wheels. Powered by gravity-fed water, the wheel operated a crank-shaft running along the top of the viaduct (in the background), which was connected to a drainage pump further up the hillside. The pump was able to raise about 250 gallons a minute through a height of 1,500 ft.

Plate 52. LAXEY MINERS, in about 1880. The surface of their hats is stiffened with hardened clay, lumps of which are also used as candle-holders. Miners had to buy their own candles, and pay to have their picks and shovels sharpened.

Plate 53. FOXDALE
MINE in 1880, which at the
time employed about 400
people.

Plate 54. NEW DAY
LEVEL ADIT, Beckwith's
Mine, Glen Rushen. It meets
the main mining shafts 250
ft. below ground.

illegal radio stations, but some members of Tynwald argued that the rights of the Isle of Man had been over-ridden by the British government by issuing an Order in Council,[1] and it was even asserted that the relationship between the governments had never been more strained.

TAXATION

The Isle of Man has a different tax structure to that of the United Kingdom. Indirect taxation on the Island and the mainland are similar and continued to be so after the introduction of Value Added Tax, but motor vehicles are taxed at a lower rate, based on engine capacity. The major difference is in the field of direct taxation, for Manx income tax is raised at a standard rate of 21·25 per cent, a good deal lower than in the United Kingdom, there are higher personal allowances, and there is no surtax, capitals gains tax, or estate duty.

Criticism has been levelled from time to time at the relatively low rate of Island taxation. The Manx case for the justification of this is based on the relative isolation of the Island and the lack of natural resources. Manufacturing industry must be encouraged by lower taxation and regional incentives higher than those available in the United Kingdom, and wealthy residents, who provide a powerful stimulus to the economy, particularly by creating demands on the construction industry, are attracted by the generally low rates of direct tax. Although revenue from Income Tax grew nearly fivefold in the decade up to 1971, the lower level of income per head in the Island compared to the United Kingdom means that the taxable capacity of Man cannot be compared with that of the mainland or even Northern Ireland. As an illustration of this, it was estimated some years ago that to produce a comparable yield of income tax and surtax with England on a population basis, the Isle of Man would have to impose an income tax rate of 60 per cent and reintroduce surtax.

1. The full debate can be read in the *Report of Proceedings of Tynwald Court* for Tuesday, 8 August 1967, 1825–98.

Plate 55. COASTERS AND PLEASURE CRAFT in Douglas harbour.

Plate 56. ANNUAL PROCESSION FROM ST. JOHN'S IN JULY. At the head of the procession the Manx Sword of State is carried before the Lieutenant-Governor, the Bishop, and other dignitaries, on their way to Tynwald Hill to hear the announcement of the laws passed in the preceding year. The rushes strewn along the processional way recall the pagan tribute to Manannan, the Celtic sea god.

THE COMMON PURSE SCHEME

This now provides a well-established method by which the Island receives its share of the total customs duties on goods used in the two countries, an essential feature being that the same rate of duty must be imposed in both areas. The origin goes back to 1890 when, as the result of the reduction of the duty on tea in England, there was a largely increased import of English duty-paid tea into the Island and consequently a heavy loss to the Manx revenue. Governor Walpole (lieutenant-governor, 1882–93) made an arrangement with Britain whereby the whole of the duties paid on tea in the Isle of Man were to be paid into the United Kingdom exchequer. Then a scheme was devised based on the average consumption of 6·35 lb. of tea per head in the Isle of Man and 5 lb. per head in the United Kingdom. These figures were based on actual consumption and took into account the visitor element in the Island—now known as the 'fiscal equivalent'. This arrangement was subsequently extended to other items and became stabilized in 1895 as the Common Purse scheme.

The scheme is based on the decennial test carried out on the Island every tenth year under the provisions of the Revenue Returns Acts, 1894 and 1895, when searching tests are made into all the articles concerned. The most recent test related to the year ended 31 March 1962, when it was calculated that the 509,869 visitors to the Island during that year were equivalent to an additional resident population of 21,279. This figure when added to the population as determined by the census gives the fiscal population of the Island (47,293 + 21,279 = 68,572) and the Manx share of the customs duties is based on the last figure. Nowadays the system has been extended to purchase tax and pool-betting duty, the allocation of the latter being based, however, on the resident population. The amount of revenue due to the Island in respect of purchase tax is also calculated on the basis of the resident population except for the tax on confectionery, ice-cream, soft drinks, and so on, which is allocated on the basis of the fiscal population. In 1965 the Finance Board was asked to consider the advantages and disadvantages of the Common Purse arrangement and after careful sifting of all the evidence it recommended in October 1966 that it should be continued.

THE MOUNTAIN LANDS AND THEIR SETTLEMENT

It has already been seen that, outside of the arable areas of lowlands and coastal plateaux, a sizeable proportion of the Island consists of waste or mountain land rising above a height varying between 750 ft. and 1,000 ft. according to conditions of soil and local climate. These areas were originally unenclosed and in many parts produced peat, while they are covered with a mixture of gorse, ling, heather, and coarse grass. Although poor, they have always had some value. During prehistoric times they were probably used for hunting. Then, during the Scandinavian period, these mountain pastures provided grazing for cattle and sheep during the summer months when there was a movement of part of the population into these *earys*, thus forming the seasonal up-and-down movements known as *transhumance*. No doubt this practice continued for some time after that; indeed it persisted in a very modified form right into quite modern times since the farmers of the lower lands often regarded the uplands as a necessary and important part of their means of livelihood. It was there that they cut and dried their peat so essential as fuel, and on these lands roamed the sturdy sheep and ponies, and sometimes cattle and horses, which provided their owners with food, clothing, and labour. Hence these waste or upland areas were regarded by the farmers as common lands.

During the Stanley regime the lords claimed possession of these areas as constituting the *King's Forest*,[1] but they also fully recognized their tenants rights as recorded in the statutes of 1417, by which time certain fees payable to the forester had been fixed for grazing and for cutting turf. Moreover, from time to time, they granted licences to individuals to enclose portions of the 'forest' to form *intack* land, usually within the transitional area between 750 ft. and 1,000 ft., thus steadily increasing the area under cultivation. No less than 22,000 acres had been enclosed in this way prior to 1860, the date at which disafforestation of the remaining area began; and when it is realized that at this date about 25,113 acres were still regarded as 'forest', it means that in the early fifteenth century the 'forest' or 'waste' was as extensive as 47,000 acres or about one-third of the whole Island. This of course reflects the restricted range of cultivation at that period.

In 1828, the unenclosed lands of the forest passed to the Crown as a result of the sale from the Duke of Atholl. Disputes regarding the enclosure of these areas still continued, becoming very serious in

1. It should be remembered that 'forest' in this sense does not necessarily imply woodland, but, like the forests of medieval England they were areas 'outside' (Latin *foris* = outside) the ordinary laws and reserved mainly for the king's hunting. Cf. J. R. Quayle, 'The King's forest', *Proc. I.M. Nat. Hist. and Antiq. Soc.* iv (1937–9), 373–80.

1855 when they led to riots, and eventually the Commissioners of Woods and Forests, on behalf of the Crown, offered to give the Manx people two-thirds of this land and retain the remainder for the Crown freed from any claims. This offer was accepted and embodied in the Isle of Man Disafforesting Acts of 1860 and 1864. The area dealt with as already seen was about 25,113 acres, and consisted of four separate tracts, namely, the Northern Mountains (North Barrule and Snaefell to Greeba), the Southern Mountains (South Barrule, Cronk ny Arrey Laa, also Foxdale and Archallagan), thirdly, the Ayre Lands, and fourthly, the Mooragh. Commissioners appointed under the Acts were to sell certain parts to provide a sum to pay compensation to those who successfully claimed rights in some parts of the forest. These commissioners also had power to set out roads and fences, the cost being met from the sales of land; thus mountain roads were constructed both north and south of the central valley. Finally, the unsold land was allotted between the Crown and the commoners.

The Commons Lands Board came into being in 1866 and all lands which had been parts of the former King's Forest and were now allotted to the people became vested in the Trustees of the Commons, one for each of the six sheadings. The lands allotted to the Crown were managed by the Crown Receiver and were finally bought by the Isle of Man government in 1949. At the present time the portions of the lands both from the Crown Allotment and the Commons Allotment which are still unsold are controlled by the Forestry, Mines, and Lands Board which was constituted by an Act of Tynwald in 1950.

SOCIAL AND CULTURAL PROGRESS

There can be no doubt that the past decades have produced profound changes which are now showing their effect in no uncertain manner. In the economic sphere it is true that mining has more or less died out and fishing has changed its character, herring fishing having shrunk to a very low ebb, but the tourist industry is still holding its own despite the diminution already discussed in the previous chapter. The influx of new residents has led to a building boom and increased prosperity in the service trades and the professions, but there is doubt in some quarters whether this rapid rate of housing development should be allowed to continue unchecked.

The improved constitutional position since the reforms of 1957–8 has considerably helped the Island financially since there is now a greater degree of flexibility, and bolder policies can be pursued. But against the advantages of today's higher incomes and living standards some people feel that the Island has suffered by the great flood of English and other influences which have nearly overwhelmed the Manx language, for the number of Manx speakers has fallen to only a hundred or so in recent years. What is quite true is that the Manx population has become more mixed as a result of the influx of new elements, and this may be seen, for example, in the fact that some of the older distinctive Manx surnames—Karran, Quirk, Kerruish, Quayle, Qualtrough, Gelling, Kinvig, Collister, Quine, Kinrade, Costain, and so on—are relatively less frequent than they used to be.

As the high tide of the visiting traffic recedes at the end of every summer season the rest of the year is spent more in accordance with the Manx people's own inclination, as may be seen from the large number of clubs and societies which exist on the Island. The definite revival of Manx national consciousness and spirit can be traced above all to the influence of the writings and other activities of Arthur W. Moore (1853–1909), for many years Speaker of the House of Keys, who completed his famous history of the Isle of Man in 1900 and who led a Manx delegation to the first Celtic Congress in 1901.[1] Others associated with him included Miss Sophia Morrison of Peel and William Cubbon of Arbory. Two existing organizations which go back to that period are *Yn Cheshaght Ghailckagh* (Manx Gaelic Society) and the Manx Music Festival or 'The Guild', founded in 1892. The former, founded in 1899, specializes in the preservation and teaching of Manx Gaelic, having as its motto *Gyn chengey, gyn cheer* (without tongue, without country). For a time between 1913 and 1917 it published a journal called *Mannin* edited by Miss Sophia Morrison. The society has had various vicissitudes and was reorganized in recent years; it organizes classes for the teaching of Manx and during the 1967–8 winter season some 100 young students were learning the language. Another organization with similar aims is called *Aeglagh Vannin* (Manx Youth Movement) founded in 1931 under the guidance of Miss Mona Douglas, and its members provide an important section of the existing Manx speakers.

1. A list of his writings can be found in William Cubbon's massive *Bibliographical Account of the Works relating to the Isle of Man*, 1 (1933), 716–20.

As a result of these efforts religious services in Manx are held periodically in Anglican churches (e.g. Kirk Braddan) and Methodist churches (e.g. Atholl Street, Peel) while the use of the language is encouraged by such other means as place-names and calendars. This surely represents a reversal of John Wesley's ill-informed stricture on the use of the language in the eighteenth century, but it should, of course, be realized that under the conditions of the modern world the possession of a separate language is, in itself, no longer regarded as the predominant feature of a distinctive nationality. General culture is promoted by the intensely popular Manx Music Festival, held in the spring.

Another organization which should be mentioned is the relatively new nationalist group known as *Mec Vannin* (Manx Gaelic for 'the sons of Man') which has points of resemblance with other groups furthering the more intensive national development of countries within Great Britain. Founded early in 1964, mainly through the efforts of Douglas Fargher, an enthusiastic speaker and teacher of Manx Gaelic, and L. Crellin, the movement has many worthy objects including the reviving and fostering of interest in all forms of Manx cultural and social activities. In the political and economic field the aims of *Mec Vannin* may be more debatable since they urge the setting up of a 'fully autonomous state'; moreover, the policy seems to contemplate the creation of an independent country, with its own coinage and economically separate from the United Kingdom whereas under modern conditions the tendency is more and more towards co-operation between nations.[1]

In connection with the quickening of interest in Manx history and culture, one of the most significant events of modern times has certainly been the establishment of the Manx Museum, Library and Art Gallery, opened in 1922, whose first curator was the famous P. M. C. Kermode. This has rapidly become the great treasure house of the Island's story, and it is also the headquarters of the Manx National Trust and of the newer branch museums at Castletown (a Nautical Museum housing the eighteenth-century armed yacht *Peggy*) and Cregneash (Manx Village Folk Museum). In the main Museum in Douglas, apart from the Library, there are various galleries illustrating archaeology, folk-life

1. It can, however, be argued that large *political* unions are characteristic rather of eighteenth- and nineteenth-century political thought and that where they have been created in this century, as in Africa, local opinion has tried and sometimes succeeded in breaking them up into smaller states.

(including the Manx farmhouse), as well as various aspects of art and natural history.

Side by side with these developments have been the struggles which have already been traced, to secure that degree of financial and political independence which would not only preserve the ancient constitution but also give the Island adequate control over its own affairs, and at the same time enable its people to contribute their due share towards the cost of maintaining those privileges which they enjoy as an integral part of the British Isles. Thus would the twin objectives of independence and interdependence be brought into harmony. In the wider sphere, the recognition of the position of Man as a distinct and separate entity within the British Commonwealth of peoples is being more and more assured, and an interesting reflection of this is the enrolment of the Manx Legislature amongst the members of the Commonwealth Parliamentary Association.

Glossary of Words Found in Manx Place-Names

A. MANX GAELIC

MANX GAELIC	ENGLISH	EXAMPLES
1 aah	ford	Ballanea (*Balley 'n aah*) = farm of the ford
2 aittin	gorse	Marashen (*Magher aittin*) = gorse field
3 arbyl	tail	Niarbyl (*Yn arbyl*) = the tail
4 ard	height, high	Cashtal yn ard = castle of the height
5 arragh	rampart	Kione arragh = end of the rampart
6 arrey	watch, lookout	Cronk ny Arrey Laa = hill of the day watch
7 aspick	bishop	Curragh aspick = bishop's curragh
8 awin	river	Cass ny h'awin = river foot (Santan Gorge)
9 baie	bay	Baie ny ooig = bay of the cave
10 barney, barnagh	gap	Ballaberna = farm of the gap
11 balla, balley	farm, village	Ballamaddrell = Maddrell's farm
12 bane (*fem.* vane)	white	Cronk bane = white hill
13 bayr	road	Bayr dowin = deep road
14 beg (*fem.* veg)	little	Ballabeg = little farm
15 beinn	peak, summit	Lhiattee ny beinnee = slope of the peaks
16 billey	tree	Ballavilley = tree farm
17 boayl	place, spot	Booilushag = bird place
18 bollagh	road, track	Bollagh jiarg = red road
19 braaid	gorge	Braaid ny glionney = gorge of the glen
20 breck	speckled	Cronk breck = speckled hill
21 broogh (*gen.* brooie)	brink, brow	Ballabrooie = bank farm; Broughjiarg (*Broogh jiarg*) = red brow
22 buigh	yellow	Rhenwee (*Rheynn wuigh*) = yellow division
23 bwoaillee	sheep or cattle fold	Booilvelt (*Bwoaillee yn vuilt*) = fold of the wether
24 cabbal	chapel	Baie yn cabbal = chapel bay
25 cabbyl	horse	Giau ny Gabbyl = creek of the horses

MANX GAELIC	ENGLISH	EXAMPLES
26 cam	crooked	Glen (Glion) Cam = crooked glen (or Devil's elbow)
27 carn	tumulus, cairn	Croit y carn = croft of the cairn
28 carnane	rocky hill	The Carnanes
29 carrick	large rock	Baie ny carrickey = bay of the rocks
30 cashtal	castle, earthwork	Balley y Cashtal = Castletown
31 cass	foot	Cass strooan = stream foot
32 cassan	footpath	Cassan cashtal = castle footpath (at Peel Castle)
33 cheu	side	Cheu yn phurt = the harbour side (North Quay, Douglas)
34 chiarn	lord	Close Chiarn = The Lord's close
35 chibbyr	well	Chibbyr y Woirrey = Mary's well
36 chirrym	dry	Close chirrym = dry close
37 claddagh	river meadow	Sulby Claddagh
38 clagh	stone	Clagh ouyr = dun stone
39 cleigh	hedge	Cleigh yn arragh = hedge of the rampart
40 close (Eng. loanword)	enclosure	Close y Chollagh = enclosure of the stallion
41 coan	hollow	Coan Shellagh = willow hollow
42 conney	gorse	Conney Mooar = great gorse place
43 cooag	cuckoo	Faaie ny cooag = flat of the cuckoo
44 cooil	corner, nook	The Cooil = the nook
45 coon	narrow	Purt Coon = narrow harbour (now Port Jack)
46 creagh (gen. cree)	boundary	Ballacree = farm of the boundary
47 creen	ripe, withered	Crow Creen (Crouw Creen) = withered tree
48 creg	rock	Creg ny baa = rock of the cow
49 creggan	rocky place	Ballacreggan = farm of the rocky land
50 croit	croft	Croit e Caley (Croit ny caillee) = the croft of the old women
51 cronk (gen and pl. crink)	hill	Ballachrink = hill farm
52 crosh (gen. croshey)	cross	Ballacrosha = cross farm
53 crossag	crossing, bridge	Crossag = crossing (Monk's Bridge, Ballasalla)
54 curragh	marsh, bog	Curragh beg = little marsh
55 darragh	oak	Cronk Darragh = oak hill
56 doarlish	gap	Doarlish Cashen = Cashen's gap
57 doo	black	Douglas (Mx Doolish) = doo, black, and glais, stream
58 doon	fort	Dhoon (Kerroo Doon) = fort quarterland

MANX GAELIC	ENGLISH	EXAMPLES
59 dowin	deep	Glendown (*Glion Dowin*) = deep glen
60 dreeym (*gen.* drommey)	back, ridge	Baldromma (*Balley Drommey*) = ridge farm; also, Dreemskerry = Skarif's ridge
61 drine	thorn tree	Baldrine (*Balley Drine*) = farm of the blackthorn
62 droghad	bridge	Droghad Fayle = Fayle's bridge
63 eairkan	lapwing	Pairk ny h'eairkan = pasture of the lapwing
64 eary	shieling, hill-pasture	Neary ('N Eary) = the shieling; Eairystane = Stein's shieling
65 eas, as	waterfall	Ballanass (*Balley 'n Eas*) = farm of the waterfall
66 eaynin	precipice	Kionehenin (*Kione ny h'eaynin*) = headland of the precipice
67 edd	nest	Burroo Ned (*Burroo 'n edd*) = nest hill
68 eean	bird	Knock-e-nean (*Knock yn eean*) = hill of the bird
69 faaie	a flat or green	Faaie heear = west flat
70 fo	under, below	Folieu = below the mountain
71 foawr	giant	Meir y foawr = the giant's fingers (remains of a megalith on Lhergydhoo)
72 foillan	seagull	Creg yn oillan = rock of the seagull
73 freoagh (*gen.* freoaie)	heather	Cronk froy = heather hill
74 gaaue	blacksmith	Mullen-e-Gaw (*Mwyllin y gaaue*) = mill of the smith
75 garee	shrubbery, wasteland	Ballagarey = farm of the river shrubbery
76 garroo	rough	Kerroo Garroo = rough quarterland
77 geay (*gen.* geayee)	wind	Gob ny geayee = mouth of the wind
78 geinnagh (*gen.* geinnee)	sand	Ballaghenny (*Balley ny geinnee*) = sand farm
79 giucklagh, giolcagh	broom	The Guilcagh = broom farm
80 glass	grey, green	Ballaglass = green farm
81 glion (*gen.* glionney)	glen	Glion Mooar = great glen (Sulby Glen)
82 gob	point, promontory	Gob ny rona (*Gob ny rayney*) = seal point
83 gorrym	blue	Gob gorrym = blue point
84 guiy (*gen.* guiyee)	goose	Loughan ny guiy = lake of the geese
85 inish (*gen.* inshey)	island	Purt ny h'inshey = island harbour (Peel)

MANX GAELIC	ENGLISH	EXAMPLES
86 jiarg	red	Bayr jiarg = red road
87 keeill (gen. killey)	church	Ballakilmartin = farm of St. Martin's church Ballakilley = church farm
88 kerroo	quarterland	Kerroomoar = great quarterland
89 keyl	narrow	Kerrookeil = narrow quarterland
90 kione	head, end	Kione droghad = bridge end
91 knock	hillock	Knock y Doonee = hill of the church
92 laa	day	See no. 6
93 lag, laggan	hollow	Lag ny killey = hollow of the church
94 lhean	broad	Slieau Lhean = broad mountain
95 lheannee	meadow	Ballalheaney = meadow farm
96 lhingey	river pool	Lhingey Vooar = great river pool (in Ballaglass Glen)
97 lhergy	slope, hillside	Lhergy Frissell = Frissell's hill slope
98 lieh	half	Lheakerroo = half quarterland
99 logh	lake	Ballalough (Ballaugh) = farm of the lake
100 loghan	pond	Loughan y shuin = pond of the rushes
101 losht	burnt	Cronk losht = burnt hill
102 magher	field	Magher breck = speckled field
103 marroo (pl. merriu)	dead	Cronk ny Merriu = hill of the dead
104 maynagh	monk	Ballamanaugh = monk's farm
105 mean, meanagh	middle	Ballameanagh = middle farm
106 meayl	bald	Slieau Meayl = bald mountain
107 moanee	turbary	Moanee Mooar = great turbary
108 moddey (gen. moddee)	dog	Cronk y Voddee = hill of the dog
109 mollagh	rough	Moanee mollagh = rough turbary
110 mooar (fem. vooar)	great	Ballamooar = great farm
111 mullagh	summit	Mullagh Ouyr = dun summit
112 mwyllin	mill	Mwyllin y Quinney = Quinney's mill
113 noa	new	Bayr noa = new road (from Brandywell to Ravensdale)
114 ooig	cave	Ooig ny seyir = cave of the carpenters
115 ouyr	dun	Slieau Ouyr = dun mountain
116 pairk (Eng. loanword)	enclosed pasture	Pairk y Chiarn = the Lord's pasture field
117 poyll	pool	Poolvaish (Poyll y vaaish) = pool of death (or, of baptism)
118 purt	harbour	Ballaphurt = harbour farm
119 reeast	moorland, waste	Rheast Mooar = great waste

MANX GAELIC	ENGLISH	EXAMPLES
120 rullick	churchyard	Rhullick ny Quakeryn = the Quakers' burial ground
121 rhenniagh (*gen.* rhennee)	fern	Bulrhenny (*Boayl Rhennee*) = place of ferns
122 rheynn	division	Renscault (*Rheynn Skeilt*) = split division
123 ruy	red	Awin ruy = red river
124 sallagh, shellagh	willow	Ballasalla = village of the willow river
125 shenn	old	Shenn Valley = old farm
126 shoggyl	rye	Glen Shoggyl = rye glen
127 slieau	mountain	Slieau Doo = black mountain
128 slogh	pit	The Sloc (*Slogh*) = the pit
129 spooyt	spout, waterfall	Spooyt Vane = white waterfall
130 strooan	stream	Strooan y kirkey = ken's stream
131 tersyn	cross, crozier	Ballaterson = farm of the cross
132 thalloo	earth, plot	Thalloo Queen = Quine's land
133 thie	house	Thie my chree = house of my heart
134 tragh	shore	Kentraugh (*Kione tragh*) = strand end
135 tramman	elder tree	Glentramman = glen of the elder trees
136 ughtagh (*gen.* ughtee)	rising ground, slope	Ughtagh brish my chree = break my heart slope
137 unjin	ash tree	Glen Unjin = ash glen
138 ushag	bird	Croit ny ushag = croft of the bird

B. NORSE

NORSE	ENGLISH	EXAMPLES
139 a	river	Ramsey (Scand. *Ramsá*) = wild garlic river
140 berg (berry)	rock, cliff	Walberry (*Valaberg*) = hawks' cliff
141 borg	small round hill	Bordall (*Borgardalr*) = fort dale (now Glen Wyllin)
142 byr (by)	homestead	Surby (*Saurbyr*) = marshland farm
143 dalr	dale, glen	Altadale (*Alptardalr*) = swan's glen (now Glen Auldyn)
144 ey	island	Kella (*Kaldey*) = cold island
145 fjall	fell, mountain	Snaefell = snow mountain
146 fors (foss)	waterfall	Foxdale (*Forsdalr*) = waterfall dale
147 gardr, gerdi	garth, farm	Fistard (*Fisksgardr*) = fish garth
148 gata	road	Gat-e-whing = Quane's road
149 gil	gill, ravine	Gilnas = ravine of the waterfall
150 gja (giau)	creek, gully	Giau yn ooig = creek of the cave
151 holmr	island	Holmtun = island town (Norse name for Peel)

	NORSE	ENGLISH	EXAMPLES
152	hyrggr	ridge	Skibrick (*Skiphryggr*) = ship ridge
153	kirkja	kirk, church	Kirby (*Kirkjubyr*) = church farm
154	klettr (clet)	rock	Clett yn stackey = rock of the stack (Calf)
155	lamb	lamb	Lambfell (*Lambafjall*) = lamb mountain
156	lang	long	Langness = long headland
157	lax	salmon	Laxey (*Laxá*) = salmon river
158	nes	headland	See no. 156
159	sandr	sand	Sandwick (*Sandvik*) = sandy creek
160	sker	isolated rock	Skerestal (*Skersstadr*) = rock farm
161	stadr	estate, farm	Leodest (*Ljotsstadr*) = Leot's or Ljotr's farm
162	stakkr (stack)	large rock	The Stack = a common Manx rock name
163	thing	assembly	Tynwald (*Thingvöllr*) = Parliament field
164	vik (wick)	creek	Fleshwick (*Flesvik*) = green spot creek

Bibliography

IN THE FOLLOWING LISTS NO DETAILED REFERENCES ARE GIVEN TO A. W. Moore, *History of the Isle of Man*, 2 volumes, London, 1900, or to William Cubbon, *Bibliographical Account of Works relating to the Isle of Man*, vol. 1, 1933, vol. 2, 1939.

The Isle of Man Natural History and Antiquarian Society, founded in 1879, publishes periodically a volume of *Proceedings*, abbreviated in the following lists as *Proc. I.M. Nat. Hist. & Antiq. Soc.* Its Field Section now publishes an occasional journal *The Peregrine*. The Manx Museum and National Trust covers all branches of study relating to the Island and publishes an annual *Journal* as well as various guides, e.g. *The Ancient and Historic Monuments of the Isle of Man*.

1. The physical and human background

ALLEN, D. E., 'The vanished forests', *The Peregrine*, II (1956).

BRACEGIRDLE, R. C., 'Post-glacial invasions of Man by the animal kingdom', *Proc. I.M. Nat. Hist. & Antiq. Soc.* VI (1963).

CHADWICK, N. K., *Celtic Britain* (London, 1963).

CUBBON, A. M., 'The Ice Age in the Isle of Man', *Proc. I.M. Nat. Hist. & Antiq. Soc.* V (1957).

—— 'Changing backcloth: the Manx environment in prehistoric and early historic times', ibid. (1959).

CUBBON, W., *Island Heritage*, p. 28 (Manchester, 1952).

DAVIES, E., 'Treens and quarterlands in the Isle of Man', *Trans. Inst. Br. Geogr.* XXII (1956).

—— and FLEURE, H. J., 'Manx people and their origins', *J. Manx Museum*, III (1937).

—— 'Anthropological survey of the Isle of Man', *J. Roy. Anthropological Inst.* XVI (1936).

FOX, C., *The Personality of Britain* (Cardiff). Originally published 1932 but has since had many editions; was mainly responsible for the conventional division of Britain into 'highland' and 'lowland' zones.

KINVIG, R. H., 'The Isle of Man and Atlantic Britain: A study in historical geography',
    Trans. Inst. Br. Geogr. xxv (1958), 1–27.
—— 'The Isle of Man', *Lancashire, Cheshire and the Isle of Man, Regions of the British
    Isles* (London, 1966).
KNEEN, J. J., *The Personal Names of the Isle of Man* (London, 1937).
ROSS, A., *Pagan Celtic Britain* (London, 1967). Although direct references to the Isle of
    Man are very limited, this important modern work gives the general background of
    the origins of Celtic language and culture.
TALBOT, T., *The Manorial Roll of the Isle of Man, 1511–1515* (Oxford, 1924).

2. The prehistory of Man

BERSU, G., 'A cemetery of the Ronaldsway culture at Ballateare, Jurby, I.O.M.',
    Proc. Prehistoric Soc. XIII (1947).
—— 'Celtic homesteads in the Isle of Man', *J. Manx Museum*, v (1945–6).
—— 'The Vikings of the Isle of Man', ibid. VII (1968), 83–8.
BRUCE, J. R., MEGAW, E. M., and MEGAW, B. R. S., 'A neolithic site at Ronaldsway,
    Isle of Man', *Proc. Prehistoric Soc.* XIII (1947).
CLARK, G., 'Prehistory of the Isle of Man', *J. Manx Museum*, III (1936), 88–94.
FLEURE, H. J., and NEELY, G. J. H., 'Cashtal yn Ard', *Ant. J.* xvi (1936), 373–95.
GELLING, P. S., 'Excavation of a promontory fort (Cronk ny Merriu) at Port Grenaugh,
    Santon', *Proc. I.M. Nat. Hist. & Antiq. Soc.* v (1952), 307–15.
—— 'Excavation at Scarlett, Castletown, (Close ny Chollagh)', ibid. v (1957), 571–5.
—— 'Excavation at Cass ny Hawin, Malew', ibid. VI (1959), 28–38.
—— 'Excavations at the Hill Fort on South Barrule', ibid. VI (1963), 313–23.
—— 'Close ny Chollagh: an Iron Age fort at Scarlett, Isle of Man', *Proc. Prehistoric
    Soc.* XXIV (1958), 85–100.
MANX MUSEUM AND NATIONAL TRUST, *The Ancient and Historic Monuments of the Isle
    of Man* (1958).
MEGAW, B. R. S., 'Manx megaliths and their ancestry', *Proc. I.M. Nat. Hist. & Antiq.
    Soc.* IV (1937).
MOORE, A. W., *Folklore of the Isle of Man* (Douglas, 1891).
—— *Manx Ballads*, pp. 2–5 (Douglas, 1896).
PIGGOTT, S., *The Neolithic Cultures of the British Isles* (Cambridge, 1954).

3. The early Christian period, 450–800

CUBBON, M., *The Art of the Manx Crosses* (Douglas, 1971).
CUBBON, W., *Island Heritage*, pp. 16–17 (Manchester, 1952).
DILLON, M., and CHADWICK, N. K., *The Celtic Realms*, History of Civilization
    (London, 1967).
GELLING, P. S., 'The Braaid site', *J. Manx Museum*, VI (1964), 201–5.
—— 'A metalworking site at Kiondroghad, Kirk Andreas, Isle of Man', *Med. Arch.*
    xiii (1969), 67–83.

HENRY, F., *Early Christian Irish Art* (Dublin, 1955).

JACKSON, KENNETH, 'Notes on the Ogam inscriptions of southern Britain', *The Early Cultures of North-west Europe*, pp. 199–213, eds. Sir Cyril Fox and Bruce Dickins (Cambridge, 1950).

—— *Language and History in Early Britain*, p. 173 (Edinburgh, 1953).

KERMODE, P. M. C., *Manx Crosses* (London, 1907).

KNEEN, J. J., *Place Names of the Isle of Man* (6 parts) (Douglas, 1925–9).

LAING, L. R., *The Archaeology of Late Celtic Britain and Ireland* (London, 1974).

MACALISTER, R. A. S., *Corpus Inscriptionum Insularum Celticarum* (Dublin, 1945–9).

MACQUEEN, J., *St. Nynia* (Edinburgh, 1961).

The Manx Archaeological Survey (Douglas). Five reports, 1909–18, giving details regarding the excavation of the *Keeills*. These reports, compiled under the auspices of a Committee of the Isle of Man Natural History and Antiquarian Society, were essentially the work of P. M. C. Kermode, and they covered all the sheadings except Rushen. A further report covering this sheading (comprising the parishes of Rushen, Arbory, and Malew) compiled and written by J. R. Bruce, was issued, with a reprint of the earlier reports, in 1969.

MARSTRANDER, C. J. S., 'Treen og Keeill', *Norsk Tiddsskrip for Sprogvidenskap*, VIII (Oslo, 1937), 287–442 (English summary, 411–31). See also article in *J. Manx Museum*, IV (1938).

MEGAW, B. R. S., 'The monastery of St. Maughold', *Proc. I.M. Nat. Hist. & Antiq. Soc.* V (1950), 169–80.

—— 'The ancient village of Ronaldsway', *J. Manx Museum*, IV (1938–40), 181–2.

—— 'Who was St. Conchan?', ibid. VI (1962–3), 187–92.

NEELY, C. J. H., 'Excavations at Ronaldsway, Isle of Man', *Ant. J.* XX (1940), 72–86.

SKINNER, F. G., and BRUCE-MITFORD, R., 'A Celtic balance beam of the early Christian period', ibid. XX (1940), 87–102.

STOKES, W., and STRACHAN, J., *Thesaurus Palaeohibernicus*, vol. II, pp. 252–5 (Cambridge, 1903).

THOMAS, A. C., *Britain and Ireland in Early Christian Times, A.D. 400–800* (London, 1971).

—— *The Early Christian Archaeology of North Britain* (London, 1971).

4. The Scandinavian settlement, 800–1266

ANDERSON, A. O., *Early Sources of Scottish History, A.D. 500–1286*, 2 vols. (Edinburgh, 1922).

ARBMAN, H., *The Vikings* (London, 1961).

BERSU, G., 'The Vikings of the Isle of Man', *J. Manx Museum*, VII (1968), 83–8.

—— and WILSON, D. M., *Three Viking Graves in the Isle of Man*, Society for Medieval Archaeology Monograph Series, no. 1 (London, 1966).

BRØNSTED, J., *The Vikings* (Penguin Books, 1965).

KERMODE, P. M. C., 'Knoc y Doonee', *Proc. I.M. Nat. Hist. & Antiq. Soc.* III (1930), 241–6.

MANX SOCIETY, *The Chronicle of Man and the Sudreys*, with historical notes by P. A. Munch, 2 vols. (Douglas, 1874).

MEGAW, B. R. S. 'An ancient cemetery at Balladoyne, St. John's', *J. Manx Museum*, IV (1938–40), 11–14.

—— 'St. Patrick's Isle: The Tara of the Isle of Man', ibid. V (1943), 116–20.

—— and MEGAW, E. M., 'The Norse heritage in the Isle of Man', *The Early Cultures of North-west Europe*, pp. 143–70, eds. Sir Cyril Fox and Bruce Dickins (Cambridge, 1950).

SAWYER, P. H., *The Age of the Vikings* (2nd edn, London 1971).

SHETELIG, H., 'Manx crosses relating to Great Britain and Ireland', *Saga Book of the Viking Club*, IX (1925), 253–74.

—— (ed.), *Viking Antiquities of Great Britain and Ireland* (Oslo, 1940–54).

WILSON, D. M., *The Vikings and their Origins* (London, 1970).

5. Life under Scandinavian rule

BINCHY, D. A., *Crith Gablach* (Dublin, 1941).

—— *Island Heritage*, pp. 82–90 (Manchester, 1952).

CUBBON, W., and MEGAW, B. R. S., 'The Western Isles and the growth of the Manx parliament', *J. Manx Museum*, V (1942), 57–62.

CUBBON, W. C., 'History of Rushen abbey', *Proc. I.M. Nat. Hist. & Antiq. Soc.* IV (1936), 98–105.

DAVIDSON, H. R. ELLIS, and MEGAW, B. R. S., 'Gaut the sculptor', *J. Manx Museum*, V (1944), 136–9.

ELLIS, H. R., 'The story of Sigurd in Viking art', *J. Manx Museum*, V (1942), 87–90.

—— 'Sigurd in the art of the Viking age', *Antiquity*, XVI (1942), 216–74.

FARRANT, R. D., *Mann, Its Land Tenure, Constitution, Lords Rent and Deemsters* (London, 1937).

GELLING, MARGARET, 'The place names of the Isle of Man', *J. Manx Museum*, VII (1970), 130–9, 168–75.

GELLING, MARGARET, NICOLAISEN, W. F. H., and RICHARDS, MELVILLE, *Names of Towns and Cities in Britain* (London, 1970).

GELLING, P. S., 'Medieval shielings in the Isle of Man', *Med. Arch.* VI–VII (1962–3), 156–72.

—— 'Norse homestead near Doarlish Cashen, Kirk Patrick, Isle of Man', ibid. XIV (1970), 74.

KERMODE, P. M. C., 'Ship-burial in the Isle of Man', *Ant. J.* X (1930), 126–33.

—— 'Knoc y Doonee', *Proc. I.M. Nat. Hist. & Antiq. Soc.* III (1930), 241–6.

KERMODE, THE REVD. R. D., 'The Vikings in Man', *J. Manx Museum*, III (1935), 23–5, 45–9.

KNEEN, J. J., *Place-Names of the Isle of Man* (Douglas, 1925–9).

MARSTRANDER, C. J. S., 'Det norske landnåm på Man', *Norsk Tidsskrift for Sprogvidenskap*, VI (Oslo, 1932), 40–386 (English summary, 333–55).

MEGAW, B. R. S., 'The Douglas treasure trove', *J. Manx Museum*, IV (1938), 77–82.

—— 'Weapons of the Viking age found in Man', ibid. III (1937), 234–7.

SMITH, A. H., *English Place-Name Elements*, vol. 1 (Cambridge, 1956).

TAYLOR, A. G., 'The monastic orders of Rushen Abbey (Savignian and Cistercian)', *Proc. I.M. Nat. Hist. & Antiq. Soc.* III (1930), 250–7.

WILSON, D. M., and KLINDT-JENSEN, O., *Viking Art* (London, 1963).

6. From the Norse kings to the Stanleys, 1266–1405

BARRATT, J. K., 'The Franciscan friary at Bymacan', *J. Manx Museum*, VI (1964), 209–13.

CAINE, P. W., 'Notes on the Manx monasteries', *Proc. I.M. Nat. Hist. & Antiq. Soc.* V (1942–6), 48–62.

CLUCAS, G. F., 'Sir William le Scrope', *Mannin*, V (1915), 257–62.

CRADDOCK, THE REVD. H. C., 'The pre-Reformation bishops of Sodor', *Proc. I.M. Nat. Hist. & Antiq. Soc.* III (1931), 321–46.

CRAINE, D., *Peel Castle* (Official Guide, 1964).

—— *Manannan's Isle*, pp. 104–6 (Douglas, 1955).

HOLMES, M. R., *Castle Rushen* (Official Guide, 1962).

MEGAW, B. R. S., 'The ship seals of the Kings of Man', *J. Manx Museum*, VI (1959–60), 78–80. Includes many illustrations.

WAGNER, A. R., 'The origin of the arms of Man', ibid. VI (1959–60), 77–8.

7. The first Stanleys

CUBBON, W., 'Watch and ward in 1627', *Proc. I.M. Nat. Hist. & Antiq. Soc.* III (1928), 258–65.

GILL, J. F. (ed.), *Statutes of the Isle of Man* (London, 1883).

MEGAW, B. R. S., 'A thousand years of watch and ward', *J. Manx Museum*, V (1941), 8–13.

WALPOLE, S., *The Land of Home Rule* (London, 1893).

8. Man during the English Civil War

CAINE, P. W., 'The second episode of Illiam Dhone', *Proc. I.M. Nat. Hist. & Antiq. Soc.* IV (1938), 136–45.

CRAINE, D., *Manannan's Isle* (Douglas, 1955).

HICKS BEECH, MRS. S., *The Yesterdays behind the Door* (Liverpool, 1956).

MANX SOCIETY, 3, *Stanley Legislation of Man* (Douglas, 1860).

—— 10, *A Short Treatise of the Isle of Man* (Douglas, 1864). A reprint of James Chaloner's history, originally published in 1656.

—— 26, *Illiam Dhone and the Manx Rebellion* (Douglas, 1877).

MEGAW, B. R. S., 'The fiery cross and the Manx "crosh vusta" ', *J. Manx Museum*, V (1941), 35–7.

MOORE, A. W., *Manx Worthies* (Douglas, 1901).

—— *Manx Ballads*, pp. 134–6 (Douglas, 1896).

9. The last Stanleys and the coming of British rule

'Bishop Barrow's historic deed', *J. Manx Museum*, II (1932), 62.

'The academy and grammar school at Castletown', ibid. III (1937), 242–5.

CRAINE, D., *Manannan's Isle* (Douglas, 1955). A collection of Manx historical essays chiefly concerned with the seventeenth and eighteenth centuries.

—— 'The Bible in Manx', *Proc. I.M. Nat. Hist. & Antiq. Soc.* V (1954–6), 540–54.

—— 'The potato riots, 1825', ibid. IV (1945), 565–77.

FARRANT, R. D., *Mann, Its Land Tenure, Constitution, Lords Rent and Deemsters* (London, 1937).

MANX SOCIETY, 12, *An Abstract of the Laws, Customs and Ordinances of the Isle of Man*, ed. James Gell (Douglas, 1867).

MOORE, A. W., *History of the Isle of Man*, 486–523; 871–909. *Privy Council Appeal Cases*, IV (1878), 294–305.

QUAYLE, J. R., 'Coinage of the Isle of Man', *J. Manx Museum*, II (1931), 14–16.

SHERWOOD, R., *Manx Law Tenures* (Douglas, 1899).

STENNING, E. H., 'The original lands of Bishop Barrow's trustees', *Proc. I.M. Nat. Hist. & Antiq. Soc.* V (1942–56), 122–45.

WALPOLE, S., *The Land of Home Rule*, pp. 202–47 (London, 1893).

10. Society and religion in the eighteenth century

ARNOLD, MATTHEW, *On the Study of Celtic Literature* (London, 1910).

—— *Carvallyn Gailckagh* (Douglas, 1891).

ASHLEY, A., *The Church in the Isle of Man* (York, 1958).

BLUNDELL, W., *A History of the Isle of Man*, 2 vols. (Douglas, 1875 and 1877).

BUTLER, W., *Memoirs of Bishop Hildesley* (London, 1799).

CAINE, P. W., 'The bishop of the Manx Bible (Mark Hildesley)', *Proc. I.M. Nat. Hist. & Antiq. Soc.* IV (1935–7), 187–94.

CRAINE, D., 'A Manx Merchant of the eighteenth century', ibid. IV (1945), 640–62.

—— 'Sorcery and witchcraft in Man', *J. Manx Museum*, IV (1939), 122–4.

CROSS, A. L., *Eighteenth-Century Documents relating to the Royal Forests and Smuggling* (Ann Arbor, 1928).

CUBBON, W., 'Maritime commerce at the end of the sixteenth century', *Proc. I.M. Nat. Hist. & Antiq. Soc.* IV (1945), 611–36.

—— 'The scriptures, carvals, etc., in the Manx language', *Bibliography of the Literature of the Isle of Man*, II. 749–836 (London, 1939).

—— *The Letters of Bishop Hildesley* (Douglas, 1904).

DOUGLAS, M., 'The traditional dances of Man', *J. Manx Museum*, V (1941), 3–7. With illustrations.

—— 'The four merchants', ibid. II (1934), 185.

—— 'Household prices 160 years ago', ibid. IV (1939), 36, 65, 85.

JARVIS, C. R., 'Illicit trade with the Isle of Man, 1671–1765', *Trans. Lancs. & Ches. Antiq. Soc.* LVIII (1945–6), 58.

KNEEN, J. J., *Place-Names of the Isle of Man* (Douglas, 1925–9).

MANX SOCIETY, 3, *Stanley Legislation of Man* (Douglas, 1860).

—— 12, *An Abstract of the Laws, Customs and Ordinances of the Isle of Man*, ed. James Gell (Douglas, 1867).

MOORE, A. W. (ed.), *The Letters of Bishop Hildesley* (Douglas, 1904).

—— *Diocese of Sodor and Man* (London, 1893).

ROSSER, J., *History of the Wesleyan Methodism in the Isle of Man* (Douglas, 1849).

WEST, J. I., 'John Wesley in the Isle of Man', *Proc. I.M. Nat. Hist. & Antiq. Soc.* VI (1956–8), 15–27.

WILLIAMSON, K., 'Characteristics of the Chiollagh', *J. Manx Museum*, IV (1939), 25–8.
WOOD, G. BERNARD, *Smugglers' Britain* (London, 1966).

11. Fiscal and political reform in the nineteenth century

CUBBON, W., 'The romance of the brig *Caesar*', *Sea Breezes, The P.S.N.C. Magazine*, XX (1936), 203–5.
—— 'The romance of the brig *Caesar* of Douglas', *J. Manx Museum*, III (1935), 63–5.
FARRANT, R. D., *Mann, Its Land Tenure, Constitution, Lords Rent and Deemsters*, chap. ii, pp. 28–52 (London, 1937).
GILL, J. F. (ed.), *Statutes of the Isle of Man* (London, 1883).
MOORE, DEEMSTER G. E., 'The effect of the Act of 1765', *Proc. I.M. Nat. Hist. & Antiq. Soc.* VII (1964–6), 35–48.
MOORE, R. B., 'The worthiest men in the land during five centuries', *J. Manx Museum*, II (1933), 143–7. Contains names of the Keys from 1417.
—— 'Petition demanding popular election of Keys (1780)', ibid. III (1937), 195–201.
WALPOLE, S., *Land of Home Rule*, pp. 248–55 (London, 1893).

12. The structure of the Manx economy

BIRCH, J. W., *The Isle of Man: A Study in Economic Geography* (Cambridge, 1964).
GARRAD, L. S., et al., *The Industrial Archaeology of the Isle of Man* (Newton Abbot, 1972).
GOVERNMENT BOARDS, *Annual Reports* of Agriculture and Fisheries; Forestry, Mines and Lands; Tourism; Highways; Harbours, Airports; Social Services.
ISLE OF MAN, *Population*, Report to the Local Government Board, 1967.
KINVIG, R. H., 'Manx settlement in the U.S.A.', *Proc. I.M. Nat. Hist. & Antiq. Soc.* V (1955).
LAMPLUGH, G. W., *Geology of the Isle of Man* (London, 1903).
Manx Herring Fishery Report. Issued annually.
MATHIESON, N., 'Manx mines during the Atholl period', *Proc. I.M. Nat. Hist. & Antiq. Soc.* V (1956), 555–70.
MEGAW, B. R. S., 'Corn-growing in Man 4,000 years ago', *J. Manx Museum*, IV (1939), 119–21.
MEGAW, E. M., 'Manx fishing craft', ibid. V (1941), 14–16.
—— 'Early Manx fishing craft', *The Mariner's Mirror*, XXVII (1941).
MOORE, A. W., *Manx Worthies* (Douglas, 1901).
QUAYLE, T., *Agriculture in the Isle of Man* (London, 1812).
SMITH, W. C., *A Short History of the Irish Sea Herring Fisheries* (Liverpool, 1923), Port Erin Biological Station, Special Publications, no. 1.
—— 'The Manx herring shoals', *Proc. Trans. L'pool Biol. Soc.* LI (1938).
Special Reports on the Mineral Resources of Great Britain, Memoirs of the geological survey. Lead and zinc ores, XXVI (1923); Copper ores, XXX (1925). Contains sections on the Isle of Man.

SYMONDS, D. J., 'Racial studies on Manx herring stocks', *Journal du Conseil permanent international pour l'exploration de la mer*, XXIX (1964), 189–204.

WORKINGTON AGRICULTURAL SOCIETY, *Reports on Manx Agriculture*, 1807 and 1808.

13. Modern times

BROWN, J. C., 'The story of Douglas harbour', *Proc. I.M. Nat. Hist. & Antiq. Soc.* V (1953), 350–7.

Centenary of the Popularly Elected House of Keys (1866–1966). Compiled by T. E. Kermeen (Clerk of the House of Keys), (Douglas, 1966).

CUBBON, W., *Bibliographical Account of the Works relating to the Isle of Man*, vol. 1, pp. 716–20 (London, 1933).

Evidence submitted by Tynwald to The Royal Commission on the Constitution (1970).

FARRANT, R. D., *Mann, Its Land Tenure, Constitution, Lords Rent and Deemsters* (London, 1937).

ISLE OF MAN WEEKLY TIMES, *How the Isle of Man is Governed: A Study in Constitutional Law and Practice* (Douglas, 1944).

MANX MUSEUM GUIDES, including *Introduction to Galleries; Cregneash Open-air Folk Museum; Castletown Nautical Museum.*

MOORE, DEEMSTER G. E., 'The effect of the Act of 1765', *Proc. I.M. Nat. Hist. & Antiq. Soc.* VIII (1964–6), 35–48.

NORRIS MODERN PRESS, *Manx Year Book and Directory* (Douglas, annually).

QUAYLE, G. E., 'Folklore of Lezayre, the King's forest', *Proc. I.M. Nat. Hist. & Antiq. Soc.* VI (1960–3), 426–30.

QUAYLE, J. R., 'The King's forest', ibid. IV (1937–9), 373–80.

Report of the Commission on the Isle of Man Constitution, 14 March 1959, 2 volumes, of which volume 2 contains the memoranda and evidence submitted to the Commission. (The chairman was Lord MacDermott.)

Report of the Departmental Committee on the Constitution, etc., of the Isle of Man, chairman, Lord MacDonnell, Cd. 5950 (H.M.S.O., 1911). Volume 2 consisting of minutes of evidence and appendices was published in 1912.

Reports of Tynwald. Memorandum prepared by the Attorney-General (Ramsey Moore) on the constitutional position of the Isle of Man with relation to the Imperial Government, 10 October 1944.

Report of the Finance Board on customs and the Common Purse arrangement (Finance Department, October 1966).

Report of the Commission on Rating and Taxation (Finance Department, 9 March 1967).

Report (Interim) of the Common Market Advisory Committee, October 1967.

Report of Proceedings of Tynwald Court, 8 August 1967, application of United Kingdom legislation by Order in Council.

SERJEANT, W. R., 'Hall Caine in Manx politics', *Proc. I.M. Nat. Hist. & Antiq. Soc.* VI (1958–60), 234–54.

Index